Faith in Development

Partnership between the World Bank and the Churches of Africa

Edited by
Deryke Belshaw
Robert Calderisi
Chris Sugden

Foreword by James D. Wolfensohn, President of the World Bank,
and George Carey, Archbishop of Canterbury

A COPUBLICATION OF THE WORLD BANK
AND REGNUM BOOKS INTERNATIONAL

The findings, interpretations, and conclusions expressed in this book are entirely those of the authors and should not be attributed in any manner to the World Bank, to its affiliated organizations, or to members of its Board of Executive Directors or the countries they represent. The World Bank does not guarantee the accuracy of the data included in this publication and accepts no responsibility for any consequence of their use.

About the Cover

The cover design shows kente cloth contributed by the World Bank Staff African American Association. Kente cloth is named after "kenten," or baskets, because the distinctive traditional designs resemble woven baskets. Design by Naylor Design, Inc., Washington, D.C.

Library of Congress Cataloging-in-Publication Data applied for.

Contents

PART 7
Faith in Development: Roles of the Churches

Foreword

Spiritual and material progress do not always go hand in hand. Some might even argue they never can. However, most people would accept that improving the lives of the entire human family must draw not only on the talents, effort, and organization of millions of people, but also on common values, such as the conviction that no one is truly well-off while others are desperately poor, and that the world's knowledge and opportunities should be available to all.

The role of the Church extends beyond the material welfare of its members, and even beyond temporal concerns altogether. But there is an important area of common ground between faith and development. In most developing countries, religious leaders are close to the poor and among their most trusted representatives. Faith communities offer health services, education, and shelter to the vulnerable and disadvantaged. Spiritual ties are often the strongest in societies otherwise rent by ethnic discrimination, conflict over resources, and violence.

Institutions like the World Bank are necessarily nonconfessional, but they have learned through long experience that economic and social reforms are fruitless if they do not reflect the views of society at large. For that reason, the Bank and its development partners, in cooperation with governments, have intensified their contacts over the last 10 years with parliamentarians, private investors, trade unionists, nongovernmental organizations, and journalists. The Bank has championed a greater role for civil society in the formulation of national policy—as for example in the development of Poverty Reduction Strategy exercises at the national level. It has worked with groups like Jubilee 2000 and Transparency International to find solutions for global issues like debt and corruption that affect the poor. And it has tried, through its engagement with the World Faiths Development Dialogue, to explore the area of common concern between the faith and development communities. The partners recognize that they have a major role in attacking the root causes of poverty and that in the case of Africa these lie both within and outside the continent. They also recognize that partnership and dialogue will lead to creative and long-lasting solutions.

This book discusses the principles and practicalities of such a partnership. It draws on an extraordinary conference, organized jointly by the Council of Anglican Provinces of Africa and the World Bank in Nairobi in March 2000, to explore closer collaboration, especially at the grassroots level. We hope it will inspire future meetings and accompanying actions, involving the full range of faith communities in Africa and other important actors, such as governments and the private sector. We also pray for God's blessings of wisdom, commitment, and courage for that partnership.

James D. Wolfensohn   George Carey
President, World Bank   Archbishop of Canterbury

Acronyms and Abbreviations

AFCAP	Africa Capacity Building Facility
AIDS	Acquired immune deficiency syndrome
CAPA	Council of Anglican Provinces of Africa
CGAP	Consultative Group to Assist the Poorest
FAO	Food and Agriculture Organization of the United Nations
GATT	General Agreement on Tariffs and Trade
GDP	Gross domestic product
HIV	Human immunodeficiency virus
IBRD	International Bank for Reconstruction and Development (of the World Bank Group)
IDA	International Development Association (of the World Bank Group)
IFC	International Finance Corporation (of the World Bank Group)
IGA	Income-generating activity
IMF	International Monetary Fund
MED	Microenterprise development
MFI	Microfinance institution
NASCOP	Kenya National AIDS/STD Control Programme
NGO	Nongovernmental organization
OI	Opportunity International
SAP	Structural adjustment program
SEEP	Small Enterprise Education and Promotion Network
SNA	System of national accounts
SSA	Sub-Saharan Africa

TFR	Total fertility rate
UNAIDS	Joint United Nations Programme on HIV/AIDS
UNCTAD	United Nations Conference on Trade and Development
UNDP	United Nations Development Programme
UNECA	United Nations Economic Commission for Africa
UNESCO	United Nations Educational, Scientific, and Cultural Organization
UNFPA	United Nations Population Fund
UNICEF	United Nations Children's Fund
USAID	U.S. Agency for International Development
WHO	World Health Organization

Part 1

A New Partnership
for the Poor

1

Introduction

Deryke Belshaw, Robert Calderisi, and Chris Sugden

Most of Africa's poor are deeply religious. Those who would serve them, or would work with them to improve their material condition, must remember that they have spiritual resources to draw on in overcoming their poverty. Why is religion so important to the poor? Why do they value the support of those with religious commitment? Certainly, religion provides consolation in the midst of misery; but typically faith is also part of the poor's personal identity, the foundation of their sense of community, and the basis of their hope.

Not only are faith communities among the poor, in many cases they *are* the poor. Like other faith communities, the Christian Church in Africa has grown impressively—from 60 million members in 1960 to 300 million today. Its development role must be taken seriously, not just because it is trusted and broad-based within Africa, but also because it is part of a global movement capable of improving the lives of the poor.

The papers in this volume were presented at the Churches of Africa/ World Bank Conference on Alleviating Poverty in Africa, which was held in Nairobi, Kenya, in March 2000. Representatives of African churches came together with senior staff of the World Bank for discussions on a topic of mutual and urgent concern: alleviating poverty in Africa. This first conference between the African churches and the Bank grew out of conversations between the President of the World Bank, James Wolfensohn, and the Archbishop of Canterbury, the Most Rev. Dr. George Carey. As a result of Mr. Wolfensohn's speech to the Lambeth Conference of Anglican Bishops in 1998, a process began that led the Council of Anglican Provinces of Africa to invite other churches in Africa to join them in a consultation with the World Bank on this complex problem.

The holding of the conference took many people by surprise, not least the participants. The 20 World Bank staff who attended (many of them country directors and sector managers) were eager to engage with the churches, and the churches found them very open to spiritual concerns and perspectives. An end-of-conference Communiqué was produced in an atmosphere of anticipation, enthusiasm, and warm cooperation.

Callisto Madavo, the World Bank's Vice President for Africa, under-scored the importance of the dialogue. "If we organize ourselves prop-erly, if we treat people as subjects rather than objects of development, if we consider not just the economic and the social aspects but also the cultural and, yes, even the spiritual, aspects of human aspirations, then we can be a valuable instrument in building a new future for Africa." The government of Kenya recognized the significance of the meeting by sending its Vice President to give a formal welcome on behalf of the nation. Harold Wackman, Country Director of the World Bank for Kenya, also added his welcome.

Participants at the conference presented a range of viewpoints, and these are reflected in the contributions to this volume. Although some of the authors have studied economics and use it in their day-to-day professional work, others bring perspectives from complementary dis-ciplines such as medicine, business studies, and theology. John Shao's keynote address summarizes the problem of poverty in Africa and emphasizes human capital formation—that is, educational programs—as a way of promoting investment and industrialization. Tokunboh Adeyemo, the general director of the Association of Evangelicals of Africa, presents a raw and self-critical analysis of Africa's crisis of lead-ership as a major cause of its poverty.

Deepa Narayan's paper, "Voices of the Poor," summarizing the World Bank's massive study, highlights a major reason for taking the role of religious organizations seriously: they are among the poor and the poor trust them more than any other organizations except their own social institutions. Nevertheless, the churches' weaknesses are also acknowl-edged. The poor view them as "survival rather than transformative institutions." Narayan's presentation was one of the most moving and talked-about at the conference. But her analysis of the research results also attracted some rebuttals, as in Vinay Samuel's response at the end of this volume.

Robert Calderisi explains the World Bank's renewed emphasis on poverty reduction, stressing that even the controversial "structural adjustment" programs of the 1980s and early 1990s were a necessary prelude to more targeted efforts to reduce poverty. The major challenge, then and now, is to recapture lost market shares in primary commodity markets. The Bank's willingness to learn from the bitter, as well as positive, lessons of past reform programs provides a basis for conciliation and cooperation on the wider agenda illustrated by the Communiqué.

The next group of authors describe ideal patterns of church development practice. Bishop Bernard Ntahoturi examines the church's role and potential in reducing conflict, speaking from his experience in Burundi. Dr. Christopher Kolade, chair of the President's Anti-Corruption Commission in Nigeria, challenges the notion that African society is culturally prone to corruption and indicates the church's key role in training servant-leaders of integrity.

Turning to the features of discrimination and material poverty, Agnes Aboum makes a strong plea for more effective action to achieve gender equality, and thus indirectly to improve living standards for children. Shimwaayi Muntemba and Mark Blackden present a World Bank understanding of how lowering gender inequality can reduce poverty and increase growth in Africa. Peter Okaalet urges the church to care compassionately for people living with HIV/AIDS while maintaining biblical moral teaching and demonstrating the value of Christian living as an "alternative" lifestyle.

Enterprise solutions for addressing poverty are addressed in three papers. Makonen Getu describes how the ideal operation of microfinance credit under Christian nonprofit management could help the poor escape from poverty using their own enterprise and effort. Yeboa Amoa, chair of the Ghana Stock Exchange, outlines the role of private finance in addressing poverty and the need for Africa to attract investment. Speaking for those investors, Gordon Johnson outlines some of the keystones of any investment and entrepreneurial strategy for reducing poverty through efficient private sector growth.

Molefe Tsele outlines the church's role in promoting social justice. Julius Oladipo gives examples of the wide range of income generation and service delivery opportunities that the church could initiate for poor people, especially the majority who live in rural areas. Finally, in his post-conference response, Vinay Samuel argues that it is only the sense of human dignity and self-worth conferred on the poor through the Christian salvation experience and world view that empowers them to respond proactively to opportunities for material improvement. The faith of the poor themselves is a significant factor in poverty reduction. Certainly, religion provides consolation to the poor in the midst of misery; but religious faith is also part of their personal identity, the foundation of their sense of community, and the basis of their hope.

A follow-up process to the Nairobi Consultation is already in place. The Communiqué has been widely circulated. It was warmly welcomed by the Meeting of the Anglican Communion Primates attended by the Minister for International Development of the United Kingdom in mid-2000. It was commended to all Anglican dioceses for study and action. It has also been agreed that HIV/AIDS issues are of supreme importance, and a consultation between the World Bank and the churches in Africa on this issue is planned for late 2001. National consultations between churches and World Bank offices in their countries are also envisaged. A one-day conference involving World Bank staff and 270 Catholic, Protestant, and Muslim religious leaders was held in Yaounde, Cameroon, in April 2001.

We hope that this volume will inspire other such exchanges and lead to practical discussions in parishes, villages, and towns across Africa on how faith and development can work together to unleash the full potential of the whole person and the whole continent.

2

Common Ground and Common Concerns: Communiqué of the CAPA– World Bank Conference

Nairobi, Kenya, 10 March 2000

Preamble

We 157 participants in the Conference on Alleviating Poverty in Africa, sponsored by the Council of Anglican Provinces of Africa (CAPA) and the World Bank, with the partnership of the Network of Anglicans in Mission and Evangelism, have met at the Kenya College of Communications Technology, Nairobi, from 6 to 10 March 2000. Our meeting had its origins in a letter from the Archbishop of Canterbury, the Most Rev. Dr. George Carey, to the President of the World Bank, James Wolfensohn, in May 1999, inviting the World Bank's participation in a CAPA training course for new bishops in Ibadan, Nigeria.

We came from 21 African nations[1] and 19 Christian denominations,[2] with representatives of the Archbishop of Canterbury and of the President of the Pontifical Council for Justice and Peace based in the Vatican. We were joined by partners in development from Australia, Germany, the Netherlands, Sweden, the United Kingdom, and the United States. The Vice President for Africa, Mr. Callisto Madavo, led the World Bank team of 20 senior staff. The Vice President of Kenya, the Hon. Professor George Saitoti, opened the conference.

We considered the roles of the Church and the World Bank in Africa, the causes of poverty, and the political, economic, and social challenges facing the continent.

Now therefore we by unanimous agreement issue this communiqué which marks the beginning of the first-ever partnership at a national and continental level between the churches and the World Bank in Africa.

We commit ourselves to work together to reduce poverty in Africa on the basis of the common ground and concerns which we have discovered through our meeting.

Common Ground and Concerns

The World Bank and the churches have recognized in mutual respect each other's role in addressing poverty issues. Standing by our own identities we share a common concern for the well-being of Africa and Africans and a mission to fight poverty by raising income and promoting empowerment, security and opportunity.

- We aspire to put people at the heart of development.
- We agree that the spiritual dimension of life is an essential component of development.
- We work with communities and seek community-driven development.
- We are committed to protecting the natural environment.
- We promote good governance and the fight against corruption.
- We are active in promoting debt relief and cancellation.
- We both recognize that we have both had our limitations and failures in understanding and in carrying out our missions of poverty alleviation.
- We seek therefore to improve our mutual understanding and hold each other to mutual accountability.

To our partnership the World Bank brings a wide and varied experience of dealing with poverty issues and widely researched information on specific aspects of poverty and public policy. It has special access to national and international decisionmakers who affect the life of the poor. It brings a global perspective and financial and professional resources to fighting poverty. The World Bank is the largest source of multilateral development assistance to Africa.

The Church brings its ability to influence constructively, based on its numbers, its position as the moral conscience of nations, its closeness to the poor, and its own accountability to God.

The churches in Africa have been shaped by the biblical story and hold it up as the source of liberation, transformation for abundant life, and human dignity of all people. The churches take spiritual issues seriously and see development as more than a secular process. Therefore, the Church seeks to hold forth humane and spiritual values to underpin social, political, and economic development. These values have kept the churches close to the poor in ways in which international development institutions and many government agencies are not. The Church represents the poor and the marginalized and can speak for them truthfully and forcefully.

Responding to *Voices of the Poor*

The World Bank's research into "the voices of the poor" confirms that the poor also feel powerless and voiceless. They know most about the experience of poverty, and place most trust in their own local institutions, including the churches. Their worsening plight indicates that they need appropriate partnership with other groups to rise out of poverty.

The World Bank has pledged to reflect these findings in an expanded approach to fighting poverty.

The Church needs to intensify and share with governments, the World Bank, and other organizations its own research on the voices of the poor based on the Church's understanding of poverty as also including religious, family, ethical, and cultural dimensions. The Church ministers to both poor and rich whom it should call to take up their responsibility and share in our mission and commitment to reduce poverty.

Such response must lead to clear actions. We now identify some of these.

Priority Areas for Joint Action

1. **Women and Assets**

   All data show the Africanization of poverty. Within Africa poverty affects women and children disproportionately. The voiceless and powerless are most often women. The most vulnerable group affected by gender inequality and access to assets are women in rural communities and informal urban settlements.

Gender equality is a moral imperative and a developmental objective in its own right. If Africa is to achieve equitable growth and sustainable development, gender inequality, often reinforced by legal and cultural structures, in access to and control of a diverse range of productive, human, and social capital assets, must be changed. Reducing gender inequality will increase efficiency and welfare.

The World Bank has a strong interest in gender programs and strategies that empower women to participate in their development and contribute to economic growth.

The Church sees the partnership between men and women as inherent in creation, its breakdown as an expression of sin, and its restoration achieved through the gospel of Christ. The Church has brought good news to women in Africa, since the majority of the members of churches are women. But part of the African Church's heritage from both missionaries and African culture are structured roles for men and women that have been perpetuated. The Church has an empowering role but has a marginalizing structure. So the Church must improve its capacity to provide space for women to express and contribute their resources and gifts in a more participatory and equal manner, and thus enable the full range of Africa's human resources to be brought to bear on the issue of poverty.

Therefore, to give full expression to the gospel:

- The Church should increase awareness about the injustices against women, empowerment programs, and gender training for both men and women.
- The Church needs to change rigid structures in its community life so as to enhance the involvement of women in leadership.

Therefore, the World Bank can work with the Church to assess the impact of programs of both institutions that are directed to rural women especially and to enable men and women to work together in mutually supportive partnership in the home and the community.

2. Children and Youth

In many African countries over 50 percent of the population is under 15 years of age. The Church has a long record of programs with children and young people and offers its expertise to the World Bank, because the plight of street children, AIDS orphans, child laborers, abused children, child-soldiers, and the right to life of unborn and disabled children demand urgent attention. The Church should encourage and support the African institution of the extended family.

3. Education and Health

Education equips communities to provide for themselves, but Africa's education is in crisis. The fall in the number of children attending school is very worrying. Twenty countries have less than half of their school-age population enrolled in primary school. There are still more boys than girls in school, and the situation is getting worse, despite the focus on girls. Literacy rates in Africa are lower than anywhere else except South Asia.

A healthy population is critical for economic productivity and improved quality of life. Access to medical services is beyond poor people. Childbearing women bear the brunt of this.

The World Bank has strong investment programs in education and health that are intended to have a direct impact on productivity and poverty alleviation. The Church has pioneered education and health services in most African countries. Churches are under increasing pressure to reassume greater responsibility for these public services. The Church cannot do this adequately without a clear understanding with governments and other development partners on appropriate roles and resources. This is an area for joint work. The Church can also partner with governments, the World Bank, and others in promoting life-skills training, civic education, education in entrepreneurship, care for the environment, and informal education for adults.

4. HIV/AIDS

HIV/AIDS is eroding Africa's achievements in its development. Two-thirds of the world's HIV/AIDS pandemic is in Africa. Though very few African governments talk about AIDS, given the scale of the emergency it is no longer just a public health issue.

The World Bank has recently declared HIV/AIDS a development crisis for Africa; has developed a comprehensive strategy to fight the pandemic; is integrating HIV/AIDS programs in all its investments and dialogue; and is designing a comprehensive project approach for countries with high prevalence rates.

The Church is committed to encourage faithfulness in marriage, and thus to enable young people to exercise abstinence before marriage and faithfulness within marriage. There is need for further work on the most culturally appropriate and effective approaches to HIV/AIDS prevention that uphold the vision of marital faithfulness.

The Church has a triple role. It is the custodian of the biblical values and virtues needed to protect the vulnerable against AIDS, and it must lead in the promotion of moral education. It can ensure that people living with AIDS are treated with respect, love, and dignity, and can be a source of pastoral care and support for them and their families. It is also a bearer of hope beyond this life.

The World Bank can partner with the Church:

- As a custodian of the values that both institutions affirm as fundamental to a healthy society, to undertake HIV/AIDS prevention programs that target vulnerable groups.
- To influence community and social leaders, Church and national leaders to break the conspiracy of silence about HIV/AIDS. The World Bank can provide data on a country-specific basis to empower the Church in making the case about AIDS to its people.
- To hold joint workshops on HIV/AIDS and the role of the Church.
- To develop microcredit enterprise schemes for those living with HIV/AIDS to sustain them and their families.
- To provide affordable antiretroviral therapy to people living with HIV/AIDS.

5. Governance, Leadership and Corruption

The Church is the one forum where leaders and followers in society can dialogue in a mutual exchange of information and support, thus empowering citizens and requiring accountability of leaders.

The World Bank and the Church can work together:

- To demand an end to corruption and a public political life based on transparency, accountability, and equal opportunities.
- To empower citizens to develop skills to recognize and acknowledge their rights and thus fight corruption.

- To improve performance in developing accountable leaders, participation of both men and women in leadership, and in addressing corruption based on tribal and political affiliation.
- To dissuade Western governments from giving tax breaks to companies that make illegal payments to corrupt African officials.

6. Enterprise, Debt, and Economic Growth

Much of Africa's economic decline stems from its loss of markets and savings. Between 1970 and 1995, this amounted to $70 billion a year, enough to pay off its total official debts in three years. Turning this around must include improving the climate for private investment, first and foremost by Africans, who presently find the best return on their investment abroad. The role of the World Bank in structural adjustment programs was much discussed, and a range of differing opinions was expressed.

Economic growth depends on *achieving higher investment*, efficiency in the use of all resources, private and public, and a sound national infrastructure. But it is public policy that will ensure that the benefits of such growth actually reach the poor. Governments and the Church must also strive to ensure that private firms behave in a socially responsible manner.

The Church has a *prophetic mission of advocacy* of honesty, integrity, and accountability, all of which are important for building confidence among investors as well as ensuring a just society. Therefore, the Church should encourage its own people with economic expertise and business experience to work with capital markets, the private sector, and the World Bank in channeling resources to the poor.

Microenterprise development is a highly effective means of channeling such resources even though it does not directly meet the needs of the very poor. The Church should encourage such initiatives led by Christian people with appropriate business expertise and work with well-established networks while introducing lending policies that reflect Christian values.

The churches and the World Bank commit themselves to increase the understanding and promotion of *fair trade* as a way of fighting poverty. The Church should encourage all its members to trade in a way that is ethical and fair, whether in North-South or South-South commerce.

The decisions on *debt relief and cancellation* in the past 12 months could prove to be an important step on the way to the solution of the debt crisis of many poor countries, especially in Africa.

The World Bank, the churches, and governments should cooperate in translating these new resources into direct benefits for the poor, building on the Bank's growing involvement in community-driven programs. Where good governance does not exist, new mechanisms should be tried to channel the benefits of debt relief directly to the poor. Debtors and creditors must continue to cooperate to find a sustainable solution for outstanding debt problems because debt repayments remain a severe burden on the economies of many poor countries.

7. **Conflict Prevention and Post-Conflict Reconstruction**

There can be no economic growth in a conflict situation. Peace depends on justice, social harmony, and spiritual fulfillment. Life must be respected as sacred. Abundant life is multidimensional.

The World Bank is not equipped to provide emergency assistance during conflict situations. However, the World Bank continues to maintain a dialogue with a country in conflict, assess when the time is right for post-conflict reconstruction, establish trust funds to provide grants to the country, and strike the balance between security issues and development.

The Church identifies the root cause of conflict in the refusal to see any "good" in "the other" and its solution in the willingness to accuse and implicate oneself and one's own group as part of the problem. Forgiveness and reconciliation, based on this analysis, is the Church's specialist field. In a conflict situation, the Church is an ongoing institution providing continuity and social stability.

The World Bank and the Church should work together:

- To address the root causes of conflicts.
- To train Church and community leaders in leadership for community harmony and in conflict transformation.
- To work together in reconstruction and rehabilitation programs that build the fabric of conflict-ridden societies.
- To enhance the role of women in the peace-building process.

The Way Forward

A joint consultative process is essential:

- The World Bank will include the churches in national consultations on economic and social policy issues and the design of poverty alleviation programs.
- The World Bank will work with the churches to understand their involvements and capacities for development work in particular countries.
- The churches and the World Bank will arrange follow-up meetings on a national basis with the broadest Christian participation possible.

Joint Action

- Where appropriate capacity can be demonstrated, or built, the World Bank and the churches will cooperate with governments in testing the channeling of development resources through Church programs. Such initiatives can include community leadership training and counseling services, conflict resolution and peace-building initiatives, centers of compassion for HIV/AIDS counseling and care, income-generating activities, rural and urban informal sector credit unions, and provision of basic services.
- Further consultations will be held within 24 months with (a) African governments, (b) the private sector, (c) other international development institutions.
- Communication and information sharing between the World Bank and the churches should be improved.
- Publication and translation into major languages of the proceedings of this conference on the Internet will be completed as soon as possible, and distribution to participants and relevant bodies within six months.
- A continuation committee to take forward the plans for joint action will be set up and empowered.

Conclusion

We have all been delighted by our mutual enthusiasm and openness to explore and develop this partnership.

We commit ourselves to develop our partnership with passion, compassion, and professionalism so that our joint work produces results for the poor. We stand together for life and dignity.

Notes

1. Benin, Burkina Faso, Burundi, Central African Republic, Democratic Republic of Congo, Egypt, Ethiopia, Ghana, Kenya, Liberia, Madagascar, Nigeria, Rwanda, Seychelles, Sierra Leone, South Africa, Sudan, Tanzania, Uganda, Zambia, and Zimbabwe.

2. African Instituted Churches, Anglican Church, Apostolic Faith Mission, Baptist Church, Church of God, Evangelical Alliances, Evangelical Church of West Africa, Evangelical Lutheran Church of Tanzania, Independent Evangelical Churches, Lutheran Church, Methodist Church, Pentecostal Church, Presbyterian Church, Reformed Church, Roman Catholic Church, United Methodist Church, Orthodox Church of Ethiopia, Eastern Orthodox Church, Greek Orthodox Church.

Part 2

Poverty in Sub-Saharan Africa

3

Alleviating Poverty in Africa

John Shao

Poverty in Africa is not a new topic for discussion or debate. Poverty in Africa is a reality that we live with on a daily basis. One does not need to venture far to see naked poverty in Africa. A few steps outside this building will be enough to bring the reality of poverty to the senses of any curious visitor.

A Widening Gap

Perhaps the most serious threat today is the widening gap between the rich and the poor both within and between nations. It has become abundantly evident that this gap is the effect of the prevailing world economic order, which in turn is based on the survival of the fittest, the profit motive, the emphasis on unlimited increase in the gross national product, a monetary system that is manipulated to the advantage of the affluent and powerful, and an extraordinary imbalance in the handling of economies when many poor nations of Africa spend vast sums on armaments. This widening gap has been dramatically revealed by structural food deficits and growing famine, mainly in the poorest countries on the continent. It has been estimated that more than 20 percent of the population in Africa lives below the minimum income of US$200 per person per year. More than half that number are on the edge of starvation. And yet there is no continent-wide food policy or structure for meeting hunger and famine in a concerted way.

In April 1974 the United Nations proposed the "establishment of a new international economic order based on equity, sovereignty, equality, interdependence, common interest and cooperation among all states, irrespective of their economic and social systems." The prevailing intention was to "correct inequalities and redress existing injustices . . . and ensure steadily accelerating economic and social development, peace and justice for present and future generations." It is fair to say today that the intention was good, but the reality is that nothing concrete came out of it. Today, we face the alternatives of either cooperation, finding a new way of relating to each other as nations, or of confrontation, leading to mutual distrust.

Within the national borders of many countries in Africa, a class of the rich has been steadily growing. Some of the riches have been accumulated in corrupt or other dubious ways. This means that within the same communities—urban or rural—it is possible these days to see people who have become so rich that they feel and look like strangers in their own villages or towns. Unfortunately, wealth has a tendency to generate power for domination, exploitation, and manipulation. The rich in African countries are by and large closer in attitude and behavior to the well-to-do on other continents than they are to their own neighbors. Furthermore, some of them become channels of exploitation from outside. If we are not careful, this growing phenomenon is bound to create great tensions within and between communities.

Financing Basic Needs

In many countries in Sub-Saharan Africa, churches have been much involved in services related to health care, education, and domestic water supply. The reason for this is partly historical and partly due to the great need for such services. Provision of medical care and education in many African countries was started by the Church through the agency of Christian mission societies during the colonial era.

The autonomous churches in Africa inherited the mission structures without the necessary resources to run them. The problem of financing these services has been exacerbated by the fact that due to the great need in our societies, the churches have had to build more hospitals, dispensaries, and schools, and to increase access to water. When a government is unable to build a clinic in a village, the people's tendency is to turn to a church for help. The proximity of the churches to the people makes it difficult for them to turn a cold shoulder to these requests.

Under colonial administration, mission societies in some African countries received financial assistance through what were termed grants-in-aid to run health care and education services under their management. There are very few governments on our continent that do the same today, and these remaining few have cut their financial grants considerably. The reason given is that the national governments are under pressure from the World Bank and the IMF to institute sharp cuts in government spending to comply with the policies of structural adjustment programs (SAPs).

We know that representatives of both the World Bank and the IMF have been countering this accusation. They have insisted that the governments of the recipient countries have not been told to cut spending on social services in order to reduce government spending. That might have been true when the policies of SAPs were first promulgated. In the last decade or so, however, definite steps have been taken to encourage governments to get out of the habit of providing free education and health care. Furthermore, we would fool ourselves to think that governments themselves would have been eager to cut military spending in favor of social services. Given the political situations in some of our countries, few African presidents would be alive today if they dared to reduce military budgets. Thus, it was the "soft" ministries that had to bear the full brunt of the cuts in government spending. The churches and the common people were deeply affected by these actions.

Basic education is a right of every child in whatever society he or she is born. When a child is denied a basic education, that child is denied the chance to reach his or her greatest human potential.

Education is a means through which social, cultural, and moral values are imparted in order to integrate children in the social milieu in which they grow up. Education can provide skills to enable children eventually to be useful in society and to provide for their own well-being. To say that a child has been denied an education does not necessarily mean that there is no school in the village. There might be a school, and yet certain children are denied the opportunity of attending because their parents cannot afford to pay the school fees for the books and school uniform.

Health care is another very important social service needed by people in every country. It should not be a luxury for the rich; it is a right of all citizens. The introduction of the cost-sharing system for medical treatment in public hospitals has led to the exclusion of many poor people.

They cannot take their children or themselves to hospitals or clinics when they need treatment. Child mortality in some sections of the population is rising. Furthermore, cuts in health care expenditure have left many hospitals in shambles: there are no drugs for the sick and inadequate equipment for medical staff. In some cases operations are cancelled because of lack of rubber gloves for the surgeons. One could recount more instances of increasing malnutrition and maternal mortality as well as lack of funds to prevent and treat diseases. It is the poor who suffer most from the austerity measures being taken by governments in the name of economic reforms.

It should be said that the churches have no political theory or economic system of their own that they would like to impose on others. But churches are made up of people just as nations and societies are made up of people. As citizens, church members have a right like everyone else to express their views on all important national or local issues. It is for this reason that I hope we will be patient and frank with one another in our discussions. It is not being argued here that all policies of structural adjustment programs are imperfect or unhelpful to the poor. Far from it; those of us who understand well the working of our countries' economies would readily concede that some SAPs are very necessary if the economic situation is to get better. The main point of contention is what features and character they should assume. A population weakened by diseases and other forms of deprivation is not likely to be in the best position to marshal the necessary intellectual and physical strength needed to compete in an increasingly healthy world. A country with inadequately educated and trained nationals stands very little chance of being a winner in an increasingly competitive world. Cutting back public spending on education, health care, water, and sanitation tends to hurt the weakest and most vulnerable sections of society—the poor, women, the aged, and children—as well the productive capacities of future generations.

Fair World Trade?

It is said that world trade is based on the principle of comparative advantage. This is a polite way of distorting the reality. The truth is that the global market is dominated and controlled by, and operates in the interests of, the industrial countries of the North. Discussions in Geneva during the GATT conference a few years ago observed that international markets are distorted by the operation of multinational corporations, government tariffs, and other restrictive practices. Is it really fair trade when pricing of commodities from Africa and the rest of the developing world is determined in the markets and/or administrations of the North Atlantic countries, while poor African countries are not involved in setting the prices for industrial goods sold to them? Can such practices in international trading be anything but unjust? The rich industrial countries are becoming richer while Sub-Saharan Africa is becoming poorer.

The economies of African countries are still agriculture-based rather than industrial; and even then, apart from raw materials and tropical foodstuffs needed in the North, these poor countries do not produce much (other than agricultural products) for world markets. Even if the African countries were able to produce regular surpluses of wheat and maize, there would be no markets for them in Canada or the United States because these countries produce more than enough of their own. Few African countries would be able to compete with the developed world in international trading. Most countries south of the Sahara will be dumping places for industrial goods, as well as some agricultural commodities, from the developed world. It is painful to say it, but the fact is that African countries could easily become the slums of the industrial world.

The fundamental imbalance between the world's rural and urban nations—between the industrial and the primary producer areas—is not yet recognized as the root cause of world economic problems and world poverty. We are still being told that the solution to present economic ills is greater investment in the already developed areas of our lands. Yet our belief is that rural development is a way of approaching economic development; it is not something different from it.

Rural development has to be tackled at two levels, national and international. At both levels it is the only way we can hope to defeat absolute poverty as well as relative poverty. For poverty and riches are two sides of the same coin in the modern world. To abolish poverty we must create wealth. But the creation of wealth, by itself, does not necessarily abolish poverty. Wealth creation has to be accompanied by practical forms of investment using part of the new wealth if poverty is to be eradicated.

At the international level the struggle for rural development is, in essence, what the demand for a new international economic order is all about. There is no simplistic answer. Aid, trade, debt relief, international credit and currency systems—all these and many other major questions of international relations are involved in the evolution of a global rural development strategy.

Structural adjustment programs must be challenged for being obsessive about the importance of market mechanisms. Instead they should finance and encourage people to develop local economies, starting with an emphasis on the production of food crops to halt declining food security and to invest hard-earned foreign currency in productive development projects.

Africa's Quest for Dignity

We are living in an unsettling period in the long narrative of humankind. History tells us that stormy weather brings out the best qualities in some and the worst qualities in others. The future of the world we live in will be determined by the nature of that balance. It would seem to me that our global community in the twenty-first century will no longer exhibit the marked differences and separate fates that have characterized past centuries. A relentless flow of images and ideas, transmitted by modern technologies, will inevitably draw each of our societies into the awareness of others in a fashion not possible just a few years ago. These images and ideas are spawning unexpected and often unwelcome reactions in country after country and region after region.

At the very time when cooperation is essential and understanding vital, xenophobia and ethnic cleansing are on the rise. Withdrawal from cooperative processes is common and political activities are reviled. Seldom in history has thoughtful, credible leadership been more needed, and seldom has the challenge to leaders been more daunting.

Those of us who live on the African continent are only too aware of the prevailing living conditions and the painful struggles we have to bear. We have access to the depressing economic statistics; we know the hardship and the anguish that these represent in our own families and communities. For us there is a chilling reality to such economic factors as low commodity prices, high interest rates, reduced bank credits, and protectionism in the global North. These do have negative impacts on the quality of life of multitudes of Africans in villages and cities, in countries large and small. These economic factors should not be ignored, and they must not be regarded as being beyond the ability of Africans to influence. In the present interconnected, interdependent world, no region is without vulnerability, yet none is without influence. The challenge to all of us is to bring these forces into some form of dynamic equilibrium. Failure to do so will be as harmful to the North, though often in different fashion, as it will be to African nations and other poor countries in the South.

Major reform, by definition, alters the status quo and often threatens the primacy of the privileged. In any community, those least willing to adapt—and often least needing to adapt—are the comparatively advantaged. This is so in the international community just as in an individual country, with the result that powerful conservative forces unite to block the reforms necessary for the introduction of effective policy adjustments. The norm in the past century, it seems to me, has been the continued supremacy of those societal elements that enjoy influence and know how to exercise it for their own benefit. This seeming invincibility of the socially and economically powerful is a manifestation of human instinct, and is found in all political systems. The question that arises is whether this inflexibility will prove to be destructive in the face of the massive and systematic changes now pulsing through the global economy. Will African countries and peoples be less resistant to change and more able to manage the necessary adjustment for their future betterment? It would seem that Africa could enjoy a competitive advantage if good leadership is offered to guide it wisely.

This is a challenge that must be borne equally by African governments, by African societies, both urban and rural, and by all churches in Africa.

Increasing Resources at the Community Level

Implicit in the choice of conference theme is a recognition and admission, however subtle, that our societies in Africa are absolutely and relatively poor and are not well set to cope with the rigors of the new millennium. As I understand the phrase, "alleviating poverty" implies decreasing poverty, and one cannot decrease poverty without increasing resources to generate more income that is also better distributed. We must address the question of increasing resources—human, financial, and material—to African communities.

Step one, therefore, must be forging a new partnership between African governments, societies, and churches in the coming century.

We need first to take into account the rapid global development and worldwide trends that will bear on the economic status of the future African population. Recognizing that the world of the twenty-first century will be increasingly globalized, we must devise new and more effective strategies for initiating and managing change aimed at improving the economic status of our people in Africa.

Of necessity, churches in Africa will have to strive to improve the economic status of our people. Yet the present global changes are so rapid that it will require a great effort even to maintain the present economic status of African people. It is like riding a bicycle. The rider must keep pedaling, otherwise he or she will fall by the wayside.

I want to underline the importance of *local participation* in poverty alleviation. We are globalizing, yes, and we must get assistance to alleviate poverty. But ultimately the fundamental mission of our church and university leadership must be to produce men and women with the knowledge, skills, and attitudes to bring about positive growth and development in African countries, societies, and institutions—development that is geared toward alleviating poverty.

There is an urgent need to establish and nurture a new partnership between church leaders and universities in producing well-educated people who are capable of addressing the issues of poverty in Africa. I want to stress that churches must seek to build a local capacity for high-quality, relevant, and egalitarian university education. We must steadily reduce our dependence on external assistance for the actions we can take to alleviate poverty. For our educational system must be— and must be understood to be—one of the most important cogs in the wheel of local societal change toward poverty alleviation.

Another important issue on which joint strategies are needed between churches and societies, and between universities and the private sector, is the need to enhance our applied research capacity in poverty alleviation issues. Only then will Africa's communities and production units and enterprises be able to apply appropriate technologies to improve production and productivity within our societies.

Ownership of the Development Agenda

One pertinent problem is that the mindset of many people in Africa and of some of their leaders has succumbed to donor dependency, which has resulted in an erosion of initiative and lack of ownership of the development agenda. This has not been conducive to addressing development challenges with dignity, confidence, determination, and persistence through hard work and creativity. The educational system has not been structured to counter this deterioration in ownership of the development agenda and in Africans' confidence in their own ability to determine the destiny of their nations.

The following have become evident:

External dependence and the erosion of confidence, dignity, and determination have diminished people's ability to effectively utilize human, physical, and mental capacities to take the initiative and to search earnestly for creative options to solve development problems. As a result, considerable potential capabilities in Africa have not been effectively marshaled and deployed for poverty alleviation.

The mindset of too many of the leaders and people of Africa has not been supportive of hard work, ingenuity, and creativity, nor has it provided a conducive environment for these attributes to emerge. There are high levels of apathy, lack of accountability, and poor self-motivation. Initiative, ingenuity, creativity, and innovativeness in society are at a low ebb. Consequently, a culture of admiring "effortless" success has become dominant, while individual initiative and the spirit of community development have not become increasingly valued.

The level and quality of education have not been adequate to meet the growing development challenges and to empower the search for solutions to the development problems confronting the nations. In particular, education has not adequately been geared to integrating the individual into the community. It also has not been able to launch Africans into entrepreneurship and remunerative self-employment.

The capacity for economic management has not kept up with the demand for macroeconomic stability and has not responded to changing conditions as quickly as it should. Generally, there has been some degree of macroeconomic instability. Policy responses to changing conditions have been slow. Other things being equal, this situation would suggest a lack of policymaking capacity to anticipate and effectively respond to changing conditions. As a result, economies do not have the long-term stability they need to attract a substantial and continuous flow of investment. Further, excessive use of administrative controls extends to nonstrategic spheres and even hinders the mobilization of capabilities outside the public sector. The excessive use of administrative controls and regulations has made it very difficult to harness positive market forces to achieve development objectives, with the result that many African economies have become weak.

The general picture in most African economies is the following:

1. The economy has remained largely untransformed. Agriculture, the backbone of the economy, continues to depend mainly on rainfall and on backward technology.
2. The productivity level in other sectors has also remained low. Available domestic resources have not been adequately mobilized or effectively utilized to promote development on a robust and sustainable basis. This low level of productivity also reflects a low degree of creativity and innovation, including low levels of utilization of science and technology.
3. The structure of the economy is still dominated by primary production, making it vulnerable to changes in international commodity market conditions and to the adoption of new industrial technologies that use significantly less raw material.

Over time, and particularly in recent years, there are signs of cracks emerging in social cohesion and national unity. Corruption and other social vices have been on the increase. This situation raises great concern. The rule of law and the voices of the people in the development process have tended to be weak. National institutional and organizational structures have not been reviewed to cope with the demands of ongoing economic and governance reforms. As a result, these structures have not supported evolving social relations that could promote the participation of all partners in development.

Conclusions

Poverty in Africa presents enormous challenges. The quest for dignity depends on how successfully Africa's people manage to struggle out of the dehumanizing poverty that afflicts the majority of them. Africa must reaffirm, in words and action, that the goal of development is first and foremost the promotion of the well-being of its people.

Africa will have to strengthen democratic institutions to ensure that its people live in freedom and peace and under laws based on the principles of justice.

Africa will need to use its own resources more effectively to accelerate economic development while ensuring that the basic needs of Africans are met and that individuals and families can free themselves from poverty, disease, and ignorance.

The challenge to African churches is to empower Africans to realize the full potential of their talents and creativity and to mobilize their contribution to the development and progress of their communities. Africa must not allow the continued degradation of its environment in the name of either development or short-term financial gain. Instead, it has to accompany development efforts with due concern for the protection of its natural environment to ensure that it can sustain present and future generations. These challenges, and others not mentioned here, are formidable. Yet they must be faced and met in order to begin the alleviation of poverty in Africa.

In his address at the inauguration ceremony of the South Commission in 1987, the late Mwalimu Julius K. Nyerere made an observation that is worth listening to carefully today. His plea to the South was to realize and develop its own potential through national and collective self-reliance. Do not be constrained by precedent or by orthodoxies, he urged; have faith in the South. Well, friends: Have faith in Africa and in Africans. Poverty in Africa can be alleviated if all partners involved play their parts appropriately.

Bibliography

Arruda, Marcos, ed. 1981. "Transnational Corporations, Technology and Human Development." Report of the 3rd meeting of the Advisory Group on Economic Matters, held in Rome, Italy, October 15–19, 1980. Geneva: World Council of Churches.

Brandt, W. 1980. *North-South: A Program for Survival.* Cambridge: Massachusetts Institute of Technology Press.

Commission on International Development (Pearson Commission). 1969. *Partners in Development.* New York: Praeger.

Dickinson, R. D. N. 1983. *Poor, Yet Making Many Rich: The Poor as Agents of Creative Justice.* Geneva: World Council of Churches.

Galtung, J. 1980. "Self-Reliance: Concepts, Practices, and Rationales." Geneva: Institute for Development Studies.

Independent Commission of the South on Development Issues. 1990. *The Challenge to the South: The Report of the South Commission.* New York: Oxford University Press.

Kurien, C. T. 1978. *Poverty, Planning and Social Transformation*. Bombay: Allied Publishers.

Morton, J. 1996. *The Poverty of Nations: The Aid Dilemma at the Heart of Africa*. New York: I. B. Tauris.

Myrdal, G. 1970. *The Challenge of World Poverty*. New York: Random House.

Nyerere, J. K. 1987. Address to the inauguration ceremony of the South Commission. Month-Pelerin, Switzerland.

4

Africa's Enigma

Tokunboh Adeyemo

An enigma is something that is hard to understand or explain. It is said that Africa is the richest of the seven continents in natural resources and yet her people are the poorest. Africa is probably the first home of the human race and yet it is the last to be developed. Africa and Africans have made many nations and peoples great, yet their own vineyards remain unkempt. How do you explain such a set of contradictions? Before attempting to solve the puzzle, let's unscramble some facts and figures.

Africa's Potential for Prosperity

First, God has blessed Africa with a varied natural environment. Africa is the second largest in land area of the earth's seven continents. With its islands, Africa covers 30,330 square kilometers, or about 22 percent of the world's total land area. This area could contain the United States, Europe, India, China, Argentina, and New Zealand together. Africa had a population of about 762 million in 1998, around 12 percent of the world's population. Generally, most of the land in Africa is good for farming or pastoralism. Given the diversity of climate, topography, and vegetation; the variety of food and commercial products; and the abundant (though underused) water supply, Africa is capable of not only feeding itself but also of being an agricultural supplier to the rest of the world.

Second, Africa is very rich in mineral resources, possessing most of the world's known minerals in significant quantities. The continent has some of the world's largest reserves of gold, diamonds, copper, bauxite, manganese, nickel, platinum, cobalt, radium, and phosphates. Found in exploitable quantities are iron ore, chromium, tin, zinc, lead, clays, sulfur, salt, graphite, and limestone. Almost every country in Africa has a reasonable amount of underdeveloped or unexploited minerals. For example, Nigeria and Angola are among the top 10 oil producers in the world. The world's largest supply of radium, used chiefly in luminous materials and in the treatment of cancer, is located in the Democratic Republic of Congo (formerly Zaire). About 20 percent of the world's copper reserves are in Zambia, Democratic Republic of Congo, Zimbabwe, and South Africa. The Democratic Republic of Congo also produces about 90 percent of the world's known cobalt, and Sierra Leone has the largest known titanium reserves. In total, Africa produces three-quarters of the world's gold, while iron ore can be found in most parts of the continent.

Third, Africa is blessed with abundant energy resources. The potential for fossil fuels, hydroelectric power, and solar energy is almost without limit. Fossil fuels are abundant, including major deposits of coal, petroleum, and natural gas. Sub-Saharan Africa is a major exporter of coal (Zimbabwe and South Africa) and petroleum (Nigeria, Gabon, and Angola). Africa owns 40 percent of the world's hydropower potential. Regarding solar power, the Sahara Desert alone covers a solar energy field area of about 9,065,000 kilometers, which could more than meet Africa's need for energy to power domestic electrical appliances. There are three other deserts: the Nubian, the Namibian, and the Kalahari. The state of Arizona in the United States has the largest solar power installation in the world. It supplies most of that state's electrical energy. Yet in size, the state is less than one-fifth of the area covered by the Sahara.

When one considers all these resources together—the land, natural and cultivated vegetation, animals, water systems, minerals, the various sources of energy—and above all, the beautiful people and their spirituality, one is stunned to learn about Africa's poverty.

Poverty in Africa

In his book *Hope for Africa*, Professor George Kinoti of the University of Nairobi categorically states that poverty is the most pressing of all of

Africa's many problems. "It is at the heart of all the important problems in Africa, be they social, spiritual or moral." According to Kinoti, Africa's poverty is manifested in five significant areas: hunger, low income, disease, dehumanization, and injustice.

Regarding hunger, one out of every three Africans does not get enough to eat. This can lead to retarded physical and mental development, disease, disability, and premature death. In Nigeria, for example, the majority of the over 100 million people cannot afford more than one meal a day. In Sierra Leone, the already bad food situation has been aggravated by rebel wars and military coups. People survive on starch alone.

Regarding low incomes, ravaged nations including Rwanda, Burundi, the Democratic Republic of Congo, Somalia, Angola, and Liberia have difficulty paying their civil servants and teachers anything at all. In a number of other countries, professionals such as nurses, lawyers, engineers, and doctors receive wages of about $300 a month. In Nigeria, university professors (many of them trained in the West) earn about $3,000 per year. As a point of contrast, Belgium has a population only 2 percent the size of Africa's, but in 1997 enjoyed a gross domestic product (national wealth) higher than all of Sub-Saharan Africa, excluding South Africa.

Regarding disease, many of the preventable and treatable diseases that have been eradicated or largely controlled in the West are still endemic in Africa, including cholera, malaria, typhoid, and meningitis. Add to the list ebola and HIV/AIDS and you have a grim situation. Patients are afraid to go to public hospitals because in many cases it is a fast way to the grave. Hospitals have no drugs, the equipment is outdated, and the staff are demoralized.

Regarding dehumanization, how can one justify the senseless killing of about 1 million Rwandese by fellow Rwandese in 1994? As a result, between 2 and 3 million Rwandese are still scattered in several refugee camps. Yet the feud is not over in Rwanda or Burundi or the Democratic Republic of Congo. Meanwhile, there is no end in sight for the problem of slavery and the struggle for autonomy in southern Sudan.

Injustice in Africa has many dimensions. In his book *Lords of Poverty* (1991), Graham Hancock reveals the injustice that surrounds the international aid business. He contends that billions of dollars of taxpayers' money sent from the West to help the poor of the Third World never reached them. Instead, the funds went to support the opulent lifestyles of officials administering the aid or to buy out collapsing multinational corporations, while whatever remained was eaten up by the corrupt and bureaucratic recipient governments.

Since political independence, which most African nations attained in the 1960s, Africa has had 56 successful military coups. Many brilliant African minds, such as Patrick Lumumba (Democratic Republic of Congo) and Tom Mboya (Kenya), have been killed in politically motivated assassinations under mysterious circumstances.

In economic and political terms, these problems have meant uncontrollable inflation, instability, economic stagnation, constant currency devaluation, and collapse of services, among other things. It's no wonder that what used to be called "brain drain" in the 1970s has become "brain flight" today, as many of Africa's best minds emigrate for economic reasons.

The Causes of Africa's Problems

In his book *What Is Africa's Problem?* (1992), President Yoweri K. Museveni of Uganda says, "One of the biggest weakening factors in Africa is tribalism and other forms of sectarianism." The late President Samora Machel of Mozambique once described tribalism as the "commander-in-chief of anti-African forces." Museveni goes on to discuss five other root causes of the continent's distress:

- Bad politics and politicians
- Communication difficulties
- Too easy a climate that leads to idleness
- Lack of aggressiveness in business
- Foreign domination, especially of the economy

In his own contribution to the debate, Kinoti (1994) identifies nine causes, namely:

- Incompetent governments
- Unjust international economic systems
- Wasteful aspects of African culture such as disregard for time
- Poor management
- Widespread illiteracy and low educational standards
- Immoral practices including tribalism, corruption, dishonesty, and laziness

- Scientific and technological backwardness
- Excessive population growth
- Human-caused environmental crises

The noted Nigerian writer Chinua Achebe (author of the novel *Things Fall Apart*) reduces all these problems into one: leadership. In his 1983 book *The Trouble with Nigeria,* he argues:

> The trouble with Nigeria is simply and squarely a failure of leadership. There is nothing basically wrong with the Nigerian character. There is nothing wrong with the Nigerian land or water or air or anything else. The Nigerian problem is the unwillingness or inability of its leaders to rise to the responsibility, to the challenge of personal example which are the hallmarks of true leadership.

He concludes the chapter by saying, "We have lost the twentieth century, are we bent on seeing that our children also lose the twenty-first? God forbid?" What Achebe says of Nigeria is equally true of all African countries with the exception of two or three that have good leaders. For decades Africa has had "bosses," and not leaders.

In 1978, following the death of the founding father of Kenya, Jomo Kenyatta, a national leadership conference was called to consider the topic "The Kenya We Want." After a week-long deliberation, the assembly unanimously concluded that "effective leadership is the most critical input in society. The measure of any nation is the measure of its leadership."

A Profile of Effective Leadership

The story of Joseph (Genesis 41:50) is well known. As a teenager of 17, Joseph started to dream and to interpret dreams. His dreams got him into trouble with his brothers, who sold him as a slave to Midianite traders. He landed a good job as an estate manager for Mr. Potiphar, an Egyptian official. But that was short-lived. On a false accusation of attempted rape by Mrs. Potiphar, Joseph was thrown into prison. While in prison he remained faithful to God and prospered. Having faithfully interpreted Pharaoh's dreams of seven years of plenty to be followed by seven years of famine, Joseph was promoted to the position of prime minister, responsible for the management of the whole economy and answerable only to Pharaoh.

That Joseph was an effective leader and manager is without doubt. Here is a man who went from prison to palace, from rags to riches, without abusing power or misusing office. He successfully managed both prosperity and poverty for the good of the people. Ten major qualifications stand out in the life and work of Joseph as a leader. These are:

- Humility (Gen. 41:16).
- Discernment (41:33, 39).
- Wisdom (41:33, 39).
- The spirit of God or fear of God (41:38).
- Diligence (41:45, 46). He went over all the land of Egypt.
- Team spirit (41:34).
- Management skill (41:47–50, 56, 57). As a competent planner, he stored grains during the time of plenty, sold them during famine (rather than giving them away free), and even planned the size of his own family (two children).
- Financial integrity (47:1–12). He brought all money collected into Pharaoh's palace, rather than sending it to his own Swiss bank account.
- Transparency (47:1–12). He walked in the light regarding the settlement of his extended family in Egypt.
- A forgiving spirit (50:15–21). He never took revenge on his brothers, who sold him into slavery, even when he had the power to do so.

In the amazing life of Joseph one sees a picture of what the Church can and should offer the governments and international development institutions like the World Bank as they work in partnership to alleviate poverty and resolve Africa's enigma. His story reminds us of men like William Wilberforce, Lord Shaftesbury, and Martin Luther King Jr., who fought for justice, human dignity, and equitable distribution of national wealth in their times. The Church produced such men and women before and it can do so again.

Prospects for the Twenty-First Century

The Bible says: "Righteousness exalts a nation . . ." (Proverbs 14:34). It also says: "Blessed is the nation whose God is the Lord" (Psalm 33:12).

I am convinced that Western civilization, open systems of government, free economies, a number of scientific inventions, and global exploration were inspired and greatly influenced by a knowledge of the Bible and the right application of its principles. I used to think that Christians have to be a majority and control political power before they can influence their nations positively. But sociologists have convinced me this is an error. They say that it takes only 3 to 5 percent of the people in any society to change it. That is, 3 to 5 percent with creative thinking, vision, and influence, who are strategically positioned—like Joseph, Daniel, and Esther, for example—are enough to bring about change.

If this is so, and given that Africa is said to have more than 50 percent of its population confessing allegiance to Christ as Lord, then there is hope for Africa in the twenty-first century. However, a large number by itself is not enough. For the Church to make a difference and become a radical agent of socioeconomic, cultural, and political transformation, it must first and foremost put its own house in order.

In closing let me tell the story of what happened in the United Kingdom during the eighteenth century. At the beginning of that century, the country was at its lowest ebb. There was gross immorality in the land. Among the kings and nobles, corruption, dishonesty, and mismanagement in public office were the order of the day. Bribery was practiced in broad daylight by all classes of people. Factories were few and primitive. The nation itself was small and weak, and many of its people were drunkards. But by the beginning of the nineteenth century, this situation had changed dramatically. The British nation became a great power that stood against Napoleon as he brought the whole European continent under his control. By the same period it had gained influence or control in South Africa, Canada, Australia, Egypt, and China. Within three generations the United Kingdom had become the dominant world power.

How did it happen? According to theologian and historian J. C. Ryle, when the United Kingdom was at its lowest, God sent a handful of anointed preachers including George Whitefield and the Wesley brothers, John and Charles. These prophetic preachers drew large crowds all over the country. Under their powerful preaching, God poured out fires of revival, lives were changed, and a new nation was born.

As the Church in Africa cleanses its house and conducts its life and witness in Christ's way, as it reaches out to society in compassion and constructively partners with other institutions of goodwill, the Lord of the nations will bring to life a new Africa where truth, justice, and peace will reign and poverty will be alleviated. So may it be in the name of the Father, the Son, and the Holy Spirit. Amen.

Bibliography

Achebe, C. 1983. *The Trouble with Nigeria*. Enugu, Nigeria: Fourth Dimension Publishers.

Hancock, G. 1991. *Lords of Poverty: The Power, Corruption, and Prestige of the International Aid Business*. London: Mandarin Press.

Kinoti, G. 1994. *Hope for Africa and What the Christian Can Do*. Nairobi: AISRED.

Museveni, Y. 1992. *What Is Africa's Problem?* Kampala: NRM Publications. Reprint, Minneapolis: University of Minnesota Press, 2000.

5

Voices of the Poor

Deepa Narayan

Poverty is like heat: you cannot see it; you can only feel it. To know poverty you have to go through it. —A poor man, Adaboya, Ghana

We eat when we have, we sleep when we don't. —A 30-year-old married man in Kebele 10, Addis Ababa, Ethiopia

It is neither leprosy nor poverty which kills the leper; it is loneliness. —Ghanaian proverb

Voices of the Poor was a large-scale study done to inform the *World Development Report 2000–2001 on Poverty and Development.* It seemed obvious that a policy document on poverty at the brink of the twenty-first century had to be informed by those who know the most about poverty— poor people themselves, the true poverty experts—so it could benefit from their voices, their experiences, and their recommendations.

There were two parts to the study. The first, *Can Anyone Hear Us?,* was a systematic analysis of more than 80 World Bank participatory poverty assessments, analyzing the statements of 40,000 people in 50 countries (Narayan and others 2000a). The second part, *Crying Out for Change,* is a new 23-country study completed last year, gathering the comments of 20,000 poor men and women (Narayan and others 2000b). So my analysis will draw on the voices of more than 60,000 poor women and men.

It is clear that the world looks quite different when viewed through the eyes of poor people. For me, personally, it has been a sobering experience.

An overriding theme is the powerlessness of poor people. Given the centrality of power relations, what has emerged from the studies is that while poverty is specific to locations, and indeed to social groups, there is a commonality of the human experience of poverty that cuts across countries, from Nigeria to Egypt, from Malawi to Senegal.

If there is one message that I would strongly convey to you, it is the dependency of the poor on the rich. This dependency leads poor men and women to conclude that despite their hard work "if you are poor you will always be poor" and "if you drink tea you will always drink tea." A discussion group participant in Kajima, Ethiopia asked: "Look at the fingers of my hand, are they equal?" The powerlessness of poor people always means that any progress or any initiatives that they take can always be taken over by the elite.

The richness of location-specific details are in the country reports. I will focus here on the persistent patterns of findings that emerged again and again.

Well-Being Is Holistic

A better life for me is to be healthy, peaceful, with love and without hunger. Love is more than anything, money has no value in the absence of love. —A 26-year-old woman, Kajima, Ethiopia

Poor people's definitions of well-being are holistic. That is, the good life is seen as multidimensional, with both material and psychological dimensions. It includes a dependable livelihood, peace of mind, good health, and belonging to a community. It encompasses safety; freedom of choice and action; food; and care of family and spirit. It is life with dignity.

Lack of work worries me. My children are hungry and I tell them the rice is cooking, until they fall asleep from hunger. —An older man, Bedsa, Egypt

Poor people are held down by multiple disadvantages: material and social deprivation, physical insecurity, and powerlessness. As one poor person in Ethiopia commented, poverty is "being tied like bundles of straw from which it is difficult to escape." Poor people talked about the psychological experience of poverty—the shame, humiliation, pain, depression, and helplessness of their condition.

Poverty is seen as an interlocking experience. Doing something often makes no difference as other things will pull you under. In Ghana it was said that if you are poor "you know what is good but you cannot do good."

The powerlessness of poor men and women comes through again and again:

When one is poor, she has no say in public, she feels inferior, she has no food, so there is famine in the house, no clothing, no progress in the family. —A discussion group of poor women, South Africa

The only way through poverty is through death. —A discussion group participant, Phweketere, Malawi

The rich are those who set the prices; the poor are those who are forced to sell their produce at the prices set by the rich. — A Tanzanian

If you don't have money today, your disease will lead you to your grave. —A Ghanaian

Also of striking importance is that while poor people are in the informal, insecure part of society, most development assistance focuses on the formal system.

Insecurity Has Increased

We have no friend but the ground. —A discussion group of older men, Mbamoi, Nigeria

Poor people said they are unable to take advantage of new economic opportunities because they lack connections, information, assets, credit, skills, and contacts. The importance of connections has inspired a new vocabulary in many languages.

In Egypt, poor people said opportunities are out of their reach. In Ethiopia, poor men and women said free-market policies have paved the way for the rich to increase their wealth. In Zambia, lack of opportunity was linked to agricultural variability; in Somalia it was attributed to the war. In Eastern Europe and Central Asia privatization was called "bribatization." In Latin America lack of opportunities was perceived to be linked to macroeconomic reform. In South Asia, poor people felt that they had more opportunities than in the past because of increased factory work, microcredit, and home-based piecework. In India, people from the lower castes perceived more opportunities because of greater social empowerment through the lower-caste movement.

Even in areas where poverty has decreased, poor people reported increased levels of insecurity and unpredictability in their lives. There were many reasons for this: among the most prominent were insecure livelihoods, breakdown of traditional social solidarity, lack of affordable health care, violence, theft, corruption, civil conflict, increasing lawlessness, and extortion rather than protection by the police. Poor people are increasingly in the informal sector, with little social or income protection.

The thread that runs through poor people's descriptions and definitions of security and insecurity is fear and anxiety: about losing a job, about not getting paid, about needing to migrate, about floods, about shelter, about falling ill, and about burial in case of death.

In the absence of law and order there is no well-being. —A Somali

Security is peace of mind and the possibility to sleep relaxed. —A woman from El-Gawaber, Egypt

The rich have protection—the poor not. —A Malawian

In one rural community in Ethiopia, life was so precarious that every young and able-bodied male had to migrate to the towns to join the army and fight in the war, just to avoid hunger.

In South Africa and Uganda, women spoke about sexual assault when reporting crimes to the police. Rural electrification emerged as a priority for women because of the link between lighting and improved security.

Gender Inequity and Domestic Violence

With increasing economic hardship and a decline in income-earning opportunities for poor men, poor women around the world report swallowing their pride and doing whatever it takes to put food on the family table. This loss of the traditional male "breadwinner" role and female "caretaker" role is traumatic for the family; it is linked to alcoholism, violence against women, and family breakdown.

When my husband died, my in-laws told me to get out. So I came to town and slept on the pavement. —A middle-aged woman, Kenya

Whether a woman wants to or not, the man controls the money and if she refuses she is in danger of being retrenched [sent away from home]. —A woman in Kabarole, Uganda

Women are beaten in the house for many reasons that may include failure to prepare lunch or dinner for the husband. She is also beaten if the husband comes home drunk or if he simply feels like it. —An Ethiopian

Men rape within marriage, but no one talks about it. —A Ugandan

Despite the fact that women are earning incomes (primarily in the informal sector), violence against women remains widespread. Physical abuse and torture is on the decline in some areas because of NGO support, work by churches, and work by women's groups in awareness raising and economic support. At the same time, social norms are starting to change, and in some places women are walking out of abusive relationships.

Gender relations are in troubled transition, at both the household and the community level. Men talked about alcohol, depression, and shame; you can no longer beat the women because they earn the money. Women talked about abuse and sometimes said that with increasing financial independence comes new confidence to take a stand. We should remind ourselves that all poverty reduction strategies affect not only community relations, but also family relations and hence gender relations.

State Institutions: Ineffective and Corrupt

We saw a food relief lorry arrive and the chief told us two weeks later that one and a half bags had been received for distribution in 166 households. — From a discussion group of poor men and women, Kwale, Kenya

The state is absent [from our lives]. —A person from Madagascar

The road was asphalted over five times on paper only. —A participant in a discussion group of poor youths, Bedsa, Egypt

We keep hearing of money that was allocated to projects and nothing happens on the ground. —A discussion group of poor men and women, South Africa

Poor people consider the role of government very important, but rather ineffective and in some cases harmful.

Poor men and women do value basic infrastructure. In fact, lack of water, roads, and so forth emerges as a definition of poverty. There have been some improvements; where available, education, health facilities, and clean water are all valued.

If we had assistance in the areas of water and electricity, it would have created a great deal of opportunity for us to improve our lives. —A group of poor men, Ethiopia

Where there is a road, development follows. —An old man, Cameroon

In evaluating institutions, poor people are very clear in the criteria they use. They can conduct sophisticated evaluations and give simple, concrete definitions of the criteria. Effectiveness, for example, was defined as "saying you are going to do something and get it done in the time." They also emphasized behavioral criteria—being friendly, respectful, willing to listen, courteous, trustworthy, professional, caring, truthful, uniting, helpful; not cheating, not lying, not corrupt or corrupting, not showing favoritism, not cruel.

Corruption in particular emerges as a core poverty issue. Problems of corruption at the local level, sometimes called petty corruption, are widespread. Such problems may seem small, but from the perspective of those with limited resources, petty corruption plays a significant role in poverty. People reported hundreds of incidents of corruption as they attempted to seek health care, educate their children, claim social assistance, get paid, obtain justice, seek police protection, and trade in the marketplace.

In addition, poor people are often subject to rudeness, insults, harassment, and sometimes assault. The behavior of service providers was mentioned again and again as an important problem.

Similarly, politicians were rated poorly everywhere:

Why should a person ask for taverns or condoms in Parliament? He should have been coming here and asking us our needs. —Participant, discussion group of men and women, Mbwadzulu, Malawi

Police were the least loved institution of all. They were singled out as impoverishing rather than helping or protecting poor people.

There were inspiring exceptions everywhere, even among local politicians, police, and government officials. There was the chief in Malawi who was available day and night; the local assembly representative in Ghana who was responsive even in the middle of the night; the sheik in Egypt who gave alms; Sister J. in Ethiopia who always helped out.

Faith-Based and Nongovernmental Organizations

Churches and mosques, as well as sacred trees, rivers, and mountains, were mentioned time and again as important and valued by poor men and women.

The church assists in times of illness and funerals. —From a discussion group of poor men and women, Khwalala, Malawi

The mosque is ours. —A Nigerian

There were, however, four problems that poor men and women articulated with regard to churches and other faith-based organizations:

- They sow seeds of disunity by reaching out only to "their flock."
- There is a lack of involvement of poor men and especially poor women in decisionmaking.
- There are some instances of corruption.
- Religious institutions are seen as survival-oriented rather than transformative institutions.

Nongovernmental organizations, where they are present, play an important role and are often highly appreciated, but poor people would like NGOs to be accountable to them. Also, these organizations are not as widely present as is frequently believed.

Resilience and Resourcefulness

These findings prompt us to ask: How, then, do poor people survive?

Whenever there is a funeral, we work together . . . women draw water, collect firewood and collect maize flour . . . while men dig graves and then bury the dead. —A discussion group from Mbwadzulu Village, Malawi

Poor people depend primarily on their own indigenous institutions and networks. Still, they recognize that there are limits to "how much one hungry man can help another." Poor women and men want to develop their own organizations so that they can effectively negotiate fair deals with government officials, traders, and NGOs. They want direct assistance, with local ownership of funds through community-driven programs. They want community groups that have control and authority over decisions.

Poor people view government as very important, and they want to work in partnership with their governments. But they are fed up with being asked to participate in projects that don't produce any benefits. In Egypt, people said they are tired of self-help initiatives; in Kenya there is too much Harambee; and in Vietnam people said, "The policy of the party is that people know, people discuss, and people do, but here they only do the last part, which is people do."

Poor men and women have shown amazing resilience, capacity for suffering, and resourcefulness against the odds. A young widow in India expressed perhaps a typical view when she said, "Even at times of crisis, I held my nerves and did not give in to my circumstances. My God has always stood with me."

These poor people have collectively challenged all of us—governments, NGOs, bilaterals—to be evaluated against criteria they deem important. Poor people want all institutions that seek to help them to be judged by whether they are "effective, trustworthy, uniting, dependable, respectful, listening, courteous, truthful, friendly, listening, not lying, not corrupt, and not corrupting."

The Main Challenge: Reaching Poor Communities

Two sets of issues emerge from this study: the systemic and the sectoral. Systemic issues:

- How to bring the voices of poor men and women to governance at the local, national, and global levels?
- How to invest in community-driven development, supporting community participation, control, and authority?
- How to invest in organizations of the poor?
- How to provide access to justice through legal aid?
- How to secure long-term financing for poor people's organizations?

  Sectoral issues and priorities:

- Given that most poor men and women work in the informal sector, how do we provide skills training, social protection, and more secure livelihoods?
- How can we bring health protection to the poor, given that the body is often a poor person's main asset?
- How can we provide access to clean water and basic infrastructure?

Within this context, what role is there for the Church? Given the scale of poverty and the poverty of governance in Africa, the churches are in a unique position to catalyze positive social change.

The Church can use its moral authority and ethical standards to influence changes in attitudes about how we should tackle the problems of poverty and injustice, gender inequity, and corruption. In order to do this, the churches must become agents of transformation, using their influence to demand better governance and public accountability. Churches can also work to help poor people obtain justice by providing legal aid. However, these efforts should not be at the cost of the role that churches have played in helping poor men and women ensure their survival.

With regard to gender inequity, this is perhaps one area where the Church is uniquely placed over other institutions, such as governments and the World Bank, to change the norms and standards by which we all live. Given the scale of domestic violence and abuse, for example, it is a moral imperative that we all act to wipe out this scourge.

Finally, we must look beyond the family and the community level to the national and the global. The Churches have taken a leading role in advocating debt relief. As we explore these issues, it is important to create mechanisms to ensure that the monies released by canceling debt go to fighting poverty and attacking the injustices that poor men and women face every day.

Bibliography

Narayan, Deepa, with Raj Patel, Kai Schafft, Anne Rademacher, and Sarah Koch-Schulte. 2000a. *Can Anyone Hear Us? Voices of the Poor.* New York: Oxford University Press.

Narayan, Deepa, Robert Chambers, Meera K. Shah, and Patti Petesch. 2000b. *Crying Out for Change: Voices of the Poor.* New York: Oxford University Press.

Part 3

Poverty and the World Bank

6

Serving the Poor in Africa

Callisto Madavo

This workshop grew from a mustard seed: a letter from His Grace the Archbishop of Canterbury to the President of the World Bank, James Wolfensohn, in May 1999 inviting us to participate in a training course for new bishops in Ibadan, Nigeria.

We nominated our External Affairs Manager to talk about Africa and the World Bank there, but a last-minute emergency prevented him from leaving Washington. When we expressed our regrets to the Bishop of Ibadan, he put us in touch with the Network for Anglicans in Mission and Evangelism (NAME), based in Oxford, and together we developed the idea of a more ambitious gathering.

This gathering also fits very well into a series of exchanges that the World Bank has been having in the last few years with faith communities around the world. This includes Mr. Wolfensohn's participation in the Lambeth Conference of Anglican Bishops in 1998 and two interfaith dialogues that our President has hosted since then.

Common Objectives

What are our interests in such a dialogue with the Church?

First and foremost, we have concern for the well-being of Africa and Africans in common. How to improve that well-being without imposing too great a burden on Africa's natural resources and environment is at the center of the development challenge.

At the World Bank, we serve mainly the material side of that well-being. The Bank's mission is to fight poverty. By tackling poverty, we mean not just raising income but also promoting empowerment, security, and opportunity. At the moment, half of Africa—some 300 million people—lives on less than a dollar a day. This is the result of both low levels of income and high levels of inequality.

We hope that if we organize ourselves properly, if we listen to the people we are trying to help, if we treat people as subjects rather than objects of development, if we consider not just the economic and the social aspects but also the cultural and, yes, even the spiritual aspects of human aspirations, then we can be a valuable instrument in building a new future for Africa.

We are a nonconfessional institution. But that does not mean that our managers and staff perform their duties cold-bloodedly. On the contrary, almost to the last man and woman among them, they have been attracted to working at the World Bank by what they see as the moral and compelling importance of improving the lives of their brothers and sisters on the planet. They want to share their knowledge and experience, plowing back into the international community the advantages they have been given. I'm proud to note that 60 percent of the people in the World Bank serving Africa are Africans. Forty percent of the Bank's Africa Region staff live and work on the continent.

We are listening more and more, to our partners and to the poor themselves. I am very pleased to be able to say that today many of our most important partners come from churches and other faith-based groups. Indeed, we have prepared for this very special year of Jubilee by working with church leaders, particularly from Africa, on building an international plan to relieve the debt of the world's poorest countries. We are striving for a plan worthy of a millennium celebration, one that places poverty at the forefront of the international agenda.

Despite the scale of the challenge we face here in Africa and in other parts of the developing world, we are optimistic. Not naively so, but optimistic nonetheless because we know that development works, and we need look no further than here in Africa for proof.

If we listen to Africans and learn the lessons of their success, this new century can be Africa's. We believe that human beings can change the world if they put their minds to it.

However, we cannot take the material for granted—even if we are urged by Christ to rise above it. The welfare of the world begins with the security and peace of every household. As Nelson Mandela has pointed out, national issues like democracy mean very little if we have trouble putting food on the table.

Priorities

We are here to listen and react to your views, so I do not want to say much more. But, in our view, here are some of the major challenges we face in Africa.

A priority is *better governance*—that is, peace and security, and more open and honest government. This implies decentralizing economic and political power, moving beyond "participation" to community-driven development, and treating people as subjects rather than objects of development.

Another priority is *releasing and using the capacities* already latent in society: opening more space for private and community initiative, allowing Africans to share their knowledge and experience more successfully, getting children back to school and keeping them healthy and challenged while there, and harnessing the Internet and distance-learning methods to serve Africa's needs.

Fighting HIV/AIDS must also be part of our fight against poverty. There is nothing in African tradition that condemns us to silence and fatalism about this. As Africans, we must stop it before it deprives us of our wealth—not just the material progress that some Africans are beginning to experience at last, but also the social and cultural fabric that makes our continent strong.

How We Can Work Together

Is our common concern for the well-being of the human race and our commitment to serving others enough to bind the World Bank and the Christian Church together in our daily work, and not just in our general sympathies?

I believe the answer is a resounding "yes."

To begin with, we have important knowledge to share with each other.

The World Bank and other development agencies such as the United Nations Development Programme (UNDP) have a history of dealing with poverty that stretches back a very long time. This will surprise some of you who associate the World Bank with the painful effects of "structural adjustment" rather than with helping the poor directly.

We lost valuable time—both in Africa and at the World Bank—in fighting poverty from the late 1970s through the early 1990s because the necessary building blocks were missing: strong economic growth and policies explicitly aimed at helping the most vulnerable in society.

But we never lost sight of our goal and we learned a great deal in those years, in Africa and elsewhere, about policies that work, programs and institutions that are crucial, and the design of social "safety nets." Furthermore, for at least 10 years now, protecting the level and improving the quality of public spending on basic health and education has been *part of* the process of economic and social reform.

In understanding public policy debates and the less obvious benefits of certain reforms, we can provide the Church with valuable and objective information that you can use to support—or challenge and refine—such changes.

For your part, you have access to the poor in ways that international development institutions and even many government agencies can never have. You represent the poor and can speak for them truthfully and forcefully. You can give them the courage to speak for themselves. That representative function is crucial even in societies that have highly developed systems of political expression.

We cannot restrict ourselves to conventional channels of public consultation when half of all Africans do not have the absolute minimum for a decent life, and need opportunities and services *now*. Yet, poverty programs that do not reflect the specific circumstances of far-flung communities will be mere pieces of paper. Those local circumstances must be explained to public officials and championed by people like yourselves who are rooted permanently in those communities.

You can also be an important sounding board on whether governments and their partners (such as the World Bank and UNDP) are dealing with the right issues—or even the right people—in analyzing and solving problems. The churches can keep governments and international agencies honest in a way that electorates cannot. We need you to be a mirror into which we can look, now and then, to test our understanding and progress. A mirror that speaks back, without fear or flattery.

And, finally, in addition to the spiritual guidance and moral comfort that you offer to your congregations, you are a source of schooling, health, and other services that the poor would lack if they depended entirely on publicly funded programs.

I have come to this subject last as I know that many of you rightly fear having the Church pigeonholed as just another NGO with which the international institutions would like to work—delivering services, but not really engaged in the broader challenge of ensuring social progress on a very broad front.

We want to work with you, directly or through governments, to improve the impact and efficiency of your efforts at the community level. But we would want to work with you *even if you were not providing such essential services to the poor.*

Promoting a Comprehensive Approach to Development

That is because one of the constraints to rapid progress in Africa is the "closed circle" in which much of public policy and planning is conducted. Even so-called participatory approaches are seldom wide-reaching enough. We need to break the mold of past approaches if we are to bring the benefits of economic growth to the front door of all Africans.

That is why we want to move toward community-*driven*, not just community-based, programs of investment where we will work with governments to force down responsibility, accountability, and as many resources as possible to the lowest level of society—ideally the village— so that programs will meet the needs people have defined for themselves and so that resources are used quickly and conscientiously.

It is also why our President, Mr. Wolfensohn, has been promoting a *comprehensive approach to development* that treats the human and social side of national progress—governance, justice, school enrollments, access to clean water, roads, the quality of the natural environment, and protecting a country's cultural heritage—with the same importance as the economic and financial aspects of development.

Here is where government plays a central role for all of us. If development is to be guided from the community level and made balanced and comprehensive at the national level, there is a need to translate local needs into countrywide priorities, assess who can do what and where, reallocate resources wisely, and ensure that those resources are used for the benefit of every single person in Africa.

That challenge sounds monumental. But it doesn't need to be if we draw on the wisdom, efforts, and goodwill of everyone in the community and acknowledge that no one can do any of this alone. It can only be done through national solidarity and a sharing of views and advantages—led by governments but involving the private sector, NGOs, the churches, trade unions, the media, and, of course, the bilateral aid donors and international institutions. The Church has a central role to play in such a partnership and in keeping it focused on the needs and capacities of the poor.

Conclusion

Let me end by saying that we want to work side by side with you in the vineyard. And this week is about making certain that we produce the same wine.

We can tell you how we are working to fight poverty. And I yearn, like most of you, for a partnership in fighting poverty that is easy and relaxed.

That is because our common cause—even though your *ultimate* cause extends well beyond our well-being in this world—is compelling and immense. And it needs as many laborers in the vineyard as possible.

Christ was fond of parables and proverbs, and we know that our own African heritage is rich in sayings that speak volumes. One of my favorites is from Côte d'Ivoire: "It takes several fingers to pick up a single grain of rice."

We have much work to do together to serve the poor in Africa. With that in mind, may God bless our conversations this week.

7

The World Bank and Africa

Robert Calderisi

A few years ago our president, Mr. Wolfensohn, visited a squatter settlement outside the Brazilian city of São Paulo where the World Bank had helped finance a water and sanitation project. While the vice governor of the state showed him around, a large group of women followed them at a short distance and waved papers in the air rather proudly. "Do you know why they are so happy?" the vice governor asked. "Because they now have running water and no longer have to drag it in buckets on their shoulders up these steep hills, I presume," said Mr. Wolfensohn. "Yes, that's true," the vice governor replied, "but that's not the reason they're showing you those papers." "Is it because they are proud to have contributed to some of the costs of the project?" "Yes," the vice governor said, "that's true, too. But what they are waving at you are their first bills for water service. It is the first time they have seen their names and addresses on an official document and the first time they feel *included* in government programs they have only heard about in the past on the radio."

Based on this and other experiences, our president has stressed how important it is that development include everyone. He has championed many ideas and causes in his first five years at the Bank, but I believe that this notion of *inclusiveness* is one of the most powerful.

I had my own experience of this a couple of months before I left Côte d'Ivoire, where I had been chief of the World Bank's Regional Mission for Western Africa in the early 1990s. A couple of young friends approached me for a small loan to start a banana project in their home village. They had jobs in Abidjan—one was a schoolteacher and the other was an information programmer—but they wanted to help about a hundred other young people create income for themselves on land that had been given to them by their parents. All they needed to get started was US$2,000 to buy banana cuttings.

I submitted this proposal to our small grants committee but they turned it down, as the purpose of our fund was to help promote efforts related to the environment, women's issues, and human rights rather than directly productive activities. I could have insisted on an exception, but that did not seem appropriate, especially as these were friends of mine, so I gave them the money from my own pocket.

A few months later, I was back in Abidjan on a visit and asked the schoolteacher, Sam, how the project was going. "Quite well, now," he said, "but I had to overcome a number of hurdles. First, I was arrested by the *sous-préfet* [the district governor], who had been told by members of the ruling party that we were agitating for the opposition rather than engaged in a real development activity. I was only released after 24 hours when I informed them that the former World Bank representative had contributed his personal funds to the project and surely you would not have done that if this was just politics. Then, still suspicious, the government sent the Minister of Youth and Sports to investigate, as he was from the region. He was so impressed by what we were doing that he decorated us with a medal in front of the whole village and promised to give us US$20,000 from one of the social funds set up after the January 1994 CFA devaluation."

I did not want to throw cold water on his excitement. Imagine how dizzy he felt—going from being in jail to being a decorated local hero in the space of a week! But, privately, I worried that the government was now doing what it had accused the young people of doing: making political capital of a personal initiative. I was also concerned that they would suddenly have more money than they could use prudently and fruitfully.

Six months later, I was back again and the news was even better. From 100 participants the cooperative had grown to more than 400. The volume and quality of production was good, thanks to technical assistance from the national agricultural extension service (ANADER), which had been streamlined with the help of the World Bank. And even the marketing was proving easier than they had imagined. People were coming by truck, or bicycle, or on foot to buy the bananas on site and transport them as far away as the capital.

"So the government's money came in handy," I said. Sam had a twinkle in his eye. "They never gave us a penny. After the 1995 elections, they forgot about us entirely," he replied. "But how did you finance all of this?" I continued. "With your $2,000 and the money we raised selling banana cuttings to new members," Sam explained.

"I'm astonished," I said. "You shouldn't be," Sam countered. "You were always telling us in your speeches that money was not the major obstacle to progress in Africa."

Now he was conveniently forgetting that he had received the seed capital free of charge, but I see this as a parable of how individual initiative and determination, good organization, well-targeted aid, and improved public services (in this case, the extension service) can combine to turn a small investment into one that makes a major difference for people. It is also an example of why World Bank staff believe so wholeheartedly in development and get a thrill out of the work they do even in the face of daunting challenges.

What Is the World Bank?

I've started with some down-to-earth stories about people rather than startling statistics or provocative statements about globalization and poverty because—occasional appearances to the contrary—giving people a step up in the world is what the World Bank is about.

To begin with, we are not a "bank" in the normal sense but a financial cooperative. We are the largest foreign aid agency in the world but we are owned by most of the world's governments and—a very important distinction—we borrow most of our money. We consist of several institutions, among them the International Bank for Reconstruction and Development (IBRD), the International Development Association (IDA), and the International Finance Corporation (IFC). And we are a source of global knowledge, not just money.

In Africa, we now draw mostly on the resources of IDA. This is the part of the Bank Group that is financed from the national budgets of about 30 countries, most of them rich, but some (like Argentina, the Republic of Korea, and South Africa) still developing. We lend up to US$3 billion to Africa on highly generous terms—interest-free, over 40 years, including 10 years' grace. By the time these funds are repaid, because of the declining value of money, 80 percent of these transfers will have been in the form of grants. Since 1985, we have been using IDA funds deliberately to help contain, rather than add to, Africa's growing debt burden.

Bank staff make up the largest group of professionals serving Africa's development. We have more than 1,400 people in the Africa Region of the World Bank, making it also the largest organizational unit in the institution. Sixty percent of Africa Region staff (850 people) are African, and 40 percent (560 people) live and work on the continent in our 32 country offices.

Sometimes we are asked why we do not give our money directly to the poor rather than to governments. Even if it were practical to do this, it would not be effective: as 300 million Africans subsist on less than US$1 a day, our US$3 billion would meet the direct needs of the poor for only 10 days of the year. So, instead, we need to invest this money in policies, projects, programs, and public debates that will help the poor improve their own lives.

Our greatest ambition is to become *less* significant in Africa—to help strengthen its economic and social institutions to such an extent that official aid will no longer be very important. We want to be a tool of Africa rather than a taskmaster (as some perceive us to be). And we are not just at the service of governments. Although our mandate is to work mainly through the public sector, our goal is to help communities and individuals obtain the knowledge and other resources they need for their own purposes.

Structural Adjustment

Now, I want to do something that, as a layman, I probably shouldn't do among clerics, that is, exorcise a couple of demons that may be upsetting you. One of them is structural adjustment. The other is debt.

First of all, "adjustment" never really happened in Africa during the 1980s, when it was feared and resented the most. Like Christianity for G. K. Chesterton, it never really failed. It simply wasn't tried. Most governments resisted the hard decisions or implemented them halfheartedly. As a result, economic recovery in Africa took a very long time and its benefits are still not widely felt.

The major adjustment of the period had nothing to do with the World Bank or the International Monetary Fund. Between 1970 and 1990, Africa lost half of its share of world markets *to other developing countries* that were able to produce and deliver the same goods more efficiently. This represented a loss of income of about $70 billion per year—enough to pay off all of Africa's official debt (US$210 billion) in just three years.

Managing shrinking public revenues in a way that would restore growth and protect basic services was the real challenge of "adjustment." This was bound to be painful. But the pain came from the massive hemorrhaging, not the blood transfusion.

The challenge for African policymakers and outside institutions was how to stop this massive loss of income and create new sources of growth and wealth. In our view at the time, even though we never expressed it clearly and continuously enough, the main solution was to try to shift economic power back to the rural areas. This meant increasing prices for farmers and reducing all the obstacles to efficient and profitable agriculture (such as overvalued exchange rates, ineffective marketing boards, export taxes, and poor rural services and roads). For us, economic reform was about more than reducing budget deficits and controlling inflation—although these, too, were important for farmers and poor people.

Adjustment was also about how resources were *spent*. In Côte d'Ivoire, for example, in the early 1990s, no one could complain that too little was being spent on health and education. In fact, 50 percent of the national budget was being invested in those two sectors. But the results for most of the population were almost imperceptible. Other countries like Zimbabwe, Sri Lanka, and Indonesia, with lower per capita incomes, had higher school enrollment and literacy rates and more clinics and schools.

These facts dragged us into internal debates that were noisy, nasty— and indispensable. With national revenues dropping sharply right across the continent and only US$3 billion to help repair the loss of US$70 billion of income per year, how could the Bank help governments choose the least painful courses of action? That was the challenge and the controversy of those years.

Often, the debate centered on the size of the public service and the salary bill. This was not because the World Bank had something against government. We were all public servants and our institution is a creation of governments. It was a product of a fast-shrinking national pie. Again, in Côte d'Ivoire, 90 percent of the budget was absorbed by government salaries, leaving almost nothing for basic materials like chalk and schoolbooks, medicines and bandages, for key public services. In a country of 12 million people, was it really right for national resources to be centered on the needs of 100,000 government employees? Even if we admitted that each of these employees supported up to 20 people, or 2 million people altogether, how could the country look after the needs of the other 10 million citizens? No one had easy answers. But it was right that Africa and its friends should consider such questions head-on.

Economic reform also had important *benefits* for society, but these were necessarily lost in the overwhelming effects of the loss of income that governments and the World Bank were trying to stem. In Côte d'Ivoire, we made an issue of the fact that Ivorian cocoa and coffee farmers had to buy their jute bags from a domestic monopoly rather than import them—as their neighbors in Ghana did—directly from Bangladesh. This practice protected 400 jobs in Abidjan but cost 400,000 farming families US$15 million a year. We also encouraged drying of these crops in the villages rather than at the processing factories in the towns. This simple change added a considerable amount to rural income. In the health sector, we promoted the use of generic medicines rather than expensive brand-name pharmaceuticals—to the great chagrin of local pharmacists—and suggested selling them in the amounts required rather than in fixed quantities of 12, 24, or 36 pills. This made an important difference to people with small incomes. This was the side of reform that rarely was heard about, but that was close to the heart of our efforts.

Debt

Now let me offer you six heretical statements on debt:

First, the World Bank wants *more*, not less, debt relief, if it can be paid for. We were not dragged into the process. In fact, our President, Mr. Wolfensohn, led the way toward a more comprehensive approach to debt reduction back in 1995–96.

Second, Jubilee 2000 has been wonderfully positive news for the Bank, not just for Africa, as it has built up political momentum for debt relief in creditor countries. It is also a striking expression of the commitment of hundreds of thousands of people in rich countries who have not "given up" on Africa.

Third, debt in itself should not be anathema. Sound borrowing is an important part of development.

Fourth, it is not clear that countries in Africa borrowed less wisely than those in other regions of the world.

Fifth, the world has been forgiving Africa's debts for 25 years. There is nothing new about this. What *is* new is the sheer scale of present efforts and the inclusion of multilateral debt.

Sixth, debt is a symptom rather than cause of Africa's slow development.

However, because Africa lost so much income in the 1970s and 1980s, debt is indeed a major problem, and the world community is doing something about it. Current plans involve debt relief for the 40 poorest countries in the world, 33 of which are in Africa. If fully funded, this relief will come to between US$50 billion and US$55 billion in the next few years—nearly as much as the World Bank has lent to Africa in the last 50 years. This may not be enough for some observers, but it is a great deal more than anyone could have predicted a relatively short while ago.

The Bank and the Christian Churches

A major reason for the confusion and fear about the World Bank's role in Africa is that we were not very effective in the 1980s in explaining the challenges we faced on the continent and the way in which we were trying to serve its people. But for the last 10 years we have been opening up to society at large, trying not to be hampered by our respect for due political processes and the primary responsibility of governments to inform their citizens of important choices in public policy. But where governments were not doing this, or the press was ill-equipped to contribute to a public debate, we had no choice but to jump-start the discussion. This could sometimes be amusing.

In 1992, I spent a weekend in a village in central Côte d'Ivoire. When I arrived on Friday evening, the town crier announced to everyone that the World Bank's Resident Representative was like the pangolin (a cross between an anteater and an armadillo) that lives in a deep hole in the forest floor. "When the pangolin comes to the surface, everyone gathers around to admire him." This was a polite way of saying: "Where have you been all this time!?"

The Bank has been dragging itself out of its hole for many years, meeting with African business groups, universities, trade unions, nongovernmental organizations, and the media. With faith communities, we have begun to work only in the last few years, and in a sense it is rather odd that this should be so. We have had so much in common, without that being clear until now. The Church is important in Africa, so it is important for the World Bank as well. You are close to the poor. You are rooted in local communities. You are normally truthful and neutral, and detached from partisan politics. And you are able to serve the material—not just the spiritual—needs of the poor directly. You can challenge governments and international institutions about their policies and actions and provide first-hand information on the needs and views of local communities.

There are a number of ways in which we can work together more closely. The World Bank has its strengths, but also its weaknesses. Even with the best of efforts, we cannot be close to the poor. Even with governments, our primary partners, our *real* influence is very limited. That is as it should be. Forty years of development experience has shown that the world—and the World Bank—cannot bribe governments into doing the right things. We must support countries that are already on the right track, not just with money but also with our advice and by setting an example. We want to spread the pollen of good ideas and practices rather than be a battering ram.

The Church can work with African governments and the World Bank to share knowledge, challenge policies or the way they are implemented, and channel funds to the poor (where faith communities have the capacity and experience to do so).

Working together will be a surer way of reaching, and helping, the poor. It will also be one way of ensuring that economic growth in Africa will be accompanied by more direct access for the poor to the skills, knowledge, health, credit, land, and other assets that they need to benefit from national progress and make it even stronger.

There will be great challenges, but also great satisfaction and undoubtedly some surprise that it took us so long to become partners!

Part 4

Reducing Conflict and Corruption

8

Conflict Prevention and Post-Conflict Reconstruction

Bernard Ntahoturi

Understanding and coping with domestic and international conflict has become a high-priority global task, particularly in the less developed countries. The media frequently carry news of unresolved and violent conflicts, and broken peace treaties or agreements. Though war and conflict are not the outcome of the human nature God intended us to have, we are unfortunately surrounded by conflictive situations at present across the globe. Conflict is defined as an expressed struggle between at least two interdependent parties who pursue incompatible goals, compete for scarce resources, and suffer interference from others in achieving their goals. Transforming a conflict into a harmonious situation depends on perceptual and/or conceptual changes in one or more parties, leading to changes in will and in relationships. Efforts should be made to challenge and transform the prevalent culture of violence into a culture of knowing that peace is a state of mind and will. Peace is indivisible from living a life of cooperation and interdependence.

One can usefully distinguish between "structural peace," which is a positive presence for human well-being in a just, free, and harmonious society, and "sustainable peace," which is a system for living together that will serve present generations and ensure stability for future ones. It is only when war, famine, and environmental collapse strike that we fully understand the necessity of peace. These shocks challenge us to change our minds, feelings, wills, and actions so that peace becomes our objective for life.

The Roots of Conflict

The Reverend Martin Luther King Jr. once said: "We have flown in the air like birds and swum in the sea like fishes, but we have failed to learn the simple act of walking the earth as brothers and sisters." This is a sad reality.

In the modern world, we live not at peace but in an armed state of readiness for, or in pursuit of, conflict, violence, and war. Even though no war may have been formally declared, at any one time many parts of the world are experiencing devastating conflict. The acceptance of conflict and war in our midst distorts our social values, so that from birth we grow into unbalanced human beings, our gentler side suppressed in favor of uncontrolled competition and violence. When the prerequisites for sustainable peace are not fulfilled, a society is unstable and prone to violence in the form of either civil conflict or external war. Any fundamental need (physical security, human identity, or social interaction) that is not adequately satisfied tends to generate conflict. The failure to meet these fundamental needs has powerful consequences because these needs address the "being," the "having," and the "doing" of each person in his or her interaction in society.

In military strategy, provision of physical security is held to involve three major concerns:

- Defense of territory from invasion and occupation
- Defense of access to strategic raw materials and markets
- Defense of society's political and social values

These issues are still at the bottom of many of the conflicts in Africa.

Other causes of conflict include:

Absolute deprivation. This leads to frustration, indignation, and distrust. The failure of a society to provide for its people's most basic needs produces strong pressures for change. Poverty and suffering are major factors in civil and local wars. Relative deprivation is a factor in growing North-South tension and in struggles over highly unequal land distribution in parts of Africa.

Ethnic dominance and rivalry. Ethnic identities are used, and sometimes intentionally strengthened, to provide a basis for the organization of rebellious action. Group loyalty is considered a virtue in every society of the world. Unfortunately, it often goes hand in hand with prejudice and intolerance.

Political repression and economic hardship. Regimes that prevent the meaningful participation of their people in the political life of the nation and especially in key decisionmaking spheres can generate mistrust and violence. Efficient repression may prolong authoritarian rule for a while, but sooner or later the people will rid themselves of their illegitimate rulers.

The mere existence of a democratic government does not guarantee the absence of conflict, but since such governments are likely to be more widely accepted, expressions of discontent are rarely aimed at challenging their basic tenets (anarchism being a notable exception). Democracy provides for a peaceful transition, through the ballot box, to an alternative government.

Economic crises—inflation, international debt, unemployment, and falling standards of living—may also generate violent expressions of social discontent. Finally, differences in religious, political, and social values can in themselves be sources of conflict, both within and between societies. But genuine differences are often exaggerated by vested interests—those holding or seeking power in a society. The powerful and wealthy, who are in a position to control the public images of who is a "friend" and who is an "enemy," sometimes foment conflict with the ultimate objective of maintaining a status quo that favors their interests.

These are the main causes of current conflicts. Secondary factors may include the effects of the colonial legacy, the global trade in arms, and the absence of Christian and humanitarian values.

Preventing Conflict

One of the supreme creations of the human spirit is the idea of prevention. Like the ideals of liberty and equality, it is a concept drawn from a reservoir of optimism that centuries of epidemics, famines, and wars have failed to deplete. It is an amalgam of hope and possibility that holds that misery is not the inevitable mandate of fate or a punishment only redeemable in another life, but a human condition that can be treated like a disease and sometimes cured or even prevented. As Jesus taught: Blessed are the peacemakers.

Awesome challenges face us: wanton killing and brutality within supposedly sovereign borders, ethnic and religious strife, millions of starving or ill-fed refugees, millions of other migrants fleeing their homes in fear for their lives or in desperate search of a better life, human rights trampled down, appalling poverty in the shadow of extraordinary wealth, and inhumanity on an incredible scale even after the end of the Cold War. These challenges call for earlier diagnoses and new kinds of therapy. Underlying causes have to be attacked sooner rather than later, before they become fulminating infections that rage beyond political containment.

According to the prevention principle, detection of preconflict stress and early intervention to head off conflict should be as honored in international relations as crisis management and diplomatic negotiation. It is peace preferred to violence, though it is more complex and controversial than that. People disagree on how to define social health and political disease. In the pursuit of some good causes conflict may appear necessary. However, prevention of conflict is a moral imperative in order to save innocent lives. It is also an economic necessity both for the countries immediately involved and for the international community, because of the exorbitant cost of war and postwar reconstruction. It is a political necessity for the credibility of international cooperation.

We have seen that the causes of conflicts that lead to human stress, community breakdown, and group violence are diverse and deeply embedded in social change. They lie in incubating prejudices and injustices that inexorably breed hatred and conflict. But these evil forces are rarely exposed early enough or fought with effective tools before predictable disaster strikes. This should be of widespread concern.

Conflict prevention does not only address the causes of tension but, more fundamentally, repairs relationships and tackles systemic problems in society. Though there are no guaranteed vaccinations to prevent conflict from starting, and no miracle cures to end them once they have started, nonetheless we cannot abandon our duty any more than a conscientious physician can abandon a difficult case. We have to protect the next generation from the aftermath of conflict by detecting, treating, and eradicating violence. It is well known that the use of force is not always the best response to violence; military intervention and sanctions, for example, often do more harm than good to the civilian population. But persuasion, education, cooperation, and prevention are the best courses for stopping violent conflict before it starts. As

President John F. Kennedy once said, "Mankind must put an end to war before war puts an end to mankind."

I am told that in the medical world, if a fatal disease threatens to spread, health experts devise control programs based on careful research and laboratory experiments, sophisticated statistical studies and models, field trials and double-blind tests that try to minimize biases and the effects of biological variants that often contaminate the best-designed studies. When deaths do occur, scrupulous postmortem analyses are conducted so that the errors and failures of the past become the building blocks for a more effective approach in the future.

Diplomatic activity should be subject to similar procedures. Nations, particularly great powers, and international organizations and institutions must become humble enough to learn from failed efforts rather than merely defending traditional practice. For example, it is unfortunate that the international community seems not to be applying the lessons of the 1994 genocide in Rwanda to the current crisis in the Great Lakes region. What is being done to prevent the genocide of 1994 from recurring in other parts of the region?

It is true that there is a shift in state relations in the direction of focusing on universal personal human rights rather than only on the rights and privileges accorded under national sovereignty. When sovereign nations fail in their obligation to protect the lives of their citizens, then the international community has the responsibility, to quote Francis Deng of the United Nations, to "hold that state accountable and if necessary to intervene to provide the needed protection and even to help find remedies to the underlying conditions that led to violence."

In particular instances, the international community should intervene in an impartial manner rather than just maintaining neutrality. Whereas neutrality focuses on warring parties, impartiality focuses on the victims as human beings, making no distinction between victims as regards race, ethnic origins, gender, and political, religious, philosophical, or other beliefs. The rights of the victims and the moral imperative of justice would take precedence over the conventional excuses for inaction of neutrality and national sovereignty.

In order to achieve that impartial mission, the international community, especially the United Nations, needs to have the necessary capacity to collect and analyze information. Otherwise, it is taken unawares by events and appropriate intervention is delayed. With the right information and analysis, the international community can prescribe effective treatment because it is able to assess both the factors that have created the risk of conflict and the likely impacts of it.

From this perspective, there are two prerequisite conditions to prevent conflict from escalating. On the one hand, the parties to the conflict need to willingly accept the proposed solution. On the other hand, the well-informed intervening third party should have the necessary support—moral, political, and financial—from the international community to carry out the agreed preventive action.

Prevention should be the mission of a wide variety of protagonists, from the statesman to the business leader, from the journalist to the international organization, from the banker to the nongovernmental organization. Everybody is concerned, given what is at stake. In matters of peace, as in medicine, prevention is better than cure. It saves lives and money and forestalls suffering. Kofi Annan, secretary-general of the United Nations, has rightly stated that "In the past 20 years we have understood the need for military intervention where governments grossly violate human rights. In the next 20 years we must learn how to prevent conflicts. Even the costliest policy of prevention is far cheaper, in lives and resources, than the least expensive intervention."

The Impact of Conflict

Though prevention is better than violent conflict, there are unfortunately few countries where conflict has been successfully prevented. In the post–Cold War era in Africa, the proliferation and intensification of internal conflicts have resulted in unprecedented human tragedies and, in some cases, have led to the partial and even total collapse of states. Men, women, and children have been uprooted, dispossessed, deprived of their means of livelihood, and thrown into exile as refugees or forced migrants.

The world has seen more conflicts in the past 20 years than at any other time in the last century. More than 50 countries have been involved in major protracted intrastate conflicts since 1980. About 35 million people are currently displaced as a result of conflict. In 30 countries more than 10 percent of the population has been dislocated, and in 10 countries the proportion is more than 40 percent. In many cases this displacement has persisted over an entire generation or longer and will have serious long-term effects.

Conflict has become a major constraint on the alleviation of poverty. A recent study by the Carnegie Commission on Preventing Deadly Conflict estimated that the cost of the seven major wars since 1995, not including the conflicts in Kosovo and East Timor, was around US$199 billion. Adding those two conflicts, the total cost rises to US$230 billion. This amount of money could easily have wiped out the international debt owed by the world's poor countries.

The legacy of conflict includes widespread population displacement; damaged infrastructure, including schools, health facilities, housing, and other buildings; reduced productive capacity; erosion of human and social capital; greatly reduced physical security; and an increased proportion of people needing social assistance in order to survive. Increasingly, landmines prevent access to infrastructure and agricultural land.

Conflict affects societies in a variety of profound and far-reaching ways that weaken their ability to complete the transition from war to sustainable peace. Many countries were poor in infrastructure and wealth even before conflict erupted; but violence and civil strife then further break down the underpinnings of the economy, undermine predictability and confidence in the future, discourage investment, disrupt markets and distribution networks, and generally thwart development potential. Social organization and family units break down and become adapted to the new environment of war and militarization. People lose trust in most institutions and in human relations in general. In brief, conflict can destroy, in a short time, social, human, and physical capital assets that took decades to accumulate. The ecological and environmental degradation resulting from deforestation by refugee camps is just one example.

Societies in conflict cannot grow, invest, or move forward to stability and renewed development. All types of conflict and civil violence have far-reaching effects on all facets of the political, social, economic, and even spiritual life of a society and nation.

Post-Conflict Reconstruction

We have seen that conflict is the product of inequity and social injustice, and that violence is the result of unresolved conflict. The aim of post-conflict reconstruction, therefore, is to restore peace, which entails a commitment to justice. This focus on justice requires that humanitarian assistance and development lay the foundation for more just relationships in society across lines of class, gender, ethnicity, age, and religion. Peace building or reconstruction as a process assists all people through solidarity, material assistance, and provision of opportunities to become full participants in the decisions that affect their lives.

Post-conflict reconstruction supports the transition from conflict and violence to peace in an affected country by rebuilding the socioeconomic framework of that society. Given the nature of intrastate conflict, the formal cessation of hostilities does not necessarily signify the completion of a transition process, although it does represent a critical point on the transitional path.

Reconstruction does not refer only to the rebuilding of physical infrastructure. Nor does it necessarily signify a rebuilding of the same socioeconomic framework that existed in a country before the outbreak of conflict. Conflict, particularly long-lasting conflict, transforms societies, and a return to the past may not be possible or even desirable.

Fragile, inequitable economies and weak governance structures often play a significant role in creating the conditions for conflict to arise in the first place. In such cases, what is needed is to establish the enabling or empowering conditions for a functioning economy and society under a framework of good governance and the rule of law. Economic development alone is not sufficient to build a cohesive society. Integrated human development, which includes the economic, social, political, cultural, psychological, intellectual, physical, and spiritual dimensions, must be introduced to help people find an alternative to violent conflict.

Since sustainable development depends heavily on peace building and visible peace dividends, especially during the fragile early period, physical reconstruction and transitional initiatives may need to be undertaken before the larger economic reform program gets fully underway. Such initiatives can build trust and sustain confidence in a war-torn population during the often rocky transition to peace. It is recommended that funds and other means for reconstruction should be disbursed rapidly and with flexible procedures, along with funds for emergency assistance. Adequacy of funding for the key tasks is also crucial. To take the cases of Rwanda and Burundi, it is clear that the failure of the international community to provide adequate support has undermined stability and development efforts to date.

It is generally accepted that a post-conflict reconstruction program has two main objectives. First, it must facilitate transition from violent conflict to a sustainable peace, that is, set up the political institutions and structures required for good governance. Second, it must support economic and social development. However, other areas must also be addressed if a holistic program of reconstruction to successfully prevent further outbreaks of conflict. These involve emotional and ethical issues. It is in these areas where many of today's conflicts have devastating impacts and where transformation and healing need to occur, and where injustice and insecurity are often manifested most strongly. If there is any role that the Church has to play in the post-conflict reconstruction process, and where it has an absolute advantage, it is precisely in this field of transformation. The Church can spread the moral values of personal responsibility, social compassion, and economic justice.

Amnesty, Forgiveness, Reconciliation: The Role of the Church

In recent years, a new method of dealing with violence and promoting post-conflict healing has been developed. It is the so-called commission for truth and reconciliation, with the most recent one set up in South Africa after the fall of the apartheid regime. Rwanda is establishing such a body after its genocide experience, and the Burundi peace negotiation in Arusha is proposing one for Burundi. The commissions invoke "truth" because a state must bring to light and account for past actions, and "reconciliation" because any society emerging from repression and enmity has to recover from its past and come to terms with a substantial legacy of conflict and confusion. One would expect a third term to be included in this conceptualization: *justice.*

In East Africa, Christian faith and life have been influenced by the East African revival movement that started in Rwanda in the 1930s. It uses a methodology based on repentance, brokenness, and telling the truth, and living a transformed life through the blood of Jesus Christ that cleanses all sins. The Balokole (or saved ones, as they were known) were supposed to separate themselves from worldly matters. They almost forgot that though they are not *of* the world, they are still *in* the world. This experience, I believe, challenges us to revisit our evangelistic methodology. The genocide that took place in Rwanda, the cradle of the revival movement, calls upon us to reconsider our theological understanding of peace, justice, and salvation or forgiveness. Questions of ethnocentrism, nationalism, and identity have to be seriously discussed. A church that identifies itself with a nation, a tribe, or an ethnic group is a church that has gone astray.

As Margot Kässmann states in "Overcoming Violence: The Challenge to the Churches in All Places" (1998), "The Church of Christ is of no nation but its unique character is precisely that it exists in all nations and is made up of people of a Nation."

The Church of God must come to grips with, and find ways to speak about, forgiveness and reconciliation as a precondition for breaking the cycle of violence. But just as Dietrich Bonhoeffer warned us about "cheap grace" as a distortion of the grace of God, so we must differentiate the biblical concept of forgiveness from "cheap forgiveness." Forgiveness and reconciliation are extremely complex processes.

Before a nation can get on with the task of nation building, or reconstruction, it has to come to terms with its past. The Church has much to contribute. It can provide theological insights about the differences between true and false forgiveness, true and false reconciliation, and true and false apologies. The Church has a unique role to play in fostering genuine reconciliation between formerly warring parties. The fact that the churches have failed to do so in some places and circumstances does not undermine the importance of the attempt. The reign of God in human affairs means first and foremost that God has taken the initiative to reconcile us, both to himself and to each other. Old enmities must be healed, for unresolved hatred can lead to further violent acts of revenge.

In this process of forgiveness and reconciliation, a heated debate centers on the question of general amnesty. It is true that acts of forgiveness and reconciliation are indispensable in the healing of a nation, but what do you do with torturers and dictators? Should they be persecuted? Exposed? Can we forgive the perpetrators of crimes when they not only refuse to repent, but continue to justify their actions as necessary for national defense purposes?

In the conflict resolution process, there are some principles that must be applied for any healing to take place. The first is that one cannot resolve conflicts, and thus make peace, unless the root causes of the conflicts are identified and dealt with. The criminals have to be identified as well. Secondly, it is not possible to attain peace unless attention is given to the justice and fairness of the process as well as the outcome of the settlement. In other words, peace without justice is a rather meaningless concept, although this is not to suggest that the pursuit of justice and the pursuit of peace are one and the same thing. Therefore, though governments are justified in granting amnesty, it should be offered under certain conditions, namely, that first and foremost the truth has to be established, and secondly, that no amnesty can be granted for crimes against humanity, including genocide. But where does this leave the Church and the ministry of justice, peace, and reconciliation?

Any Christian talking about forgiveness and reconciliation in a world of violence must recognize that there is often an almost unbearable tension between the need to call for justice and the conviction that healing and wholeness of life require that we do not hate our enemies. In the Bible, peace (*shalom*) is a vision of how things and people ought to be and a call to transform society. This clearly implies that the first contrast is not between peace and violence, but between peace and injustice, since it is the violence born of injustice that is the major hindrance to the existence of peace.

People, as well as structures of society, need to be transformed. People who are caught in oppressive structures need to be liberated from the antivalues and false perspectives inculcated by those structures. The peacemaker, as a result, is involved in a mission of conversion—converting people to a new understanding and way of life. This conversion is based on God's love and frees one from old patterns of thought and action. The Church, therefore, should provide leadership in this mission of resisting the structures of oppression and working for the liberation of powerless and oppressed people.

Conclusion

Any program for conflict prevention or post-conflict reconstruction should aim at restoring peace, which is not only a situation where conflict, war, and violence are absent, but the expression of harmonious relations between people and between the human community and the environment. Former president Julius Nyerere of Tanzania once said:

"Peace is more than an absence of war. It is a positive quality, with three essential components: relations of harmony and mutual respect among people in a society, human cooperation for the common good, and justice based on the concept of equality." Without justice in our social, economic, religious, and political relationships, peace is impossible. The question upon which the whole future of peace for Africa and the world depends is this: Are the present wars and conflicts a struggle for a just and secure peace, or only for a new balance of power? We must be courageous and struggle, not for a balance of power but for a community of power, not for organized rivalries but for an organized common peace.

I will conclude by echoing former U.S. president George Bush: "We have a vision of a new partnership of nations that transcends the Cold War. A partnership based on consultation, cooperation, and collective action, especially through international and regional organizations. A partnership united by principle and the rule of law and supported by an equitable sharing of both cost and commitment. A partnership whose goals are to increase democracy, increase prosperity and increase peace."

9

Corruption in Africa: Causes, Effects, and Counter-Measures

Christopher Kolade

This paper addresses the specific issue of corruption in Africa, but it is important to remember that corruption is a global issue. It is present to some degree in every country, and exerts an influence on the lives of people everywhere. Studies by bodies such as the World Bank and Transparency International have suggested that developing countries, especially in Africa, tend to be in the top league of so-called "corrupt societies." Corruption increases in strength wherever systems for ensuring effective accountability are weak, as they tend to be in many developing economies. By the same token, the fight against corruption also tends to be most successful when there are both the desire and the will to establish and operate accurate systems of accountability.

Many definitions of corruption are possible, because a wide variety of activities and transactions are affected by it. For this discussion of high-level corruption in Africa,[1] it may be appropriate to adopt a two-part definition that sees such corruption, first, as the abuse of an influential position for private gain and, second, as the exploitation of a system for securing unmerited advantage. The first part of this definition relates to holders of influential positions (in the public or private sector) who have access to the people's shared resources because they are custodians and stewards of those resources. The second part relates to people who lobby such officeholders for access to preferential or undue advantage. Both groups are agents of corruption.

The emphasis on "access" in our definition is of particular significance in the African context. In most African countries some of the basic essentials of life are in short supply, particularly opportunities for securing education, medical treatment, financial loans, and so forth. For this reason, the distribution of resources is managed mainly by allocation, and this fact confers enormous power on those who hold management positions. Unless they are conscientious and faithful in carrying out their responsibilities, there is an almost inescapable tendency for corruption to creep in and take hold within the system. This kind of corruption, therefore, usually reflects the way in which authority is exercised in a society.

Leadership and Power in African Communities

The tussle for leadership positions has been a strong feature of governance in African countries. Military takeovers of government have been frequent, and even democratic elections have often turned out to be life-and-death exercises. One of the reasons for this is that the leader is usually looked upon as one who should wield power and authority to personal advantage. Politicians compete for public office not so much to serve all the people as to win positions of power and privilege.

This focus on the power and privilege elements in leadership is misleading because it underplays the importance of the links between *responsibility, authority* (that is, power) and *accountability*. The leader accepts a responsibility and is given the authority to make things happen in pursuit of the desired outcome. The leader must be prepared to be judged on the basis of the quality of that outcome. The misuse of authority will frequently frustrate the objectives of responsibility, and almost certainly prevent faithfulness in accountability. In other words, it is important to stress the fact that the leader's authority is conferred upon him to empower him to fulfill the responsibilities of the office, and not to create private gain for himself and his friends.

The traditional concept of leadership in many African societies was community-based, and was reflected in the chieftaincy institutions that exist under different names in various countries. No doubt they were, and some still are, positions of considerable authority to which members of the community accord immense respect. In truth, however, such positions are "responsibility posts," and the respect accorded the leader is in recognition of the responsibility burden that he carries. Like the leader described in the Bible, he is "God's *minister* [that is, servant] to do us good," and this is what entitles him to our respect and obedience (Romans 13:4–5).

Moreover, before anyone was accepted as a leader in these traditional African societies, they usually went through a recognized period of "apprenticeship" during which they matured in both experience and wisdom, acquiring the skills required for their leadership role. As a result, they enjoyed both the respect and the confidence of their followers, and their judgment was hardly ever questioned, since they were regarded as people whose leadership ability had been tested and established.

From the outset, such leaders were expected to use the authority of their position to ensure equity in the availability of opportunity to all members of the community. That was their responsibility, and they were held accountable for performing it. The prevalence of corruption in any society usually reflects the degree to which leaders have allowed their performance to drift from the promise implied in their acceptance of positions of authority and influence in their community or country.

Culture, Corruption, and Poverty

Two Cultures

There is a school of thought that attempts to excuse bribe-taking in Africa on the grounds that the giving of gifts in return for favors is integral to the culture of most African societies. This is erroneous on several counts, as it ignores the following prevailing norms in traditional gift-giving:

- The gifts are modest in proportion, and are to be given for favors received, not for favors expected.
- The gifts may be accepted, but should never be demanded.
- Each party to the exchange considers it a matter of honor to ensure that their own part of the exchange has been faithfully performed.

Traditional African culture, properly practiced, demanded that both leaders and followers honor their obligations and meet the expectations of their positions. The leaders accepted the obligation of using their position to ensure the welfare of their followers, especially those whose low levels of influence or access placed them at a disadvantage.

Today, however, a culture of corruption has developed. Among other things, the notion is accepted that decisionmaking requires some "oiling of the wheels" before results can be produced. Now, transactions occur on a platform of preferential advantage, paying scant attention to the equalization of opportunity or to the concept of rewards being justified by the volume and quality of work or the acceptance of risk.

Corruption contributes to the perpetuation of poverty in a significant way mainly because it weakens the performance of both leaders and followers. In every modern African situation, it is easy to see that the gap between rich and poor continues to widen: the rich get richer (often indecently so), while the poor become progressively less able to fend for themselves. Whatever productive capacity they may have is effectively captured and controlled by those in power. Any effort to relieve poverty will be effective only if the system can be sanitized sufficiently for the influences of corruption and the concentration of power to be substantially diminished.

Enabling Conditions for Corruption

As noted above, high-level corruption tends to flourish where accountability is weak. A close examination of some African situations reveals that, even where systems for promoting accountability existed initially, they have been deliberately weakened over several decades because of the highly centralized system for exercising executive power. Elected legislators tend to represent vested interests rather than voter interest, and many of them see their presence in Parliament as an opportunity to siphon public resources into private pockets. They do nothing, therefore, to correct the institutional weaknesses that exist, and they perpetuate public policies that generate economic rents. Where the government is not elected the situation is far worse, as members of government suspend the constitution and put themselves outside the controls by which society normally manages itself.

The people "in power" are able to carry on in this way because civil society itself is weak and underdeveloped. Levels of education are low, and this discourages the recognition and expression of individual rights and obligations. Per capita income is similarly low, and poverty promotes the tendency for individuals to see themselves as dependent upon the goodwill and favor of those who allocate the community's resources. Even the individual's capacity to be productive is weakened because government controls the terms and conditions under which personal initiative may be productively exercised. Government is also able to "move the goalposts" arbitrarily and without notice, creating a sense of continuous uncertainty and instability. The country is thus mired in a situation of institutionalized corruption.

Institutionalized Corruption

The main features of institutionalized (or systemic) high-level corruption include the following:

- Officials or managers of institutions have wide discretion but little accountability.
- Policies are poorly designed, articulated, and communicated, and they are implemented with manifest indifference to their impact and cost-effectiveness.
- Formal rules remain in place, but they are superseded by informal conventions. Even where a code of conduct has been published, hardly anyone reads it or refers to it.
- The remuneration of public servants is low and inadequate, thus encouraging individuals to seek other (often illegal) ways of making ends meet.
- Officials delight in creating multiple layers of red tape, setting up "tollgates" that create delays and increase frustration and insecurity for other stakeholders.
- The consequences of being caught and punished for corrupt behavior are low relative to the benefits. This is because leaders and supervisors shy away from asserting their proper disciplinary authority.
- Individuals wanting to perform their functions with efficiency and integrity find themselves isolated and endangered: they are perceived as potential whistleblowers.
- External instruments of restraint (such as, for example, an independent judiciary) are deliberately marginalized and weakened. Military governments actually enact laws with "ouster" clauses denying citizens the right to judicial redress where needed.

Fighting Corruption

Although institutionalized corruption is prominent in many African countries, it flourishes mainly because individuals continue to indulge in, or acquiesce in, corrupt practices. It has been well said that "corruption is controlled only when citizens no longer tolerate it." There are indications that this idea is gaining acceptance, not only by the international community but also by local societies in quite a few African countries. In Nigeria, for example, two organizations, Transparency in Nigeria and Integrity, have become particularly active in recent years. Through their activities a number of seminars and conferences have been held, with public and private sector participation, both local and international. A Code of Business Integrity has been publicly launched, and a growing number of private sector companies have signed it. The Nigerian press and electronic media are proving particularly dynamic in staging a fight against corruption.

However, significant success will not come until the citizens of African countries are effectively mobilized to regain their "voice" and recapture their role as the real decisionmakers in the governance of their countries. Combating corruption requires credible progress on at least three fronts. First, the individual citizen must be empowered. Second, private firms must acknowledge and carry out their proper role. And third, governments must become truly responsible and accountable.

Empowering the Individual Citizen

Citizens must be better able to manage themselves and to make their appropriate contribution to the progress of their society. For this, the quality of civic and moral education must be upgraded and made more relevant, in order to enable citizens to recognize and acknowledge their rights as well as nondisruptive ways of claiming those rights. Past deprivations have often led citizens to feel that they must take the law into their own hands and demand their rights with violence.

At the same time, citizens must come to understand that they have obligations to fulfill. Society at large needs the lawful productive effort of its members for continued economic good health. The freedom of the press (to take one example) also will be strong and sustained only when individual citizens give it support. Citizens need to become better educated about the processes of democratic or representative government and the role that they must play in keeping their representatives conscientious and accountable.

Awakening the Business Sector

Business enterprises in African countries often fail to recognize the economic strength they have and the ways in which that strength should be expressed. I recently made the following suggestions to a gathering of Nigerian executives:

- A company should be clear about the values and standards that are to be identified with its operations and its people.
- Acceptable styles of management should be clearly articulated, preferably in a code to which the corporation's executives are required to subscribe.
- Systems should be established for monitoring actual practice regarding all the standards that are prescribed.
- Transparency in business dealings should be well defined. It should be based on the open and frank sharing of information that is relevant to the pursuit of the company's objectives.
- Companies should reexamine and dismantle systems and practices that tend to contradict their rhetoric and go against the values and standards that they have established.
- Organizations should develop routines for giving specific recognition and reward to those who act effectively in accord with the values that are being promoted. By the same token, they should be consistent and decisive in applying sanctions to undesirable performance.
- Companies should take their social responsibility obligations seriously, making sure that they offer support to the development of society, while ensuring that they do not participate in violating the values reflected in the traditional culture of the people.
- Top management has the special responsibility of ensuring that it consistently "walks the talk." Example is always the best confirmation of purpose.
- Companies should collaborate to adopt and express strong positions on the rampant corruption in business relationships. For example, they should take concerted action to expose and oppose all attempts to operate "rent" or "toll" systems that promote extortion and defeat productivity.
- Appropriate sanctions should be devised and applied to members of business societies or chambers of commerce that violate the standards of business integrity that these associations seek to promote.

Making Government More Responsible and Accountable

African societies will continue to depend on government to do a number of important things. These include:

- Making laws that reinforce and consolidate the agreed objectives of society

- Clarifying public rules and processes for the general understanding of the citizenry
- Establishing systems that encourage and facilitate the examination of decisions and actions of public officials
- Ensuring the effective enforcement of the relevant laws and sanctions (which apply to all citizens, from the head of government on down)

Governments need to consider a number of issues worth their serious attention in combating corruption and alleviating poverty. To begin with, they must establish (or restore) professionalism in the public service while strengthening the discipline of financial management. The capacity for effective policymaking should be expanded, with creation of oversight agencies to ensure the effective enforcement of statutes. Governments must move urgently to ensure the independence of the judiciaries. And, finally, they must take steps to enable civil society to engage in participatory governance.

Building a Climate of Integrity: Role of the Church

Empowering the people to fight corruption must be the main focus of activity if present situations are to be effectively corrected. In pursuit of this objective, a culture of mutual trust and integrity needs to be built. A new and more responsive style of leadership must emerge, and systems of advocacy against corruption need to be strengthened.

People should be encouraged to exercise their rights and meet their obligations within the rule of law, while ethical values (justice, honor, integrity) and standards that have fallen into disuse must be reestablished and communicated forcefully. Government needs to restrict its role and decentralize power to the representatives of the people who are at the frontline of initiative and action. And, finally, everyone has to be reminded that individual accountability is both desirable and inescapable (Romans 14:12).

The Church is one forum where both leaders and followers in society can still meet without feeling threatened with the loss of their authority or psychological integrity. The Church, therefore, should be able to provide opportunities for open and meaningful dialogue through which servant-leaders can learn from followers in a mutual exchange of information and support.

Note

1. "High-level" corruption, where high office is abused both to acquire wealth illegally and to secure client support, can be usefully distinguished from low-level corruption, where a distorted moral economy allows petty theft of property and employees' time, and cheating in a wide variety of transactions, to become the unchallenged norm. This chapter concentrates on the first type of corruption.

Gender Inequity and the AIDS Pandemic

Part 5

Gender Inequity and the AIDS Pandemic

10

Gender and Poverty in Sub-Saharan Africa

Shimwaayi Muntemba and C. Mark Blackden

If Sub-Saharan Africa (SSA) is to achieve equitable growth and sustainable development, one necessary step is to reduce gender inequality in access to and control of a diverse range of assets. Evidence suggests that reducing gender inequality—a development objective in its own right—increases growth, efficiency, and welfare. This paper principally addresses the linkages between gender-based asset inequality and poverty in SSA. It complements the paper by Agnes Abuom in this volume (see chapter 11), which focuses principally on gender issues in education and health.

Gender Inequality in Access to and Control of Assets

Evidence throughout Sub-Saharan Africa points to gender disparities in access to and control of the critical assets necessary for poverty reduction.[1] In all cases, women's more limited access to and control of these assets hampers their efforts to reduce poverty and diminishes the effectiveness of poverty reduction more generally. Many of these disparities are well documented, as shown in the examples below.

Land

Having access to land and other land-based resources is a crucial factor in determining how people will ensure their basic livelihood. The vast majority of the people in Africa rely on land and land-based resources for their livelihoods. An enormous variety of rights to natural resources can be found in countries and communities throughout SSA, and these rights are firmly embedded in complex socioeconomic, cultural, and political structures. With increasing scarcity of land and water resources, the rights of individuals—especially women—and households to these resources are being eroded.

Women's rights to arable land are weaker than those of men. Women's rights to land vary with time and location, social group (ethnicity, class, and age), the nature of the land involved, the functions it fulfills, and the legal systems applicable at the local level. In many societies where women used to enjoy direct rights to land, these rights have been eroded. Increasingly, the most women can enjoy are "use rights" to land owned by husbands or sons. Their rights may cease on the death of the male owner. Data indicate the near absence of women from land registers, where such registers exist in SSA; fewer than 10 percent of those who obtained land certificates were women.[2]

Technology

Those involved in development and transfer of technology often assume that the process is gender-neutral and benign. Yet this is often not the case, as for example when the technology does not fit the physical and sociocultural conditions of end users, or when end users face specific socioeconomic constraints in applying the technology (box 10.1).

BOX 10.1 Gender-Blind Technology Development

When varieties of rice developed during the Green Revolution in Asia were introduced in Africa, they were not readily adopted. Women, key actors in rice harvesting, would not adopt them because they had to bend down to pick up the semidwarf rice panicles.

A high-yielding, disease-resistant bean was introduced in Ghana in the early 1990s. This variety required longer cooking time, thus consuming more fuelwood, which added to women's workload. Also the bean could not make thick gravy and the color was unacceptable, and its adoption was therefore rejected. Researchers adopted a participatory process to improve the final variety.

An oil press introduced in Kenya and Tanzania met with limited acceptance because of its large size and the high level of energy required to use it. Tests had been carried out with men.

Source: SPAAR 1999.

Lack of awareness of the gender roles of household members results in the development of technology that is inappropriate for its end use and user. More systematic use of gender analysis and participatory approaches can contribute greatly to addressing these problems early in the cycle of technology development and transfer (Muntemba and Chimedza 1995).

Capital and Financial Services

Data on gender differences in access to financial services are scarce. Available estimates suggest that the poor in general have little access to finance, and that women in particular have less access than men. Women's World Banking, a global network providing financial services for women entrepreneurs, has estimated that less than 2 percent of low-income entrepreneurs have access to financial services. In Africa, women receive less than 10 percent of the credit to small farmers and 1 percent of total credit to agriculture. In Uganda, it is estimated that 9 percent of all credit goes to women. In Kenya, only 3 percent of female farmers surveyed, compared with 14 percent of male farmers, had obtained credit from a commercial bank (figure 10.1). Similarly, in Nigeria only 5 percent of female farmers compared with 14 percent of male farmers had received commercial bank loans (Baden 1996).

Women face gender-specific barriers in accessing financial services, including lack of collateral (usually land); low levels of literacy, numeracy, and education; and lack of time and cash to undertake the journey to a credit institution. Women do form the largest percentage of those reached by microfinance, but they receive very small loans (most are in the range of US$50–$300). In some cases the few men reached by microfinance receive in aggregate a higher proportion of total loan value than the more numerous women (for the Ghana case, see Quainoo 1999).

Labor

Men and women have different access to employment (paid labor); while family labor, including that of women, is often controlled by husbands. Competition from other household tasks limits women's farming activity. Labor remuneration also differs along gender lines, as the total income share received by men is more than twice the share received by women (figure 10.2). African households can be viewed primarily as social institutions for mobilizing labor, in which there are

FIGURE 10-1. Gender Gap in Access to Credit among Farmers in Two African Countries

Percent

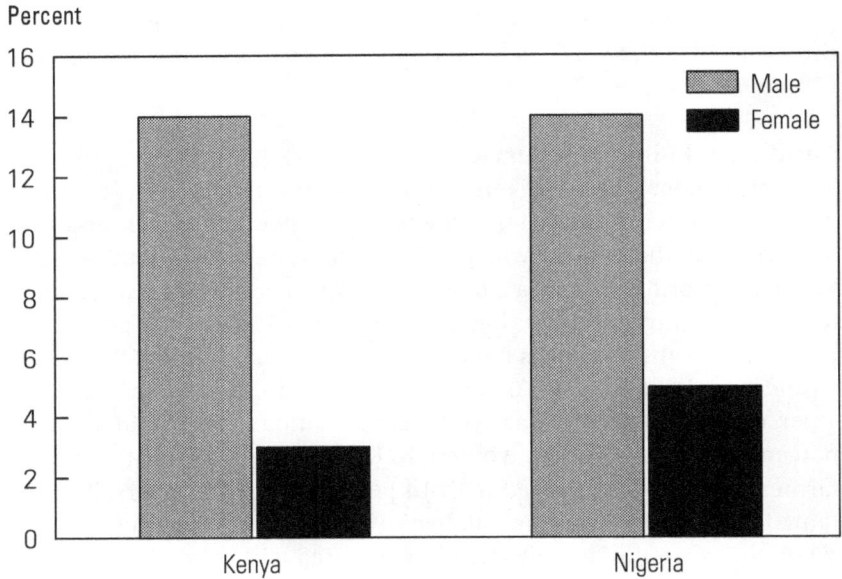

Source: Baden 1996.

strong differences between household members in their social command over labor that are directly related to their positions in the household hierarchy.

Education
Between 1970 and 1994, girls in Africa made more rapid strides than boys in completing primary education, thus narrowing the gender gap (figure 10.3). This improvement has not benefited the poor as much as the nonpoor, however. Differentials persist at all levels of income, suggesting that social and cultural factors play a stronger role than income in determining female participation in education. Domestic chores, notably caring for younger children and fetching fuel and water, are one of the main factors limiting girls' access to schooling.

FIGURE 10-2. Distribution of Earned Income by Gender in Selected African Countries
(percent)

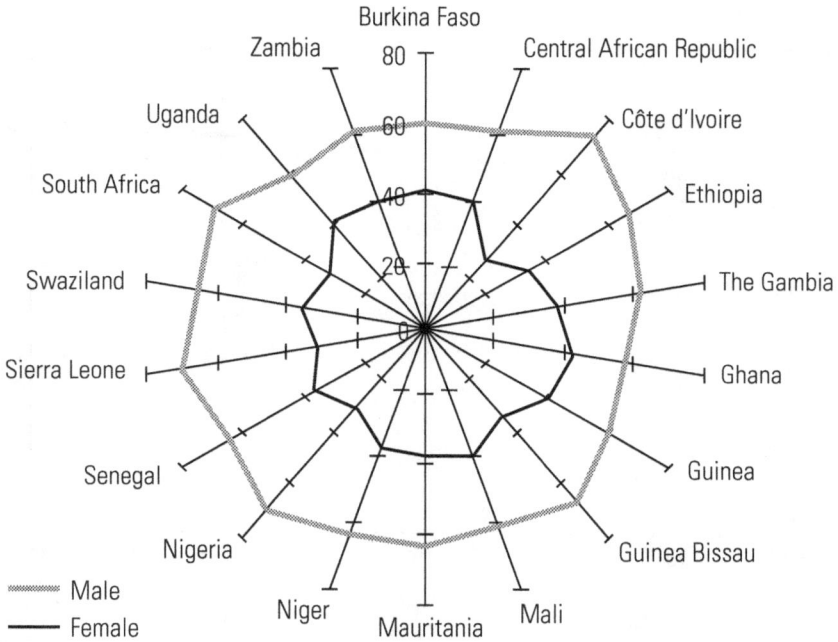

Source: Fofack 1998, cited in Blackden and Bhanu 1999.

Health

African men and women face an array of health problems, though their needs and priorities are quite different. This is seen, for example, in the enormous gender differential in the region's sexual and repro-ductive burden of disease, as measured by deaths and disability-adjusted life years.[3] Africa's total fertility rate (TFR) in 1997 was 6.0. Women in Africa generally report an ideal family size of five or six children, and they have more children than women anywhere else in the world. Maternal mortality rates in SSA remain the highest in the world: between 600 and 1,500 maternal deaths for every 100,000 births in most SSA countries. Africa accounts for 20 percent of the world's

FIGURE 10-3. Gender Gap in School Enrollment Ratios, Sub-Saharan Africa, 1970–94

Female-male ratio (percent)

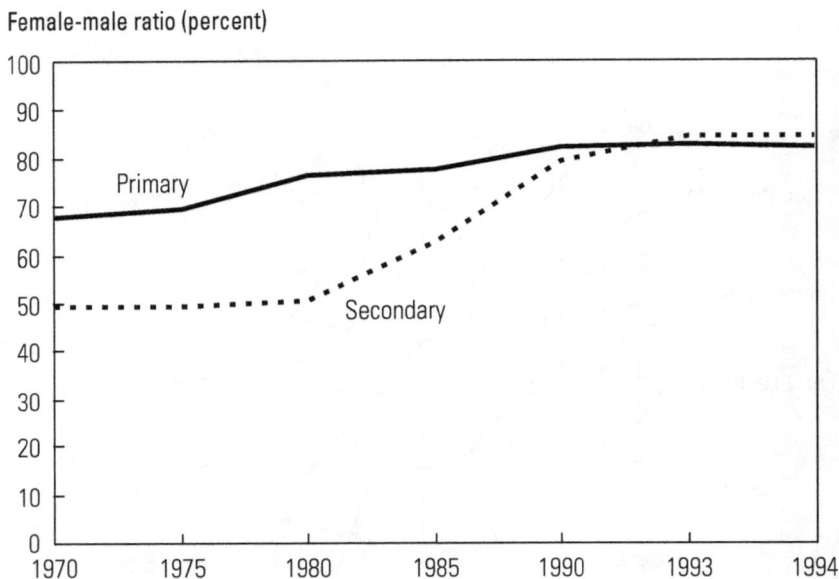

Source: Blackden and Bhanu 1999.

births but 40 percent of the world's maternal deaths. In SSA, the median age at first marriage ranges from 17.0 to 19.2 years. In 17 SSA countries recently surveyed, at least 50 percent of women had their first child before age 20. These are the highest percentages of any global region.

HIV/AIDS

HIV/AIDS is a significant—and worsening—health, economic, and social issue for Sub-Saharan Africa. Recent research points to complex interlinkages between poverty, sexual behavior, inequality (particularly gender inequality), and the AIDS epidemic. The fact that gender inequality both causes and is caused by AIDS is a matter of grave concern.

Of the 30.6 million adults and children with HIV/AIDS around the world, 20.8 million live in SSA. The current adult prevalence rate in the region is 7.4 percent. Of the world's 11.1 million women with AIDS, 82 percent live in Africa. Women under 25 years of age represent the fastest-growing group with AIDS in SSA, accounting for nearly 30 percent of all female AIDS cases in the region. Data for eight African countries indicate that HIV prevalence is twice as high among women aged 15–24 as among men of the same age (figure 10.4).

In particularly severely affected countries in southern Africa, human development gains achieved over the last decades are being reversed by HIV/AIDS. In Zambia and Zimbabwe, 25 percent more infants are dying than would be the case without HIV. Given current trends, by 2010 Zimbabwe's infant mortality rate is expected to rise by 138 percent and its under-five mortality rate by 109 percent because of AIDS. In Botswana, life expectancy, which rose from under 43 years in 1955 to 61 years in 1990, has now fallen to levels of the late 1960s.

FIGURE 10-4. HIV Prevalence among Men and Women in Selected African Countries

Percent

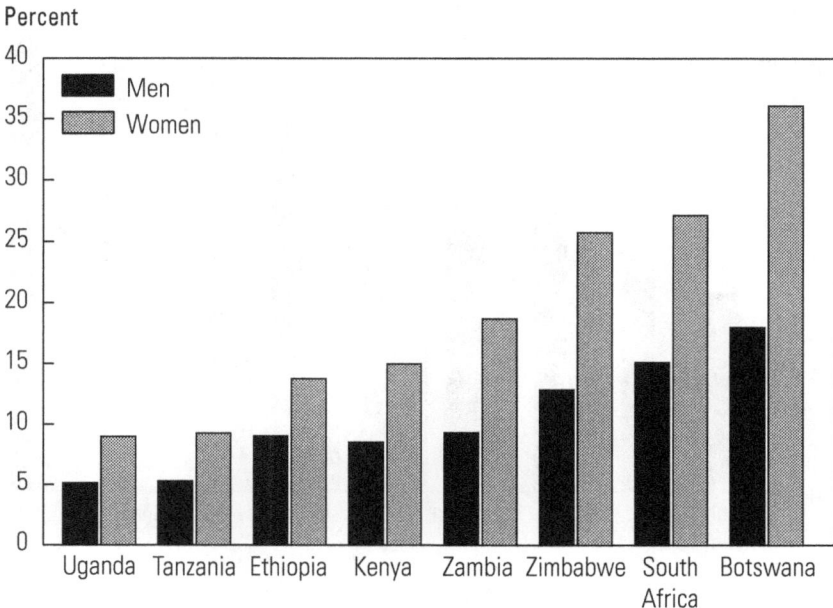

Source: Joint United Nations Programme on HIV/AIDS.

Time

Analysis of men's and women's time allocation captures the interdependence between the "market" and "household" economies. It is well documented that women work longer hours than men throughout SSA (figure 10.5), and this clearly demonstrates the time pressures faced by women. Much of women's productive work is unrecorded and not included in the system of national accounts (SNA). For example, it is estimated that nearly 60 percent of female activities in Kenya are not captured by the SNA, compared with only 24 percent of male activities. Children are closely integrated into household production systems, and the patterns that disadvantage girl children begin very early. Poor households need their children's labor, sometimes in ways that also disadvantage boys.

FIGURE 10-5. Productive Hours Per Day by Gender in Selected African Countries

Hours per day

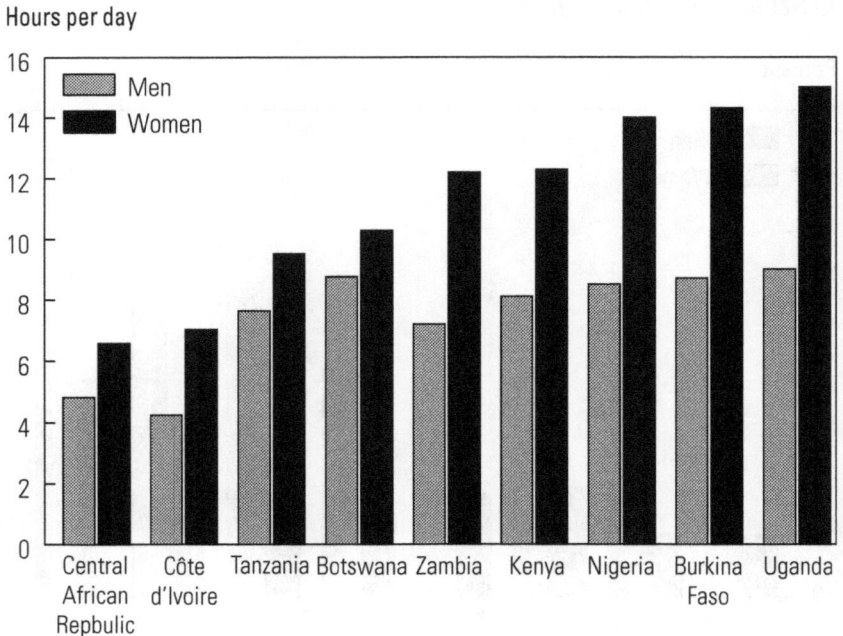

Source: Blackden and Bhanu 1999.

Participation and Voice

Women in Africa are consistently underrepresented in institutions at the local and national levels, and have little say in decisionmaking. Gender barriers limit women's participation and reinforce power gaps. Almost half of the 15 African countries reporting to the Inter-Parliamentary Union showed no change or negative change in the level of women's representation between 1975 and 1997. Women in Sub-Saharan Africa constitute 6 percent of national legislatures, 10 percent of bodies at the local level, and 2 percent of national cabinets. Half of the national cabinets in SSA have no women at all. While governments have made international commitments at the Cairo, Copenhagen, Beijing, and Istanbul conferences, and by signing the Convention for the Elimination of All Forms of Discrimination Against Women (CEDAW), few have made systematic efforts to institutionalize these commitments and translate them into practical strategies. Figure 10.6 shows data for men's and women's representation in the parliaments of 14 SSA countries.

Structural Roles of Men and Women in African Economies

A distinguishing characteristic of SSA economies is that both men and women play substantial economic roles. Data compiled by the International Food Policy Research Institute indicate that African women perform about 90 percent of the work of processing food crops and providing household water and fuelwood, 80 percent of the work of food storage and transport from farm to village, 90 percent of the work of hoeing and weeding, and 60 percent of the work of harvesting and marketing (Quisumbing and others 1995). Time allocation data throughout SSA confirm women's preponderant role in agricultural activities, as noted above. There are marked subregional variations in men's and women's shares of work; in much of the Sahel, men predominate in agriculture, including in the food sector.

One way to capture the dynamics of the varied contributions of men and women to the productive economy is through the "gender intensity of production" in different sectors. In Uganda, for instance, men and women are not equally distributed across the productive economy, as agriculture is a female-intensive sector while industry and services are male-intensive (table 10.1). According to this estimate, men and women each produce about half of the country's gross domestic product (GDP).

FIGURE 10-6. Participation of Men and Women in Parliaments of Selected African Countries

Percent

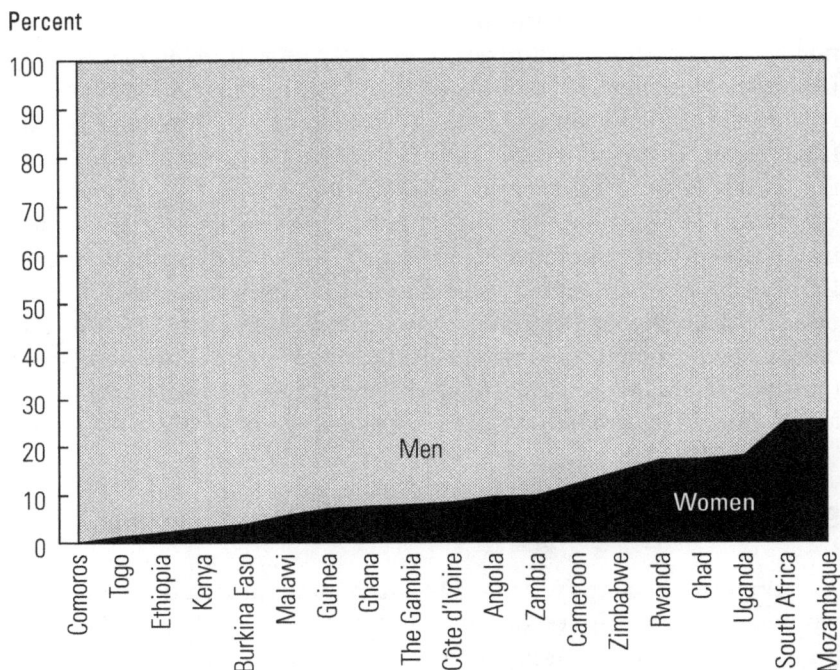

Source: International Parliamentary Union 1997.

Micro-level analyses portray a consistent picture of gender-based asset inequality acting as a constraint to growth and poverty reduction. Extensive micro-level data and case studies—and emerging macroeconomic analysis—show systematically how gender differences in access to and control of these assets directly limit African agricultural growth and prospects in terms of supply response, output, and labor productivity (box 10.2). The agricultural growth that SSA does not achieve because of gender inequality is not marginal to the continent's needs as it has detrimental consequences for food security, nutritional status, and vulnerability to poverty. Given many African countries' chronic food insecurity and vulnerability, these differences are too important,

TABLE 10.1 Structure of the Productive Economy in Uganda
(percent)

Sector	Share of GDP	Share of exports	Gender intensity of production	
			Female share of employment	Male share of employment
Agriculture	49.0	99	75	25
Food crops	33.0	n.a.	80	20
Traditional exports	3.5	75	60	40
Nontraditional agricultural exports	1.0	24	80	20
Industry	14.3	1	15	85
Manufacturing	6.8	n.a.	—	—
Services	36.6	n.a.	32	68
Total/average:	100.0	100.0	50.6	49.4

— Not available.
n.a. Not applicable.
Source: Elson and Evers 1997.

and their impacts too severe, to ignore. Measures specifically designed to overcome these gender-based barriers to agricultural growth deserve urgent policy attention, a point reiterated in the recently published study *Can Africa Claim the 21st Century?* (box 10.3).

Comparative cross-regional macro data on gender differences in education and formal employment also provide a basis for assessing the impact of gender inequality on growth. Between 1960 and 1992, Sub-Saharan Africa, together with South Asia, had the worst initial conditions for female education and employment and the worst record for changes over the 30 years. Total years of schooling for the female adult population in 1960 was 1.1 years on average. Gender inequality in schooling in 1960 was also very high in SSA, with women having barely half the schooling of men. Females in SSA experienced the lowest average annual growth in total years of schooling between 1960 and 1992 (an annual increase of 0.04 years, raising the average years of schooling of the adult female population by a mere 1.2 years). Females experienced a slower expansion in the growth of total years of schooling

---

BOX 10.2 Gender and Missed Potential Growth in Four African Countries

Burkina Faso: Shifting existing resources between men's and women's plots within the same household could increase output by 10–20 percent.

Kenya: Giving women farmers the same level of agricultural inputs and education as men farmers could increase yields obtained by women by more than 20 percent.

Tanzania: Reducing time burdens of women could increase household cash incomes for smallholder coffee and banana growers by 10 percent, labor productivity by 15 percent, and capital productivity by 44 percent.

Zambia: If women enjoyed the same overall degree of capital investment in agricultural inputs, including land, as their male counterparts, output could increase by up to 15 percent.

Source: Blackden and Bhanu 1999.

---

than males. Women also have a weak position in formal sector employment. In 1970, the female-male ratio of formal sector employment was among the lowest in the developing world, and the share of female formal sector employment increased by only 1.6 percentage points between 1970 and 1990.

Based on these trends, comparison between SSA and East Asia indicates that gender inequality in education and employment reduced

---

BOX 10.3 Can Africa Claim the 21st Century?

"Women are one of Africa's hidden growth reserves, providing most of the region's labor, but their productivity is hampered by widespread inequality in education and access to resources. Thus greater gender equality can be a potent force for accelerated poverty reduction."

Source: World Bank 2000: 2.

SSA's per capita growth in the 1960–92 period by an estimated 0.8 percentage points per year, and it appears to account for up to one-fifth of the difference in growth performance between SSA and East Asia. While this is far from the overriding factor, it is an important constituent element in accounting for SSA's poor economic performance.

Implications for Policy

Analysis of the gender dimensions of poverty and growth in SSA leads to the following principal conclusions:

- Both men and women play substantial roles in SSA economies, but they are not equally distributed across the productive sectors, nor are they equally remunerated for their labor. This means that different sectoral growth and investment patterns make different demands on men's and women's labor and have different implications for the division of labor and the distribution of income.
- The market and household economies coexist and are interdependent as revealed in time allocation data showing the "double workday" of women. This means that short-term intersectoral and intergenerational tradeoffs (and positive externalities) may be very significant for asset-poor and labor-constrained individuals and households.
- Gender inequality in access to and control of a wide range of human, economic, and social assets persists in SSA, and constitutes a key dimension of poverty. This gender-based inequality directly and indirectly limits economic growth in SSA and diminishes the effectiveness of poverty-reduction efforts.
- The poor in general, and poor women in particular, have little or no voice in decisionmaking, and their different needs and constraints do not inform public policy choices and priorities. This means that proactive measures are needed to ensure inclusive participation and the formulation of inclusive policies and programs.

In our view, this analysis contributes to a fuller understanding of the causes of poverty and indicates in turn different policy responses and investment priorities to reduce poverty. These are summarized in table 10.2.

TABLE 10.2 Framework for Integrating Gender into Poverty-Reduction Strategies

Principal issues	Policy implications	Key operational tasks
Structural Economic Roles of Men and Women in Africa : Toward Economic Inclusion		
• Men and women both have structural—and different—roles in SSA economies • Men and women are not evenly distributed across economic sectors • Cultural and social factors shape these roles more than strictly "economic" ones	• "Sectoral growth patterns make different demands on men's and women's labor and have different implications for the gender division of labor and income" (Elson and Evers 1997) • Constraints, opportunities, incentives, and needs (COIN) differ for men and for women	• Target sectors for growth and strengthen productivity where the poor (women) work, e.g., ensure greater policy attention to "nontraded" sectors, notably subsistence agriculture and the urban informal sector • Respond to different COIN
Interdependence of Household and Market Economies : Minimizing Tradeoffs		

• The "market" and "household" economies coexist and are interdependent, as time allocation data reveal
 	
• "Time" is a scarce factor of production, and "time poverty" is a major constraint for women
 	
• Labor productivity (especially of women) is very low in both the market and household economies
	• There is risk of short-term intersectoral and intergenerational tradeoffs within asset-poor and labor-constrained households, e.g., between growth (raising incomes) and human development (investing in education)
	
	• Constraints, opportunities, incentives, and needs (COIN) differ for men and for women
	
	• There is considerable scope for raising labor productivity
		• Carry out balanced and concurrent investment in both market and household economies to minimize tradeoffs and maximize externalities through priority to sectoral investment to raise (female) labor productivity:
		  Water supply/sanitation
		  Labor-saving technologies, focused on food processing and transformation
		  Intermediate means of transport
		  Domestic energy

Persistent Gender-Based Asset Inequality: Linking Gender and Poverty Reduction

- Gender inequality persists in access to and control of the full range of human, economic, and social capital assets necessary for development and growth:
  - Human capability
  - Economic assets, resources, and opportunity
  - Security and power
  - Voice and participation

- Gender inequality directly and indirectly limits economic growth
- Gender dimensions of poverty include women's greater vulnerability and risk aversion
- Women have greater vulnerability to and burden from HIV/AIDS
- Gender equality is a development issue in its own right
- Political commitment to gender equality is crucial

- Promote greater "voice" for women in decisionmaking at all levels with focus on governance and conflict prevention
- Enhance female education and literacy, skills training
- Focus on HIV/AIDS, especially prevention and orphan care
- Invest in directly productive assets for women: financial services, agricultural technology, and inputs
- Address sustainable land and property ownership/use rights for women as part of legal reform

Analytical Issues: Completing the Picture

- Data issues, including the "invisibility" of much of women's work, limit analysis and understanding of gender/ poverty interactions
- Complexity of household structures and relations limits household-level analysis in poverty-monitoring and trend analysis

- "Incomplete" picture of total productive activity masks dynamic interactions and potential for synergy across sectors
- Female-headed households are not necessarily poorer
- Larger households are also not necessarily poorer

- Include non-SNA work in country analysis
- Develop country-specific time budgets for men and women
- Develop gender/women's budget initiatives
- Use benefit incidence analysis of public expenditures
- Disaggregate poverty data and analysis by gender

A Different Poverty Agenda: Gender-Inclusive Poverty Reduction

Public policy and partnerships with civil society both have a major role to play in promoting gender-inclusive growth and poverty reduction. A key challenge for public policy is to undertake concurrent actions across a range of sectors that explicitly minimize these tradeoffs and raise labor productivity in both market and household economies. We identify five priority areas for policy response and investment that are of importance for policymakers and opinion leaders.

1. **Enhancing the participation of the poor (especially poor women) in economic decisionmaking.**
   There is an important role for public policy in reaching out to the poor, and especially in building up women's skills and capabilities. Promotion of participation requires a corresponding commitment to make available the resources needed to build up women's long-term capacities to make themselves heard. A promising approach, related to economic management and priority-setting, is the development of "women's budgets" or "gender budget initiatives." Africa has led the way in this area. Women's budgets examine the efficiency and equity implications of budget allocations and the policies and programs that lie behind them. This should enable public spending priorities to focus on investment in rural infrastructure and labor-saving technologies, as described below.

2. **Concurrent investment in the household economy and in raising labor productivity.**
   Public policy can have a significant impact on the heavy time burden of domestic work through investment in the household economy. Infrastructure to provide clean and accessible water supply is especially critical in view of its multiple benefits. Labor-saving domestic technology related to food processing is likely to have a greater immediate impact in raising the productivity and reducing the time burdens of many women. Transport interventions need to reflect the different needs of men and women, so as to improve women's access to transport services (including intermediate means of transport) commensurate with their load-carrying responsibilities (figure 10.7). These investments in the household economy are likely to have substantial payoffs in increased efficiency and growth in the market economy.

FIGURE 10-7. Gender and Transport Burdens in Three African Countries

Tonne-kilometers per year

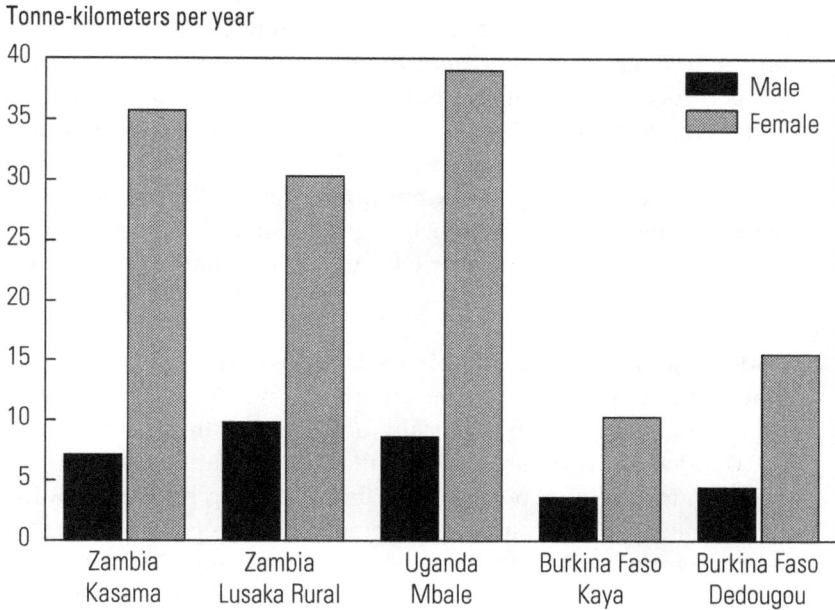

Source: Barwell 1996.

3. **Concurrent investment in human capability.**
   Investment in basic education and literacy, especially for girls, is paramount, as is appropriate investment in health care, especially reproductive, maternal, and child health. The strongly positive linkages associated with better health and education are well documented in Agnes Abuom's paper (see chapter 11) and will not be further addressed here.

4. **Concurrent investment in gender-inclusive growth.**
   Agricultural strategy, in particular policy, research, extension, and technology, needs to support the livelihood strategies of smallholder households. The key policy priority is to break through the asset poverty of women. Agricultural institutions (notably research extension services and institutions providing credit) need to treat women farmers as priority clients and develop outreach systems to

them. The right mix of assets, including land, labor, technology, and financial services, is critical to ensure that women can fully contribute to Africa's growth and development. Policy needs to focus on the food crop sector, where there is an urgent need for more women-focused integrated packages, including research, extension, and technology development. This would influence choices about which agricultural technologies are developed, which crops and tasks are prioritized, which extension messages are developed and delivered, which research priorities are pursued, and, most importantly, how these will be carried out in ways that reach women effectively.

5. **Making gender issues visible in data and analysis.**
    Statistics and indicators on the situation of women and men in all spheres of society are an important tool in promoting gender equality. Gender statistics have an essential role in eliminating stereotypes, in formulating policies, and in monitoring progress toward full equality. Key tasks are the systematic disaggregation of data by sex, integration of intrahousehold and gender modules in statistical surveys and poverty analysis, expanded use of gender-budget initiatives and use of benefit incidence analysis, greater use of country-focused time budget surveys, and the inclusion of the household economy and home-based work in national accounts data.

Notes

1. We define "assets" broadly to include directly productive assets (principally labor, land, agricultural inputs, financial services, and infrastructure); human capital assets (education and health); and social capital assets (focusing on household relations and participation). We use a variety of sources of evidence for gender disparities, including Blackden and Bhanu (1999) and other documents included in the bibliography.

2. An example is Cameroon. See World Bank 1995.

3. Disability-adjusted life years are an indicator of the time lived with disability and the time lost due to premature mortality, and represent an effort to combine mortality and morbidity in a single indicator. It is used as a basis for calculating the "global burden of disease," from which these estimates are drawn.

Bibliography

Baden, Sally. 1996. "Gender Issues in Financial Liberalization and Financial Sector Reform." Paper prepared for DGVII, European Commission, Brussels.

Barwell, I. 1996. "Transport and the Village: Findings from African Village-Level Travel and Transport. Surveys and Related Studies." Discussion Paper 344. World Bank, Africa Region, Washington, D.C.

Blackden, C. M., and Chitra Bhanu. 1999. "Gender, Growth, and Poverty Reduction: Special Program of Assistance for Africa 1998 Status Report on Poverty." Technical Paper 428. World Bank, Washington, D.C.

Blackden, C. M., and Elizabeth Morris-Hughes. 1993. "Paradigm Postponed: Gender and Economic Adjustment in Sub-Saharan Africa." Technical Note 13. World Bank, Poverty and Human Resources Division, Technical Department, Washington, D.C.

Budlender, Debbie, ed. 1998. "The Third Women's Budget." Cape Town Institute for Democracy in South Africa (IDASA), Cape Town.

Cleaver, K. M., and G. A. Schreiber. 1994. "Reversing the Spiral: The Population, Agriculture, Environment Nexus in Sub-Saharan Africa." Directions in Development Series. World Bank, Washington, D.C.

Elson, Diane, and Barbara Evers. 1997. "Gender-Aware Country Economic Reports. Working Paper No. 2: Uganda." Prepared for the Development Assistance Committee/Women in Development (DAC/WID) Task Force on Programme Aid and Other Forms of Economic Policy-Related Assistance. World Bank, Washington, D.C.

Fofack, Hippolyte. 1998. "Overview of Gender Issues in Labor Force Participation in Sub-Saharan Africa." Background paper for the 1998 SPA Status Report on Poverty in Sub-Saharan Africa. World Bank, Africa Region, Washington, D.C.

International Parliamentary Union. 1997. *Men and Women in Politics: Democracy Still in the Making—A World Comparative Study.* Geneva.

Klasen, S. 1998. "Gender Inequality and Growth in Sub-Saharan Africa: Some Preliminary Findings." Background paper for the 1998 SPA Status Report on Poverty in Sub-Saharan Africa. World Bank, Africa Region, Washington, D.C.

Martin, Doris, and Fatuma Hashi. 1992a. "Law as an Institutional Barrier to the Economic Empowerment of Women." AFTSP Working Paper 2. World Bank, Africa Region, Washington, D.C.

———. 1992b. "Gender, the Evolution of Legal Institutions and Economic Development in Sub-Saharan Africa." AFTSP Working Paper 3. World Bank, Africa Region, Washington, D.C.

————. 1992c. "Women in Development: The Legal Issues in Sub-Saharan Africa Today." AFTSP Working Paper 4. World Bank, Africa Region, Washington, D.C.

Moser, Caroline O. N. 1996. "Confronting Crisis: A Comparative Study of Household Responses to Poverty and Vulnerability in Four Poor Urban Communities." Environmentally Sustainable Development Studies and Monographs Series 8. World Bank, Washington, D.C.

Muntemba, Shimwaayi, and Ruvimbo Chimedza. 1995. "Women Spearhead Food Security: Science and Technology an Asset?" In U.N. Commission on Science and Technology for Development, Gender Working Group, *Missing Links: Gender Equity in Science and Technology for Development.* Ottawa: International Development Research Centre, in association with Intermediate Technology Publications and UNIFEM.

Quainoo, Aba Amissah. 1999. "Financial Services for Women Entrepreneurs in the Informal Sector of Ghana." Studies in Rural and Micro Finance 8. World Bank, Africa Region, Washington, D.C.

Quisumbing, Agnes, Lynn R. Brown, Hilary Sims Feldstein, L. Haddad, and Christine Peña. 1995. "Women: The Key to Food Security." Food Policy Report. International Food Policy Research Institute, Washington, D.C.

SPAAR (Special Program of African Agricultural Research). 1999. "A Gender Sensitive Agenda for the Special Program of African Agricultural Research." Prepared by the Gender Working Group for the 19th SPAAR plenary session, Gaberone, Botswana.

Tibaijuka, Anna. 1994. "The Cost of Differential Gender Roles in African Agriculture: A Case Study of Smallholder Banana-Coffee Farms in the Kagera Region, Tanzania." *Journal of Agricultural Economics* 45 (1).

World Bank. 1995. "Cameroon: Diversity, Growth, and Poverty Reduction." Report 13167-CM. Population and Human Resources Division, Central Africa and Indian Ocean Department. Washington D.C.

————. 1997. *Confronting AIDS: Public Priorities in a Global Epidemic.* World Bank Policy Research Report. New York: Oxford University Press.

————. 2000. *Can Africa Claim the 21ˢᵗ Century?* Washington, D.C.

11

Women's Issues in Health and Education

Agnes Abuom

By the 1990s an international consensus had emerged that poverty alleviation should be the overarching goal of both economic and political development. Initially, it was hoped that poverty could be alleviated though economic growth alone. Poverty was seen as a short-term hardship, one that would disappear as nations developed and grew in economic terms. But poverty is now recognized as a major threat to very significant sectors of countries' populations, with worrisome consequences for the security of nations and the economic well-being even of those people with surplus income and good access to services. It is also increasingly apparent that national economic growth per se is not a sufficient condition for poverty reduction. For one thing, the causes of poverty are multidimensional. Poverty can be viewed as including not only the shortage of disposable income but also deprivation in other economic and social areas: in education, in life expectancy, and in a whole spectrum of factors that affect a person's standard of living and quality of life.

This new consensus should inspire development policy in Africa where, by many estimates, two-fifths of the population live in poverty, and the number and proportion of poor people are increasing. For example, 37 of the 48 countries in the United Nations Development Programme's category of "low human development countries"—those with low literacy, low income, and low life expectancy—are located in Africa (UNDP 1999). So are 33 of the 48 countries on the U.N. list of "least developed countries" (UNCTAD 1999).

In pursuing the challenge of poverty reduction, each African country has to ask which strategy is most likely to be effective. Since 1990 the World Bank has proposed the need for three main elements: labor-demanding growth, investment in health and education, and safety nets for poor and vulnerable groups. Increasingly, a fourth element—good governance—is being advocated as well, since governments still control a significant share of national resources and shape the policy environment for private economic agents and civil society.

Since 1997, many African governments have been specifically incorporating poverty alleviation and improved social welfare into their policies. Most see the issue of poverty reduction as a national challenge. A recent example is Botswana, where in 1997 the government published a study on the impact and alleviation of poverty (FAO 1998: 16). In Kenya, the National Poverty Eradication Plan provides a national policy and institutional framework for taking urgent action against poverty in the country. The plan presents a vision for the early twenty-first century, when Kenya hopes to halt the current increase in the incidence of poverty and then to eradicate it gradually (Kenya 1999). The Kenyan plan underscores the government's determination to address the poverty challenge not only as a political necessity and moral obligation, but also on grounds of sound economic principles that recognize the critical role and potential contribution of the poor to national development.

The question that can be posed at this juncture is: Why revisit the issue of poverty alleviation, with special emphasis on women, when previous attempts and recommendations have had limited impact? The answer is that churches and various religious groups, African governments, the international financial institutions including the World Bank, and nongovernmental organizations all have today the benefit of hindsight. They have identified a host of factors underlying their previous failures. These include, among others: (a) lack of common consensus; (b) insufficient political will by governments to implement the recommendations; (c) failure to involve the private sector; and (d) failure to sensitize the public about the importance of enhancing women's capacities in economic development and genuine participation by women in decisionmaking processes.

This paper provides a critical analysis of past and current knowledge about African economies, with particular emphasis on the state of women's health and education. While the economic and political conditions of African women are examined at length, the paper also offers a menu of possible interventions to stem the tide of poverty in general, and among African women in particular.

Africa's General Economic Performance

After 20 years of decline, African economies may be growing once more. According to the most recent estimates, the region's overall economy registered a rebound in 1998 with a growth rate of 3.3 percent per year, well above the 2.9 percent growth in 1997 and also above the population growth rate of 2.8 percent per year (UNECA 1999). Average GDP growth in Africa increased from 2.6 percent in 1994 to 3.8 percent in 1995 and 4.5 percent in 1996; this contrasted to the 2.1 percent annual average for the first five years of the 1990s. Strong growth in export earnings underpinned the recovery, which also owed much to better weather conditions and to ongoing policy reforms in a number of countries. In 36 countries of the region, economic growth exceeded population growth rates, allowing a modest improvement in average per capita incomes for the first time in many years (UNECA 1999).

However, even if the growth of the past few years could be sustained through the current decade, that would not reverse the marginalization of the region or make much dent in widespread poverty; indeed it would do little more than recover the ground lost during the past two decades. The challenge for policymakers is to turn this recovery into a stronger and sustainable economic take-off, with the aim of attaining the 6 percent growth target set by the United Nations. In the past four years or so, only a handful of countries have managed to sustain growth rates reaching or surpassing this target.

In addition, democratization is having a profound impact on political and economic dynamics across the continent. Since 1990, more than 42 multiparty presidential elections have been held, with 21 of them being the first such elections in the respective countries. In 35 countries, opposition parties have been legalized. Most governments' acceptance of responsibility, coupled with encouraging participation by civil society, has contributed to modest gains in building critical capacities needed for economic development.

However, during the recent past, civil conflicts have occurred in a host of African countries, causing severe human suffering and material destruction and tearing the very social fabric. Most of the people affected are in the vulnerable groups in society, especially women and children. This implies that there will be no quick fixes or panaceas imposed from outside; rather, the process of creating an environment of self-fulfillment and peace will be long-term.

Impacts of "Economic Recovery Programs" in Sub-Saharan Africa

No single subject in development economics provoked as much discussion in the 1980s and 1990s as the costs and benefits of structural adjustment programs (SAPs). In fact, SAPs were a watchword of the 1980s, particularly in Sub-Saharan Africa. The programs have been much analyzed and debated by academics, policymakers, churches, and NGOs alike, with a view to assessing their effectiveness in eradicating poverty, promoting human development, and fostering economic growth.

The SAPs incorporated such measures as currency devaluation, removal of subsidies on certain producer and consumer goods, reduction of government spending, promotion of public enterprises, and cost recovery and cost containment in the social services. Under these programs, governments' budgets have been drastically curtailed, resulting in profound deterioration of social and economic infrastructures and often undermining the basis of economic recovery itself. More often than not, SAPs overlooked the distributional aspects of development and the effects on the living standards of vulnerable groups. Proponents of SAPs argue that the social costs during the period of adjustment are both transitional and necessary in order to revive economic activity, and thus wage employment and self-employment, and so reduce poverty. In fact, most if not all of the countries that have embarked on SAPs or "economic recovery programs" were adversely affected before adjustment by rising energy prices, falling commodity prices, balance of payment problems, and rising debt burdens.

There is, therefore, a raging debate about the effectiveness of SAPs in attaining their objectives of restoring economic balance and growth, as well as about their impact on employment, personal incomes, and living standards as measured by nutrition and health or even education. It is argued here that SAPs in most cases have not taken account of their social effects and that this has been a major cause of their failure; also, that it is the design of the programs and the speed and sequencing of the reforms that have caused the current controversy.

Viewed in this light, it is apparent that short-term approaches to structural adjustment have to be replaced by approaches that fully envisage the long-term requirements of development. In other words, SAPs have to be integrated into long-term development planning objectives.

While discussing the impact of the economic recovery programs on women's education and health, it is important to recognize that the problems cannot be attributed to the International Monetary Fund and the World Bank alone. Other key actors, including governments, churches, and individual households, have contributed to the current situation as well. Naturally, each group will have a different opinion as to the culprit for the problems. Nonetheless, without apportioning blame or passing judgment on any particular group, the intention here is to be more inclusive and accommodative, with a view to achieving, more or less, a common consensus.

The Programs' General Impact on Women

Poverty among women is growing faster in Sub-Saharan Africa than in any other developing region. Women in Africa, as a group, are less educated, earn less, own less, control less, and are less well represented in most economic and political spheres than women elsewhere. Poor women already on the margins of the economy suffer most during the implementation of economic recovery programs. For instance, cutbacks in state programs of health care, child care, and elder care imply that women are expected to take up extra responsibilities in these areas. Moreover, women's own health is in jeopardy due to their critical roles in production, childbearing and child rearing, and household management. When unemployment worsens and subsidies on essential goods and services are cut, it is again poor women who suffer most.

For instance, closely associated with people's health status is their level of nutrition. As a result of the debt crisis and the economic recovery programs, a large number of African countries have had to eliminate or reduce subsidies on food. This has led to higher food prices, which in turn have contributed to falling standards of living in the urban areas. In this respect, declining levels of nutrition were reported in a number of African countries particularly in the 1980s (UNECA 1990), and to some extent in the 1990s. Also, deregulation of prices in internal retail markets, it is argued, has contributed to inflation. With women's limited resources, this has reduced their purchasing power and has made it more difficult for them to meet their families' basic needs.

Education Profile

In 1990 five international agencies—the United Nations Children's Fund (UNICEF), the United Nations Development Programme (UNDP), the United Nations Educational, Scientific, and Cultural Organization (UNESCO), the United Nations Population Fund (UNFPA), and the World Bank—sponsored a landmark international meeting in Jomtien, Thailand, called the World Conference on Education for All. It recommended two goals: universal primary education for all and gender equality in enrollments in primary and secondary education.

Today, many governments and organizations, including the World Bank, have adopted the two recommendations as objectives.

Investment in appropriate education leads to accumulation of human capital, which is the key to sustained economic growth and increased incomes. Sound education develops a person's capacity for learning, for interpreting information, and for using knowledge of local conditions. Furthermore, through its potential effects on economic productivity and on other aspects such as health, education influences a person's well-being. And since the majority of agricultural subsistence producers are women, appropriate education for women could be expected to improve agricultural productivity and incomes as well as women's employment opportunities and decisionmaking influence within the household.

Female education is recognized as one of the critical pathways for promoting social and economic development. Many studies suggest that the education level attained by girls has a significant influence on the health and nutrition of children born to them later. For instance, a study conducted in 45 developing countries found that the average mortality rate for children under five was 144 per 1,000 live births when the mothers had no education, 106 per 1,000 when they had primary education only, and 68 per 1,000 when they had some secondary education (World Bank 2000: 17). Figure 11.1 illustrates the generational impact of educating a girl.

Nonetheless, in many SSA countries there continues to be substantial discrimination favoring boys' education over girls'. The inequality in primary and secondary school enrollment rates is shown in table

FIGURE 11-1. Generational Impact of Educating a Girl

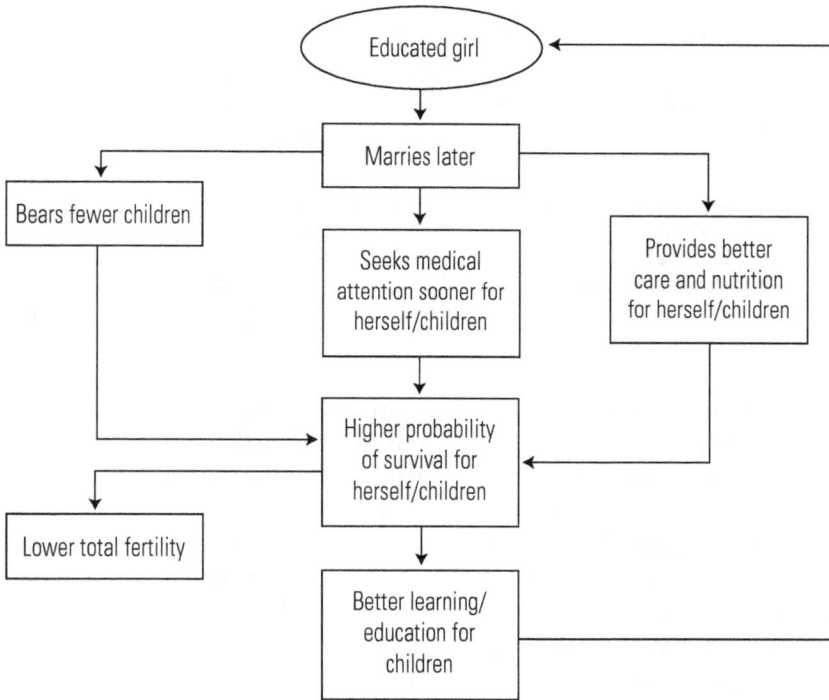

Source: Based on Herz and others 1991.

11.1. The gross enrollment ratio for girls in primary school throughout SSA rose from 66 percent in 1980 to 74 percent in 1996; this is a substantial increase, but the ratio for girls is still significantly lower than for boys in primary enrollment. The secondary school data show that although significant improvement was registered in female enrollment ratios between 1980 and 1996, they still lag behind male ratios.

It is important to point out that the overall statistics for SSA in table 11.1 mask wide variations between countries. For instance, although Mauritius and South Africa have achieved nearly universal primary enrollment, a significant number of other African countries still have primary enrollment ratios for girls that are less than 50 percent.

TABLE 11.1 Primary and Secondary School Gross Enrollment Ratio in Sub-Saharan Africa, 1980–96

(percent)

Educational level	Male			Female		
	1980	1990	1996	1980	1990	1996
Primary	87	80	86	66	65	74
Secondary	19	25	32	10	20	26

Note: School gross enrollment ratio is the total number of students enrolled in school, regardless of age, expressed as a percentage of the total school-age population.

Sources: For 1980 and 1990, World Bank 1998: 338–43. For 1996, African Development Bank 1999: 11.

In a number of African countries, dropout rates at the primary level are higher for girls than for boys, indicating that the gap in actual enrollment and hence completion of primary education is even wider than is reflected in the enrollment ratios in table 11.1.

Tables 11.2 and 11.3 present regional summaries of youth and adult illiteracy rates between 1980 and 1997. The combination of an increased absolute number of children (both male and female) who are out of school and low primary completion rates implies that the formal education system in Sub-Saharan Africa is likely to be inadequate as a mechanism for overcoming illiteracy. Both tables present a gloomy picture, particularly for women, whose adult illiteracy rates are significantly higher than those of men. Although female adult illiteracy declined between 1980 and 1997, it remains at 50 percent in SSA and is not likely to fall much below 40 percent without new interventions from governments, the private sector, churches and other religious groups, and NGOs.

The Roles of Women in Political Participation and Decisionmaking

Political participation is a key issue for women because it is both an indicator of their social status and a tool to improve their situation in society. In many African countries, women have the right to vote and they do vote. However, the mere act of voting cannot be regarded as a measure of political consciousness or participation. In many instances, poor rural and urban women are mobilized by political parties to vote.

TABLE 11.2 Youth Illiteracy Rates, 1980 and 1997

(percent)

Region	Males aged 15–24 years		Females aged 15–24 years	
	1980	1997	1980	1997
Sub-Saharan Africa	34	20	55	29
Middle East and North Africa	26	14	52	27
Latin America and Caribbean	36	25	64	48
Europe and Central Asia	1	1	5	2
East Asia and Pacific	11	7	11	6
South Asia	5	2	15	4

Source: World Bank.

TABLE 11.3 Adult Illiteracy Rates, 1980, 1995, and 1997

(percent)

Region	1980		1995		1997	
	Male	Female	Male	Female	Male	Female
Sub-Saharan Africa	42.8	70.8	35.1	54.2	34.3	50.0
Middle East and North Africa	45.0	73.8	28.0	50.0	26.9	50.0
Latin America and Caribbean	17.9	22.5	12.2	14.0	12.0	14.0
Europe and Central Asia	—	—	—	—	2.0	6.0
East Asia and Pacific	19.6	42.0	9.0	24.3	9.0	22.2
South Asia	47.2	75.5	37.1	64.2	36.0	63.0

— Not available.

Note: Applies to people 15 years of age and above. Literacy is defined as the ability to read and write. A person who can, with understanding, both read and write a short, simple statement about his/her everyday life is literate.

Sources: African Development Bank 1999; UNESCO 1995; World Bank 1996, 2000.

In 1997, there were about 130 million illiterate adults in SSA (about 43 percent of the total adult population), compared with about 33 million (13 percent of the total adult population) in Latin America and the Caribbean (World Bank 2000: 230–33). The estimates in tables 11.2 and 11.3, although not exhaustive, indicate how vast is the illiteracy problem (although the rapid fall in SSA youth illiteracy to well below the levels in Latin America and the Caribbean should be taken as an encouraging sign).

In such situations, women vote in high numbers, but they do not participate in any other political activities. Though a few women in some countries of Africa are now actively involved in formal politics, the overall situation of women in regard to political participation is still unsatisfactory.

Women are also underrepresented in senior public offices. In some African countries a few women have been appointed to responsible positions in sectors such as culture, social welfare, and women's and youth affairs. A number of factors hamper women's ability and willingness to run for office. The first is the typical style of electioneering, which is often marred by violence. The second is financial limitations. Third is the unethical and derogatory language typically used against women candidates. Fourth is lack of relevant capacity and experience.

Table 11.4 presents gender gaps in political participation ratios for selected African countries in 1996. The table shows that only eight of the countries had over 10 percent of government positions filled by women, and only the Seychelles attained the 20 percent level during the period. Stark as these data may appear, the figures may underestimate the true picture. This is because the figures are only a snapshot and refer to the state of affairs some four years ago; in the meantime, some situations have worsened. In Kenya, for instance, there was no woman holding a ministerial post in early 2000.

Nonetheless, since the International Year for Women was declared more than two decades ago, the struggle for women's liberation and empowerment has made some progress. In fact, the last decade has witnessed the establishment of a number of women's research groups, organizations, and programs, such as the Association of Women for Research and Development, FEMNET, the African Center for Women, the United Nations Fund for Women, and the Federation of African Women in Education. We also have the Gender and Economic Reforms in Africa program, which was initiated in 1996 in collaboration with African women's organizations and researchers. Its stated purposes are to provide critical analysis of economic reform processes in Africa from a gender perspective, and to develop alternative approaches that ensure gender equality and economic justice. All these groups, and others, have worked hard to sensitize people about the importance of gender equality in the economic development process. Such efforts are commendable but still have a long way to go.

Table 11.4 Gender Gaps in Political Participation in Selected African Countries, 1996

| Country | Rank[a] | Percentage of government positions held by women[b] | | |
		All levels	Ministerial level	Subministerial level
Botswana	3	13.5	7.7	15.4
Burundi	22	5.4	10.3	0.0
Cape Verde	7	11.1	13.3	8.3
Côte d'Ivoire	16	7.1	8.3	6.8
Eritrea	14	7.8	18.8	4.2
Ghana	10=	9.6	10.3	9.4
Kenya	20	5.8	3.4	6.6
Lesotho	2	14.6	0.0	18.2
Malawi	23	4.3	3.6	4.7
Mauritius	9	9.8	0.0	12.6
Mozambique	4	12.8	4.0	14.7
Namibia	6	11.4	8.7	12.3
Niger	8	10.9	14.3	10.0
Nigeria	18	6.2	7.7	5.6
Rwanda	19	5.9	3.8	6.5
Senegal	21	5.6	6.7	4.2
Seychelles	1	20.8	33.3	18.3
South Africa	17	7.0	1.0	7.5
Sudan	24	1.7	2.4	1.3
Swaziland	15	7.5	0.0	13.6
Tanzania	10=	9.6	10.5	8.9
Uganda	12	8.9	10.5	8.1
Zambia	13	8.4	7.7	8.4
Zimbabwe	5	11.6	8.3	14.0

a. Countries are ranked by the "all levels" proportion.
b. Includes elected heads of state and governors of the central banks.
Source: UNDP 1999: 239.

In most churches in Africa today women constitute the majority of members, up to 90 percent. In such circumstances, religious leaders can use churches to sensitize their members about the importance of empowering women in the processes of economic, political, and social development. It is also clear that the Church is now active again in providing formal education in many countries.

African governments should take into account that women are equal partners with men, that their participation in politics and in decisionmaking forums is critical for development, and that women are an economic resource whose contributions should be sufficiently acknowledged and enhanced. If we take the position that women are underused human resources, then that potential must be developed and appropriately utilized to accelerate national economic recovery.

Health Profiles

People's health depends on effective poverty alleviation, clean water, adequate and balanced nutrition, decent housing, good sanitation, and sound basic education, especially for girls. Even more important than any of these factors, indeed a sine qua non for a good health sector, is a sound, robust, and vibrant national economy. This is because no matter how hard the health authorities may try, a per capita average health budget of less than US$10 for SSA cannot provide adequate health care for individuals.

The health sector continues to bear a disproportionate burden of the ongoing socioeconomic crisis. The average expenditure on the health sector in SSA in the late 1990s rarely exceeded 5 percent of GDP (UNDP 1997; World Bank 2000). In many African countries, poor service conditions have demoralized most of the health professionals, leading to the exodus of doctors, nurses, and medical technicians. Together with declining public health expenditure, this has led to the virtual collapse of modern health services.

Table 11.5 indicates that between 1970 and 1997, significant progress was made in reducing infant mortality rates in Sub-Saharan Africa. The table indicates that between the two periods, the infant mortality rate in SSA declined from 142 to 91 per 1,000 live births (a reduction of about 36 percent). But this rate is still high in comparison with other developing regions, that is, the Middle East and North Africa, Latin America and Caribbean, East Asia and Pacific, and South Asia.

The majority of Sub-Saharan Africa's population is currently not reached by health services. For instance, health profiles indicate that in 1990 there was one doctor for every 18,488 people in Sub-Saharan Africa. This compares to one doctor for every 344 people in the industrial nations, one for every 5,767 in all developing countries, and one

TABLE 11.5 Regional Infant Mortality Rates, 1970–97

(per 1,000 live births)

Region	1970	1980	1992	1997
Sub-Saharan Africa	142	115	99	91
Middle East and North Africa	139	95	58	49
Latin America and Caribbean	85	60	44	32
Europe and Central Asia	—	41	30	23
East Asia and Pacific	84	55	39	37
South Asia	138	119	85	77

— Not available.

Sources: UNECA 1999; World Bank 1994, 2000.

for every 4,968 worldwide. In the same year, one nurse served 6,504 people in SSA compared with 4,715 people in all developing countries (UNDP 1996: 161; World Bank 1994: 215). The maternal mortality rate in SSA was 971 per 100,000 live births compared with 471 in all developing countries and only 31 in the industrial countries (UNDP 1997: 60).

African women, particularly rural women, are often the most vulnerable population in terms of ill health and malnutrition. They are affected by frequent pregnancies and by traditional dietary customs, which often forbid women to eat foods that are rich in protein. The scarcity of doctors, especially in the rural areas, means that women in most cases receive services too late or not at all. The high costs, under cost sharing or privatization, of medical treatment and drugs contribute to the problem.

It is obvious from the foregoing that virtually all indicators of morbidity and mortality are higher in Africa than in the rest of the world. This includes Sub-Saharan Africa's average life expectancy of 45 years, which is about 25 years lower than the average for the industrial nations and 13 years lower than the world average (UNECA 1999). Needless to say, disease and ill health lower people's productivity, depress the GDP, and increase poverty.

The issue of high fertility in Africa and its critical relation to maternal and child health, poverty, and sustainable development has been discussed at length in a number of forums. The most recent of these include the third African Population Conference held in Dakar, Senegal, in December 1992 and the International Conference on Population and Development held in Cairo, Egypt, in September 1994.

Table 11.6 provides a regional summary of the total fertility rate (TFR)—the number of children the average woman has in a lifetime. Sub-Saharan Africa still lags behind other regions in its demographic transition. Although the TFR for SSA as a whole declined somewhat from 6.5 in 1970 to 5.5 in 1997, the rate is still very high in comparison with the other developed and developing regions. Three other regions, Latin America and Caribbean, Middle East and North Africa, and East Asia and Pacific, managed to reduce their TFRs by around one-half between 1970 and 1997.

Indeed, the high fertility rate in SSA is a large contributor to the ill health of both mothers and children. Pregnancies among young women are common, posing health risks to the young mothers and often stifling their chances for advancement as the first pregnancy will usually require them to leave school. In rural SSA it is estimated that 25 percent of all women between the ages of 15 and 44 get pregnant each year, compared with only 10 percent in the industrial countries. Perhaps even more striking is the fact that 50 percent of all women in the region who start bearing children at a tender age die by age 50 from fertility-related causes. The above figures reflect the need for family planning services, which at present are still insignificant.

In fact, few women actually use any effective form of contraception. In Kenya, for instance, among both men and women, contraceptive use is higher in urban than in rural areas. The differential use by level

Table 11.6 Total Fertility Rate, 1970–97

(births per woman)

Region	1970	1980	1992	1997
Sub-Saharan Africa	6.5	6.6	6.1	5.5
Middle East and North Africa	6.8	6.2	4.1	3.7
Latin America and Caribbean	5.2	4.1	3.0	2.7
Europe and Central Asia	2.5	2.5	2.2	1.7
East Asia and Pacific	5.7	3.0	2.3	2.1
South Asia	6.0	5.3	4.0	3.5

Sources: World Bank 1982, 1994, 2000.

of education is striking. Less than 20 percent of married women with no education are using some method of family planning, compared to 35 percent among those who have completed a primary education and 52 percent among those with some secondary education (Kenya 1999: 49). This again underscores the importance of education. Nonetheless, it must also be noted here that the issue of family planning methods has yet to be resolved among various religious and church groups in the region.

The Church and Women's Issues

Although a majority of church members are women, the relationship between the Church and women is contradictory. On the one hand, the Church empowers women, and on the other, it has been slow in applying the revolutionary message of good news for women within its own structures. Women tend to be marginalized within Church structures insofar as decisionmaking and leadership are concerned.

In many respects, the Church has been one of the few civic institutions that have empowered women. It is in the church context that women's organizations such as the Mothers Union, the Women's Guild, and others have thrived. Through these organizations, women have engaged in delivery of social services at the micro level as well as in purely welfare activities. Around churches one finds women's groups undertaking all types of interventions related to, for example, domestic water supply, credit, and sewing, often basic work for the survival of households. Many of these activities are supported through the churches.

As regards health and education, some churches fund and run quality private schools as well as hospitals and community-based health care services. It is estimated that up to 70 percent of modern health care is now managed by churches in some African countries. The pressure is high on churches to increase their involvement in education and, as a result, a number are venturing into university education.

The issue of decisionmaking in the churches is complex and contested. Many churches still do not have women in their top leadership or active in decisionmaking. Further, management and leadership styles in many churches do not facilitate women's participation, let alone empowerment. However, increasingly churches are ensuring that women participate more. One such method is providing quotas for women to attend church meetings.

A Framework for Action

A rethinking of policies must recognize and directly address the structural constraints and institutional hiatus that pervade African economies. Needless to say, there is no universal recipe that will solve the problem of how to alleviate poverty. Rather, a menu of mutually reinforcing actions, phased over a long period of time, is called for. Governments *must* take the lead as facilitators and providers of an enabling environment to curb poverty, while the international donor community also has an important role to play by evolving policies and programs that can help African countries strengthen their national economic base.

Today, much is known about what is needed to alleviate poverty, particularly among women: access to credit, land redistribution, investment in basic needs (such as education and health), promotion of the informal sector, and sound macroeconomic policies. Nonetheless, too little attention has been given to ensuring that such actions are taken. It must be underscored here that provision of education and health care alone will not reduce poverty; complementary macroeconomic policies and physical investments are also needed.

How can an enabling environment be created that ensures that state policies, market forces, civil activism, and community mobilization will all contribute to the alleviation of poverty? What political and economic reforms are needed to ensure pro-poor policies and pro-poor markets?

A political and economic strategy for poverty alleviation must encompass the following six essential elements, among others:

Political Empowerment for Poor People

People must organize for collective action to influence the circumstances and decisions affecting their lives. To advance their interests, their voices must be heard in the corridors of power. For instance, as a major part of the rural workforce, women are the primary stakeholders in rural investment projects—whether aimed at poverty alleviation or agricultural and rural development. Their full participation in the development process is essential to achieve a sustainable impact. Increased efforts must therefore be made to involve all beneficiaries in the planning and implementation of projects to ensure that projects respond to their expectations, and to gain concerted commitment.

Gender Equity

In a number of African countries, various indicators—the practice of prenatal sex selection, higher mortality rates for very young girls than for boys, and lower rates of school enrollment for girls, among others—suggest that "son preference" is curtailing the access of girl children to education and health care. To this end, the value of girls to both their families and the larger society must be expanded beyond their definition as potential childbearers and caretakers. Changed attitudes must be reinforced through the adoption and implementation of educational and social policies that encourage girls' and women's full participation in the development of the societies in which they live.

A strategy for broad-based growth is needed, particularly (but not exclusively) in the rural areas, where more than 80 percent of poor men and women live. It must be stressed here that poverty among women, especially rural women, requires special attention.

Often, women's rights to land are put at risk by widowhood or divorce, and lack of land jeopardizes women's incomes and economic well-being. To this end, legislation should be enacted to remove formal legal obstacles to women's effective rights to land for income generation purposes. Similarly, governments must seek to remove constraints within customary law systems.

Partnership for Change

All agents in society—churches, the media, community-based groups, private companies, political parties, academic institutions, professional institutions, and others—need to come together in partnership to address human poverty in all its dimensions. For instance, churches need to give clear guidance on the issues of HIV/AIDS and on how to lower the current fertility rate and hence population growth rates. So far, the messages from the churches on these issues have been contradictory.

The health hazards caused by female circumcision are well documented and include obstructed labor, hemorrhage, infections, and even maternal and infant deaths. In this regard, governments are strongly urged to prohibit female genital mutilation wherever it exists and to give support to efforts among NGOs, community-based organizations, and various religious groups to eliminate such practices.

Sound Intersectoral Linkages

Provision of a country's health services calls for satisfactory coordination between the ministry of health and all other ministries, departments, agencies, and churches whose activities impact the health sector. Such linkages are not yet strong in a number of African countries. For instance, closer collaboration is needed between ministries of health; ministries of education; ministries of agriculture and rural development; ministries responsible for water, sanitation, and housing; NGOs active in the area of water supply; mission hospitals; and traditional medical practitioners. In the same vein, provision of a country's educational services calls for coordination between the relevant key players.

Reliable Statistics

Governments are urged to create comprehensive data on the situation of the girl child with particular reference to the urban poor, rural poor, school dropouts, and adolescent mothers, so that these statistics can be used for appropriate national planning.

An Enabling and Responsible State

The state needs to foster the peaceful expression of people's priorities and ensure democratic space for brokering the interests of society's many groups, that is, by encouraging private-public partnership and promoting participation. Furthermore, the state must be transparent and accountable and must resist pressures from the economically powerful.

There is no gainsaying the nexus between democracy and development. New democratic governments are hard pressed to simultaneously repay debt obligations and maintain popular support. To this end, the international donor community and institutions could help African governments meet such obligations by instituting, among others, measures such as debt relief and/or debt cancellation so that substantially more resources could be released and directed toward rebuilding and sustaining critical sectors in the national economies.

Political and economic initiatives at the highest level will be needed if this framework for actions is to be realized. A general recommendation to African leaders, policymakers, churches, NGOs, and the donor community on the issue of women's health and education is in order, stressing realism, vision, seriousness, and discipline in whatever they do. This is a goal that all of us should be determined to pursue with a view to putting the continent on a sustainable development path—in both the short and the long term.

Conclusions

What new approach might help? A stronger and more genuine partnership between African governments and the international donor community is now called for. The failure by many African governments to critically define poverty reduction as their central objective has been a major shortcoming; donors, including the World Bank, must accept some responsibility for this failure because of their willingness to lend despite weak commitment by those African governments to poverty reduction. The international financial institutions are also urged to adopt a gender perspective in dealing with African countries, and to lend support to governments' initiatives to improve domestic policies.

In sum, the time has come for African governments, the international donor community, NGOs, and community-based organizations alike to address the challenges of poverty reduction with specific emphasis on women by placing strategic focus on key issues, responding to the existing and impending crisis in the Africa region. An attempt has been made in this paper to indicate effective solutions in that direction.

Bibliography

Abuom, Agnes. 1998. "The Persistent Problem of Debt: A Gender Perspective." In *Proclaim Liberty*. Nairobi: Christian Aid.

African Development Bank. 1999. *Selected Statistics on African Countries*. Vol. 19. Abidjan.

Cleaver, K. M., and G. A. Schreiber. 1994. *Reversing the Spiral: The Population, Agriculture, and Environmental Nexus in Sub-Saharan Africa*. Washington, D.C: World Bank.

FAO (Food and Agriculture Organization of the United Nations). 1998. *State of Food and Agriculture 1998*. Rome.

Herz, Barbara, K. Subbarao, Masooma Habib, and Laura Raney. 1991. "Letting Girls Learn: Promising Approaches in Primary and Secondary Education." Discussion Paper 133. World Bank, Washington, D.C.

Kenya. 1999. "National Poverty Eradication Plan 1999–2015." Nairobi.

Martin, M. 1997. "A Multilateral Debt Facility: Global and National." In *International Monetary and Financial Issues for the 1990s*. Vol. 8. New York and Geneva: UNCTAD.

North-South Institute. 1999. "Toward Participatory Economic Reforms in Africa: A Quest for Women's Economic Empowerment." Ottawa.

Summers, Lawrence H. 1994. "Investing in All the People: Educating Women in Developing Countries." EDI Seminar Paper 45. World Bank, Washington, D.C.

UNCTAD (United Nations Conference on Trade and Development). 1999. *The Least Developed Countries 1999 Report.* New York and Geneva.

UNDP (United Nations Development Programme). Various years. *Human Development Report.* New York: Oxford University Press.

UNECA (United Nations Economic Commission for Africa). 1990. *The Human Dimension of Africa's Persistent Economic Crisis.* Edited by A. Adedeji, S. Rasheed, and M. Morrison. New York: Hans Zell.

———. 1999. "Economic Report on Africa 1999: The Challenges of Poverty Reduction and Sustainability." Addis Ababa.

UNICEF (United Nations Children's Fund). 1999. *The Status of the World's Children 1999: Education.* New York.

World Bank. 1994. *World Development Report 1994.* New York: Oxford University Press.

———. 1996. *World Development Report 1996.* New York: Oxford University Press.

———. 1998. *African Development Indicators 1998/99.* New York: Oxford University Press.

———. 2000. *Entering the 21st Century: World Development Report 1999/2000.* New York: Oxford University Press.

12

Reducing Poverty
by Combating AIDS

Peter Okaalet

It has been stated that an estimated 9 out of 10 people with HIV/AIDS live in situations marked by poverty, discrimination, and a subordinate status for women and children. Moreover, according to the World Health Organization and other authorities, poverty increases the vulnerability of human communities to HIV/AIDS. If we are to seriously address HIV/AIDS, then, we need to seriously address poverty and other related issues. In other words, by combating poverty we shall automatically be combating HIV/AIDS.

The World Council of Churches states that AIDS has become an issue affecting development. The pandemic imposes a heavy burden on the health care systems of communities, and the cost of treatment is often completely disproportionate to the incomes of the affected families. Therefore, HIV/AIDS needs to be addressed on its own merit.

I agree with this view. Indeed, we need a multipronged approach to fight both HIV/AIDS and poverty. To start with, poverty has always been a development issue. It has always been felt that if we address the development issues like the economy and education, other areas will automatically fall in place. This view may have to change. Now, health in general and HIV/AIDS in particular must be seen as development issues in their own right.

Every community on earth is feeling the effects of HIV/AIDS. I would argue that HIV/AIDS is actually leading to greater poverty than existed before the infection. In other words, a stable case of poverty is made worse by the onset of HIV/AIDS and its associated ill effects on individuals, families, communities, and nations.

Consider, for example, a case where a bank manager who is the bread-winner for his family suffers from HIV/AIDS-related diseases. By the time he dies he has spent most of the family's resources on medical care. His survivors now face a lower standard of living than they are used to. To cope with their lower status in the society and to relieve anxiety and depression associated with poverty, some family members may turn to using mind-altering drugs. They may inject drugs intravenously, thus predisposing and exposing themselves to HIV/AIDS infection. And they may resort to other high-risk behavior, such as prostitution, in order to make money to fill the void left by the breadwinner.

Poverty creates living conditions that promote disease. Without decent protection, many of the poor are exposed to severe weather, as well as to bacteria and viruses carried by other people, hence the high rates of infectious diseases among them. The chances are that the bank manager's family may slide from affluence to relative poverty to absolute poverty or destitution within a very short time, because HIV/AIDS and poverty form a vicious circle. Each stage of both poverty and HIV/AIDS is worse than the previous one.

By addressing HIV/AIDS now, therefore, we shall also be addressing a severe form of poverty that is exacerbated by the pandemic.

Understanding Poverty

Diverse Concepts of Poverty

When a person is reduced to poverty, he or she cannot afford the basics of life. As a result, poor people may be denied literacy, good nourishment, and good health. We need to distinguish the different types of poverty:

Relative poverty. Having fewer resources or less income than most others within a society or country.

Food poverty. Food consumption below a normative minimum level of nutrition that the human body needs for healthy growth and maintenance.

Income poverty. Lack of adequate income or expenditure to meet minimum basic needs. It is always measured in terms of income or expenditure.

Absolute poverty. Defined in monetary terms by a fixed standard such as the international one-dollar-a-day poverty line, which compares poverty levels across different countries. Someone in absolute poverty lacks basic human facilities such as adequate and nutritious food, clothing, housing, shelter, and health services. This is the most pervasive form of poverty, and it is what we need to guard against even as we fight the HIV/AIDS pandemic.

Vulnerability. A condition of risk. People not currently considered poor can become poor, while those at some milder level of poverty can move into extreme and/or absolute poverty. People who are not poor may become poor due to a number of factors; at present, one of the major factors is HIV/AIDS infection.

Indicators of Poverty and Well-Being

According to the UNICEF document "Challenges for Children and Women in the 1990s," there are two standard indicators of absolute poverty (UNICEF 1991). The *head count index* shows the percentage of a country's people living below the poverty line. It does not, however, show how far below. The *poverty gap* gives the percentage increase in total consumption that would be necessary to lift all the poor in a given country above the poverty line.

The World Bank distinguishes between "the poorest" and "the poor." *Extremely poor* people have annual incomes below US$275 per person. *Poor* people have annual incomes below US$370 per person. The World Bank estimates that there are 120 million extremely poor people and 185 million poor people in the world. The rest of the world's population is in the vulnerable category.

Another tool sometimes used is the Human Development Index, an attempt by the United Nations Development Programme to consider life in more than a single dimension. It measures human development as a composite of three basic variables: life expectancy at birth; educational attainment (measured as a function of both adult literacy and average mean years of schooling); and real GDP per capita (in purchasing power parity).

The State of the Poor

Whether we are talking of relative poverty, food poverty, or absolute poverty, we need to remember that poor people face many constraints in life. They include:

- Low status in society
- Poor infrastructure

- Declining government services
- Lack of income-earning opportunities
- Insecurity
- Political unrest
- Inability to access resources
- Lack of political power
- Illiteracy

Illiteracy means that the poor cannot obtain information that might help them to better their lot. They are deprived, as well, of good nutrition and a clean living environment, vaccinations and curative drugs, and testing and counseling services for HIV/AIDS.

Dignified living can be viewed as a basic human right. Dignity is the ability to meet socially perceived minimum basic needs. These needs are:

- Reliable food security
- Land holding/ownership
- Ownership of basic household items
- Peace
- Decent housing
- Adequate disposable income
- Access to knowledge and health

HIV/AIDS in Kenya

Poverty in Kenya

Kenya is ranked the eighth-poorest country in Africa. Most of the land is arid or semi-arid, and crop failure is common.

Income inequality is pronounced in Kenya. The richest 10 percent of Kenya's population received 47.7 percent of national income in 1998 (a rate of inequality nearly as high as Brazil's, where the richest 10 percent had 51.3 percent of income). According to a 1998 Kenyan government survey, more than 50 percent of the poor are located in 17 of the country's 60 districts. Around 15 percent of the poor live in four districts: Makueni, Siaya, Kitui, and Bungoma.

Women from poor households had a total fertility rate of 6.6 children per woman, compared to 6.1 children for their nonpoor counterparts. Only 14 percent of youth from poor households had completed secondary school, compared to 27.3 percent of nonpoor youth (Kenya 1998).

Incidence and Pervasiveness
The first reported case of HIV/AIDS in Kenya was in 1983 or 1984. Within the last 15 years or so, HIV prevalence has been increasing by leaps and bounds. Kenya's National AIDS/STD Control Programme estimates that in 1998, adult HIV prevalence stood at 13.9 percent (NASCOP 1999).

Last year the president of Kenya declared HIV/AIDS a national disaster. The situation is so bad that in some areas AIDS patients occupy 50 percent of hospital beds. The disease has not spared our schools. Some statistics indicate that almost 20 percent of schoolchildren in Kenya are HIV-positive. The death toll in the uniformed forces is alarming. This disease is not only destroying our past; it is also destroying our future.

A recent workshop on HIV/AIDS curriculum development organized by MAP International, a nongovernmental relief organization, was attended by tutors drawn from theological and pastoral training institutions in Kenya. I asked the participants: What makes us believe that HIV/AIDS is "real"? Here are some of the responses I received:

- "I have lost a relative to this disease—my cousin, in fact."
- "We lost a student to HIV/AIDS in our school two weeks ago."
- "I have buried several people who are said to have died of this disease."
- "The fact that we are here, attending a workshop on developing a curriculum on HIV/AIDS, means that this disease is for real!"
- "I understand from reliable sources that about 50 percent of the bed-space in the hospitals in the western part of Kenya is now occupied by HIV/AIDS patients."
- "There is already an escalation of the number of orphans in Kenya—as is true in other nations of Sub-Saharan Africa."

These responses point to one fact: AIDS is *real*. Its effects are already being felt in our midst, even infecting and affecting the church and the theological institutions in our society.

The Impacts of HIV/AIDS
The HIV/AIDS pandemic can no longer be ignored. It is a threat to humanity with wide-ranging and devastating demographic and economic impacts.

The *demographic impact* is marked by lives lost, especially of young people between the ages of 15 and 49. There are increasing childhood deaths, and a growing number of orphans. AIDS will have a significant impact on population size.

The *economic impact* of AIDS includes, on the one hand, losses to firms. In 1995 AIDS-related expenses came to US$45 per employee per year. By 2000 these expenses are expected to increase to US$120 per employee per year.

AIDS also has a severe impact on agriculture and the rural economy. Eighty to 90 percent of all Kenyans live in rural areas and make their living from agriculture. AIDS has affected commercial agriculture by decreasing the supply of both skilled and unskilled labor and by driving down the productivity of those who are working.

Equally dire has been the impact on smallholder farmers. The ravages of the disease have meant a decrease in the acreage under cultivation (for example, on sugarcane and vegetable farms) and corresponding loss of income.

The macroeconomic impact of AIDS results in part from the medical expenses associated with HIV/AIDS treatment. These include palliative care, which can run US$20 per patient per year, and the cost of dealing with opportunistic infections, ranging from US$30 to $200 per patient annually. Antiretroviral therapy costs between US$10,000 and $20,000.

Going beyond medical expenses, the macroeconomic impacts of the disease also include absenteeism, declining labor productivity, increasing training costs for new recruits, increasing labor turnover costs, and the cost of mortality.

Combating HIV/AIDS

Root Causes: What Drives the Pandemic?

Transience and loneliness are factors in spreading HIV over large populations and geographic areas. People on the move include migrant workers, refugees, and long-distance drivers. Prisons are another setting in which HIV can spread rapidly.

Violence contributes to the spread of HIV. Cases of rape and abduction are common in conflict situations.

Poverty fuels a sex industry in which commercial sex workers spread HIV, and is also associated with alcoholism and drug abuse.

Cultural and traditional practices that can foster the spread of HIV include wife inheritance, sharing of wives, "widow cleansing," rituals such as circumcision, and superstitious practices such as adult men having sex with virgins.

Finally, the *stigma of HIV/AIDS* leads to fear, shame, silence, and denial, all of which stand as obstacles to prevention and treatment of the disease.

Preventing Transmission

HIV/AIDS infection can be prevented in various ways.

1. Interventions to prevent transmission through heterosexual contact:
    *   Promoting abstinence before marriage
    *   Promoting faithfulness to one partner
    *   Promoting the availability and use of condoms in special circumstances
    *   Controlling other sexually transmitted diseases

2. Interventions to limit mother-to-child transmission:
    *   Preventing infection in women
    *   Reducing transmission during childbirth
    *   Reducing transmission through breastfeeding
    *   Reducing number of pregnancies
    *   Antiretroviral therapy

3. Promotion of a safe blood supply.

4. Combined interventions.

5. The role of individuals. Individuals must undergo behavior change, thus:
    *   The HEAD: "Don't be like the people of this world, but let God change the way you think" (Romans 12:2, CEV).
    *   The HEART: "Trust in the Lord with all your heart and lean not on your own understanding . . . !" (Proverbs 3:5, NIV).
    *   The HANDS: "Who may ascend the hill of the Lord? . . . He who has clean hands and a pure heart" (Psalm 24:3, 4).

6. Challenge of community mobilization efforts:
    *   Keep land ownership alive at the community level
    *   Achieve long-term sustainability
    *   Strengthen household economic resources

- Respond to village-driven needs
- Implement relevant monitoring and evaluation systems at the community level
- Support changes in sexual behavior

Resources and Institutions to Fight the Pandemic

When faced with a problem of the magnitude of HIV/AIDS, we sometimes forget that we have resources available for the fight. These include:

- Government
- Nongovernmental organizations
- Community-based organizations
- U.N. agencies, including UNAIDS, WHO, UNICEF, UNFPA, UNDP, and the World Bank
- The churches and other religious bodies
- Universities, colleges, schools, and other institutions of learning
- Workplaces, e.g., insurance companies, banks, and industries
- People living with HIV/AIDS

All these need to be unified as a common front to fight the scourge. However, this has not been the case in the past.

Why Have Past Approaches Too Often Failed?

According to UNAIDS, the Joint United Nations Programme on HIV/AIDS, past approaches have often failed because of:

- Lack of political commitment
- Failure to involve communities and churches/religious bodies, which have been given limited roles in policy and planning
- Reliance on short-term quick fixes that are not sustained
- Focus on single-shot interventions
- Top-down approaches
- Donors' many contradicting agendas
- Conspiracy of silence (mainly cultural and traditional beliefs), due to the stigma attached to HIV/AIDS
- Denial of the problem

For the fight against HIV/AIDS to succeed, we need some minimum common actions in each country. These actions must unfold at three levels: the political level, the institutional level, and the community level, involving the mobilization of all for the health of all.

The Church's Involvement in Combating HIV/AIDS

Edward Dobson, a U.S. pastor quoted in "Facing AIDS: The Challenge and the Churches' Response," captures the feelings of most church people when he asks: "Given the inadequate knowledge and even ignorance about HIV/AIDS in our churches, how many people will die in the next two years? What are we going to do to help our people?" (World Council of Churches 1997).

In fact, the Church can do a great deal, and should be in the forefront of the fight against HIV/AIDS, because:

- It has a long history of presence, proclamation, and persuasion
- It has well-developed structures
- It is self-sustaining
- It has a captive loyal audience that meets every week
- It has predictable leadership
- It cuts across geographical, ethnic, national, gender, and other barriers
- It has grassroots support and understands the language at the grassroots level
- It gives hope beyond the grave
- It has the Bible, a manual with tested and proven effectiveness in changing behavior and morals

Giving Hope: The Christian Response

The whole message of the Bible is about HOPE, LOVE, and the FUTURE. This what humankind is looking for. The Church is the custodian of this message.

Psalm 31:24: Be strong and take heart, all you who hope in the Lord.

Psalm 33:22: May your unfailing love rest upon us, O LORD, even as we put our hope in you.

The Church can lead by:

Understanding hope by knowing facts about HIV/AIDS:

Proverbs 23:18: There is surely a future hope for you, and your hope will not be cut off.

Discovering hope in the HIV/AIDS epidemic through our biblical foundations:

Romans 15:4: For everything that was written in the past was written to teach us, so that through endurance and the encouragement of the scriptures we might have hope.

Psalm 119:114: You are my refuge and my shield; I have put my hope in your word.

Psalm 130:5: I wait for the LORD, my soul waits, and in his word I put my hope.

Spreading hope by mobilizing the church to perform HIV/AIDS ministries:

Psalm 9:18: But the needy will not always be forgotten, nor the hope of the afflicted ever perish.

Developing hope by changing feelings and attitudes about HIV/AIDS:

2 Timothy 2:25: Those who oppose him he must gently instruct, in the hope that God will grant them repentance leading them to a knowledge of the truth.

Sharing hope through pastoral care to families and communities affected by HIV/AIDS:

2 Corinthians 1:7: And our hope for you is firm, because we know that just as you share in our sufferings, so also you share in our comfort.

Offering hope through HIV/AIDS pastoral counseling:

Psalm 62:5: Find rest, O my soul, in God alone; my hope comes from him.

Giving hope to parents and youth for AIDS-free living:

Psalm 71:5: For you have been my hope, O Sovereign Lord, my confidence since my youth.

Ministering hope through home-based care to people with AIDS:

Romans 12:12–13: Be joyful in hope, patient in affliction, faithful in prayer. Share with God's people in need. Practice hospitality.

Romans 15:13: May the God of hope fill you with all joy and peace as you trust in him, so that you may overflow with hope by the power of the Holy Spirit.

Conclusion

In September 1999, representatives of Christian development organizations and UNAIDS gathered in Gaborone, Botswana, to discuss collaboration around HIV/AIDS issues. The gathering adopted an "Affirmation of Presence and Continuity" that states in part:

> We are in an evolving epidemic of HIV/AIDS. Loss and death are real for all of us. Through the strength of fellowship we must face our fear of death. Only then can we celebrate life fully—now, and after death.

We have a vision of the Church as a servant with the courage to truly participate in communities so as to realize shalom. We look forward to rethinking and reworking of the relationships and ethos of participating in community, care and change. We also look forward to a movement beyond ourselves and beyond our boundaries. We together are on a "JOURNEY INTO HOPE" . . . !

May this be our commitment, too, as we seek ways and means of reducing poverty through combating HIV/AIDS.

Bibliography

Kenya. 1998. "Economic Survey." Nairobi.

NASCOP (Kenya National AIDS/STD Control Programme). 1999. "AIDS in Kenya." 5th ed. Nairobi.

UNICEF. 1991. "Challenges for Children and Women in the 1990s: Eastern and Southern Africa in Profile." UNICEF Eastern and Southern Africa Regional Office, Nairobi.

World Council of Churches. 1997. "Facing AIDS: The Challenge and the Churches' Response." WCC Study Document. Geneva.

Part 6

Poverty, the State, and the Private Sector

13

Public and Private Sector Initiatives to Combat Poverty

Yeboa Amoa

What is poverty and what initiatives by governments and the private sector are required to combat poverty? As has often been noted, an important step toward addressing any problem is accurate diagnosis.

Poverty has many dimensions or characteristics. The appendix to this chapter provides a list of such characteristics in relation to poverty in Ghana. In summary, poor communities are characterized by low incomes, malnutrition, ill health, illiteracy, and insecurity. There can be consumption poverty, asset poverty, and limited human development. There is also a sense of powerlessness and isolation. These different aspects interact and combine to keep households and, at times, whole communities in persistent poverty.

What causes poverty among individuals, communities, and nations? The factors include:

- Harsh terrain or physical environment
- Lack of natural endowments
- Environmental degradation
- Human exploitation, selfishness, greed
- Oppression and absence of good governance, that is, "state failure"
- Persistent wars or civil strife
- Lack of finance, low productivity, unemployment
- Disease, physical incapacity
- National economic mismanagement
- The "ugly face" of capitalism, that is, "market failure"
- Illiteracy, lack of technical know-how
- Lack of justice and fairness
- Sheer laziness

Possible Government Initiatives

With these poverty characteristics and causal factors in mind, let us consider some initiatives that governments could take to address poverty. The literature asserts that a wide range of government policies can affect poverty and inequality to some degree. In the short run, with a given level of national income generating a significant amount of public revenue, fiscal policy is generally regarded as effective in reducing poverty and enhancing equity, with expenditure policy viewed as more effective than tax policy. Furthermore, the composition of expenditure not only influences income distribution, but also can have an impact on economic growth.

The Agricultural Sector

Generally speaking, Africa cannot feed itself. Agricultural production is suboptimal. For example, in Ghana it is about 20 percent of capacity. Yet 66 percent of the population of Ghana live in the rural areas and are engaged in agricultural activities. Unstable food production and a weak marketing infrastructure significantly contribute to household food insecurity and to high levels of malnutrition in Africa. These problems indicate the presence of the severest forms of poverty.

Currently, major concerns include lack of technological change and innovation in crop cultivation, livestock raising, fishing, and forestry production and in agro-processing; the limited adoption of efficient production methods coupled with a heavy reliance on rainfall, with insignificant land under irrigation; weak producer organizations; and lack of access to markets.

One of the major ways of accelerating poverty reduction consists of offering subsidized extension services to poor farmers and agro-processors. Agricultural extension is a nonformal educational process aimed at improving the living standards of rural households by providing appropriate skills, knowledge, and attitudes that will bring about changes in behavior.

The time has come for Africa to move away from rain-fed agriculture to irrigation farming. These irrigation development components, however, should be mainly small-scale schemes targeted at rural families.

Development of Rural Feeder Roads

While urban poverty is real, the fact is that a large proportion of the poor in Africa are located in remote and inaccessible regions, beyond the reach of health or extension services and distant from markets for their farm inputs and produce. The Upper East Region of Ghana is so inaccessible due to the poor road network that it is called "overseas"! And yet in Ghana, the farthest point from Accra, the capital, is not more than 700 miles away. The provision, improvement, and expansion of feeder road networks serving deprived communities in African countries is therefore a high priority for poverty reduction. To be effective and cost-efficient, such projects should concentrate on regravelling, rehabilitation, and surfacing of roads. Advisory services should be obtained from local and international consultants for engineering designs of feeder roads to be rehabilitated as well as for maintenance management.

Such projects can have an impact on poverty by:

- Increasing agricultural production through easier access to inputs such as fertilizers, pesticides, extension services, and credit
- Reducing the need for head loading, which will particularly benefit women
- Creating employment on road works for the rural community through the promotion of labor-based construction and maintenance
- Reducing the cost of transporting goods and people
- Creating employment through expansion of farming
- Giving remote rural communities greater access to social services such as health and education
- Minimizing rural-urban migration, leading to a reduction in urban poverty
- Deepening democracy by enabling political activists to visit rural communities

Social Services

Spending on education and health, particularly basic education and primary health care, builds human capital that can contribute both to economic growth and to the alleviation of poverty in the long term. An important justification for public spending on basic education is its effect on individual lifetime incomes, usually measured as a rate of return based on the increased incomes generated by public expenditures on education. Many studies have found that the rate of return is highest for primary education, followed by secondary and tertiary education. One should note that these studies were done mainly in communities experiencing economic growth; that is, opportunities were growing sufficiently to employ the increases in human capital productively.

Public spending on health, especially primary care, is generally justified by its role in reducing disease in the productive years of people's lives. Many studies have concluded that the most cost-effective health care programs are preventive in nature, because they increase both individual productivity and the number of productive years in people's lives more cost-effectively than does curative medicine.

The productivity of overall government spending on education and health has improved in Africa, but the average level of efficiency has declined relative to Asia and the Western Hemisphere. Inefficiency in African countries appears to be higher at higher levels of per capita spending and may be the result of the high share of total spending going to government wage payments. This is particularly acute in the health sector, where provision of essential drugs and maintenance of facilities are underfunded. Not only is the composition of public expenditures unfavorable in Sub-Saharan Africa (SSA), but the incidence of spending on education and health has been found to be unfavorable to the poor. For example, the poor have been shown to benefit less than the rich from education expenditures in selected SSA countries. These results imply that higher overall spending on education and health will not necessarily improve the well-being of the poor unless measures are taken to address inefficiency, especially where the level of spending is already high.

Recent empirical analysis provides evidence that public spending on *primary* education has a greater positive impact on enrollment rates than *total* spending on education. The same is true for the effect of primary health care spending on child and infant mortality relative to total health care spending. Spending on primary education and primary health care is more likely to improve social indicators and increase individual productivity and incomes, thereby reducing poverty in the long term.

Education. One of the major goals that governments should adopt to combat poverty in Africa is the achievement of functional literacy and numeracy. People who complete a basic education earn significantly more than people without schooling, it has been found. In principle, therefore, basic education should be made universal, free, and compulsory. There should also be functional literacy programs aimed at reducing adult illiteracy rates.

The objectives of basic education sector improvement programs should include the following:

- Improvement in the quality of teaching and learning.
- Improved access and participation, especially for girls and other disadvantaged groups.
- Improved management of the education sector.
- Development of indicators to measure and monitor the progress of basic educational programs. These indicators would include education's share of gross domestic product (GDP) as well as gross enrollment ratios

To achieve universal enrollment in basic education, the critical growth rate is that of primary school enrollment. To achieve full enrollment of the school-age population, the primary school growth rate would have to exceed the population growth rate. As stronger economic performance, rising public tax revenues, and reduction of parental fees with public subsidies permit, considerable additional expenditures should be made to achieve the objectives of the basic education program.

Health services. African governments should work to:

- Increase geographical and financial access to health services for all their citizens
- Provide better-quality care in all health facilities and outreach centers
- Improve efficiency at all levels of the health sector
- Foster closer collaboration and partnership between the public health services, private providers, and other sectors
- Increase overall resources in the health sector yearly and ensure equitable and efficient distribution

To achieve these objectives, African governments would need to rehabilitate and expand health facilities, provide the needed logistics and equipment, put in place capacity-building initiatives that will ensure efficiency, and improve the quality of care in health facilities.

A key way to increase the life expectancy at birth of Africans is by reducing infant and under-five mortality as well as maternal mortality (since maternal survival increases child survival). Other child survival initiatives would include improving the immunization programs run by health ministries.

Poverty reduction initiatives in health should focus on health care at the community level. Primary health care services, it is suggested, should consist of curative services at health centers, outreach services to rural communities, referrals to district hospitals, special programs aimed at the poor and vulnerable (such as nutrition supplementation programs for malnourished children), family planning programs, and health promotion programs at the family level.

In addition to providing these basic services, the government would have to reduce the financial burden on the poor by providing fee exemption packages to them. Thus, any patient declared poor would not have to pay the cost of health care. The government should also provide for other vulnerable groups, defined as children under five, pregnant women, and the aged. In principle, these groups also should not pay the cost of their health services. Other categories to be considered for exemption would be tuberculosis patients and HIV/AIDS patients.

The enhancement of expenditure on the poor and vulnerable can be achieved by, among other things:

- Increasing the overall resources going to the health sector by charging higher fees to richer groups so that the health sector generates more of its own funds
- Pooling donor resources to the health sector through the common basket approach
- Strengthening financial management practices in the health ministries
- Building capacity through continuous in-service training in clinical skills, and through financial management and better procurement practices.

Water supply. Clean water has to be made available at the community level. To this end, strategies have to be designed to ensure the sustainability of delivered facilities and emphasize, among other things:

- Promotion of women's roles in decisionmaking about water facility delivery, waterborne disease eradication, and so on
- Participation in the formulation and implementation of development programs at the community level
- Human resource and productivity management (easier access to water makes increased time available for economic activities), and
- Private sector promotion and support by the public sector

Water supply and sanitation facilities to communities should include (as the core):

- New boreholes
- Borehole rehabilitation
- New hand-dug wells
- Hand-dug well rehabilitation
- Pipe systems for small communities
- System conversion
- Rain harvesting
- Pipe systems for small towns
- School/institutional water systems

There should also be complementary training programs for local consultants, contractors, mechanics, pump caretakers, and so forth.

Social welfare. The effects of poverty and poverty-related conditions include social problems such as child abandonment, malnutrition, high child mortality, disablement, the phenomenon of street children, juvenile crime, parental irresponsibility and divorce, neglect of the elderly, destitution, prostitution, teenage pregnancy, drug abuse, lack of access to medical and health care, and general deprivation. In principle, therefore, social welfare services are needed to assist and empower vulnerable or disadvantaged individuals to improve their socioeconomic situation.

Vulnerable groups include people with disabilities, especially children with disabilities, out-of-school youth, children in need of care and protection, and the elderly and destitute. These groups constitute a high percentage of the poor, and most of them are unable for various reasons to participate meaningfully in the mainstream of development without subsidized support.

African governments have accepted the principles of the Western welfare state for ensuring the integration of the most vulnerable groups into the mainstream of society. The accepted poverty reduction objectives include increasing access by the poor to an equitable share of the benefits of development and improving the living standards of the elderly. Activities to achieve these objectives should include the following:

- Increasing access by the poor to economic services and employment opportunities
- Developing effective mechanisms to benefit the socially and economically disadvantaged
- Enabling communities to articulate their needs
- Improving the quality of vocational and technical rehabilitation and training

It is also widely accepted in principle that the main objective of the social welfare component of governments' poverty eradication programs should be to ensure equal opportunities for the vulnerable by:

- Providing employment skills training to people with disabilities and out-of-school youth, including street children
- Helping the disabled obtain assistive devices like prostheses and orthoses
- Providing tools and seed capital loans to enable trainees to set up microbusinesses
- Placing children in need of care and protection in orphanages, day care centers, or primary schools, with natural or foster families, and ensuring their well-being
- Giving care and social assistance to the elderly and destitute through facilities at hospitals, homes, and so forth

These challenges would require:

- Orphanages, day care centers, and special schools for handicapped children, whether deaf, blind, or mentally retarded
- Vocational rehabilitation centers or training institutes
- Rehabilitation centers for juvenile delinquents
- Integrated community centers for teaching employment skills
- Arrangements for apprenticeship to master craftworkers in communities

Especially in the poorer African countries, such facilities are provided, if at all, by NGOs, churches, and other faith-based organizations.

Population management. Many African countries face the challenge of supporting continued population growth with dwindling resources (financial, managerial, ecological, technological, etc.). This aggravates national poverty indicators, and governments must adopt strategies for dealing with the situation.

The last national population census in Ghana, for example, showed that the population had almost doubled in 24 years. The current population is estimated at approximately 18.9 million, with an annual growth rate of about 3 percent. The government of Ghana adopted an explicit National Population Policy in 1969.

The main goal of this policy is to ensure that the country achieves and maintains a level of population growth that is consistent with national development objectives. The impetus is to promote the population's quality of life, especially vulnerable groups as defined above. In order to provide a basis for assessing, monitoring, and evaluating the overall performance of the policy, a number of measurable targets have been set for all major program areas. These are:

• Phased reduction over a specific period of the annual rate of population growth and the total fertility rate
• Achievement of specified rates of contraceptive use
• Reduction of infant mortality rates over time
• Enhanced access to quality reproductive health care, including prevention and management of reproductive tract infections, sexually transmitted diseases, and HIV/AIDS
• Greater capacity to integrate demographic factors into national development planning and policy formulation

A critical assessment of the policy after 20 years of implementation, however, found that fertility levels are still high; the population growth rate had increased rather than decreased; and child, infant, and maternal mortality rates are still high. This may be due to a number of reasons. Among them are the adoption of a "top down" approach to policy formulation and the lack of a strong body to coordinate both the family-planning and the non-family-planning components of the policy.

More recently, the Ghanaian National Population Council has adopted fertility management as its medium-term policy objective. In line with the action program adopted by the 1994 International Conference on Population and Development, a comprehensive reproductive health program has been developed. This is being implemented by the Ghanaian Ministry of Health, by NGOs such as the Planned Parenthood Association of Ghana and the 31st December Women's Movement, and by religious groups, among others. Private sector participation is ensured by the involvement of the Private Medical Association of Ghana and the Ghana Social Marketing Foundation.

The Design of Institutional Structures, Strategies, and Programs

National poverty prevention. Effective poverty-reduction efforts require well-designed institutional structures, strategies, and programs. At the highest level, cabinet subcommittees could be placed in charge. The following account of the situation in Ghana is illustrative.

In Ghana an Inter-Ministerial Committee on Poverty Reduction chaired by the minister of finance is responsible for overall policy direction and coordination of all donor assistance and related programs. The committee has a technical arm, the Technical Committee on Poverty, whose chairman is the director-general of the Ghana National Development Commission. The technical committee does the following in relation to poverty reduction:

- Disseminates information
- Establishes policy guidelines for district development plans
- Monitors programs
- Develops training aids and programs for capacity building in designing poverty reduction initiatives at the subnational level
- Administers, manages, and coordinates all programs
- Fosters linkages among NGOs involved in the diverse donor-funded poverty initiatives

Below this there is a decentralized and participatory development planning system that extends deep into the community level in 110 local district assemblies.

The main goal of the long-term national development policy is to transform Ghana into a middle-income country by 2020. The broad strategy for poverty reduction emphasizes rural development, expansion of employment opportunities for the rural poor, and greater access by the rural and urban poor to basic public services. The main approaches to reducing poverty consist of focusing central budget expenditure on poverty reduction and fostering decentralized participatory development through local communities, which allocate a District Assemblies Common Fund and a Social Infrastructure Fund. Various multilateral and bilateral agencies have identified or are providing financial and technical support for specific programs that interest them. Under these programs, resources can be channeled directly to poor groups and communities through the district assemblies and the NGOs and community-based organizations that implement them.

For sustainable poverty reduction to occur, the emphasis must be on direct income enhancement for the poor by raising the value productivity of self-employment and wage labor. There is scope for varied partnerships mixing public and private institutions, NGOs, community-based organizations, and faith-based organizations, depending on their capacities and accountabilities. Linkage from the local level to the intermediate and national levels in the public sector can be critically important, especially where physical infrastructure is deficient.

Other necessary government roles. The government also has important roles to play in several areas where absent or weak institutions may create impediments to successful pro-poor economic growth. These areas in African countries usually include land tenure, the rule of law (especially commercial law) and law enforcement, and public incomes policy.

An obvious weakness in many African countries is the land tenure system, with its bewildering uncertainties, complexities, confusion, and hierarchies of owners and interests. Laws regulating land acquisition for development purposes need to be streamlined and the processes expedited (especially screening of claimants as well as compensation payment). Once the compulsory land acquisition regime is enhanced, then prospective entrepreneurs can be assured of greater speed in accessing land as well as security of tenure. Leaseholds can have an advantage in reconciling the claims of traditional authorities with the reduction of risk for developers.

Because law is the cornerstone of civil society, strategic management considerations require governments to review and update the legal regime comprehensively, repeal all obsolete laws, and pass laws to facilitate development. For example, in Ghana the Companies Code of 1963 does not recognize the use of computers in the registration and transfer of share titles. We need to legitimize the use of computers for record keeping in business and commercial transactions to provide for and recognize the evidentiary value of records so generated. There are other laws that need to be enacted, such as laws of trusts and bankruptcy laws.

The following examples from Ghana are illustrative. The Exchange Control Act of 1961 is still in force though the philosophy underlying it is clearly out of date. Furthermore, Ghana wants to encourage development of the capital market as a complementary avenue for the private sector to raise capital. Yet the regulations under the Exchange Control Act place nonresident owners of listed securities and the listed companies themselves at a disadvantage in relation to unlisted securities and unlisted companies. Again, current investment tax laws favor bank deposits as well as Treasury bills and are biased against equity issuance. Thus, interest income from bank deposits and Treasury bills in the hands of individuals is tax-exempt. But individuals must pay 10 percent tax on dividend income—no matter how small such income may be.

Enhancing the legal environment goes beyond continuous review of legal provisions; the courts themselves need reforming in relation to their procedural rules. Ghana's High Court Rules, for example, were passed in 1954. In addition to the facilities in the courts as they relate to the actual trial process, the recording of evidence, secretarial support for the judges, and the quality of judges' libraries need improvement; judges and magistrates currently write down evidence and legal arguments themselves in longhand. The judiciary needs to update to keep up with the fast-changing financial and technology sectors in which it operates.

Greater deregulation calls for clear definition of parameters for the ever-widening private sector and the creation of regulatory bodies for those monopolies that are being privatized. Poor incomes and remuneration policies in Africa have made it difficult to retain sufficient legal, managerial, and information technology expertise. The success of the institutional strengthening effort will depend on available human resources and their professionalism and motivation.

Inadequate remuneration and the brain-drain problem are a consequence of the general reluctance and/or inability in Africa to pay realistic prices for most economic factors. Governments, and sections of the general public, have tended to resist the payment of reasonable rates for health services and utilities until the agencies providing those services are near the point of total collapse. A reasonable charge should translate into a reasonable source of income for the employees providing services, in addition to covering plant maintenance and replacement costs. This way lies sustainability for those agencies and their services. Access problems for the poor should be addressed through poverty-reduction strategies rather than by maintaining nonviable prices and incomes.

There needs to be greater insistence on law and order enforcement, as for example through road traffic regulations and bylaws on sanitation. Law and order enforcement requires good governance, and vice versa, so that corruption can be stamped out.

Possible Private Sector Investment Initiatives

Most of the initiatives considered above would require private sector inputs or involvement to succeed, although many of them concern provision of public goods. The private sector participants might include professional individuals or firms, which could be involved in the design, implementation, monitoring, assessment, and evaluation of those public sector activities. Or they could be private business interests establishing and operating enterprises in the primary sector (agriculture, minerals, forestry), secondary sector (processing and manufacturing), and tertiary sector (services). Many of them could be taking advantage of an improved investment environment to set up new businesses. The level of private sector investment is generally related to seven items: natural endowments, policy, law, institutions, technology, human resources, and the milieu, or business climate. I want to concentrate on one of the imperatives for successful private sector investment in Africa: appropriate responses and winning attitudes on the part of the private sector.

Seven Aspects of African Business Success

Stop, look, and listen. There is much that is happening around us in the business and economic fields that should interest us. But we Africans are typically so busy going about our daily existence that we cannot even pause to think about these events and their implications. Sometimes we are too busy criticizing people in authority and impugning institutions—city council, municipal authority, village development committee, utility services providers, or the government itself. Let us also stop, look, listen, and think about the economic circumstances around us and how to make the best use of them.

For example, about 50 percent of people in African countries are under the age of 15. This creates opportunities for operating schools and other businesses related to children, especially where it is clear that government alone cannot provide for all the educational needs of its citizens. Furthermore, we should take note of the ever-expanding market opportunities both within and outside Africa. For instance, cassava and pawpaw have a surprisingly large market in Europe, while the craze for African textiles and styles has led to the export of these products to some of the major U.S. department stores. In Ghana, cement, refined sugar, handkerchiefs, toothpicks, and sandpaper could all be made from local raw materials, but they are imported. Most of these are easily within our reach; none of them requires space-age technology.

Foresight, planning, and preparation. In order not to burn their fingers, private sector investors should require planning and preparation before venturing into worthwhile projects.

Reliance on professional advice and help. "Penny-wise, pound-foolish," it has been said. Sadly, many businessmen and women are not prepared to spend money on professional advice for their businesses. They want to do everything themselves, or to use cheap, inefficient, unskilled or semiskilled labor. They use a court clerk instead of a lawyer to prepare a legal document. They want to bribe a judge or use a "military connection" instead of obtaining sound legal advice or obtaining a court judgment to solve a legal problem. They want to engage relatives, who have no qualification for the tasks involved, instead of hiring competent people.

African entrepreneurs should learn to seek and rely on professional services. They should also learn to make and keep proper books, accounts, minutes, and records! If for two years or so a businessman has not prepared year-end accounts, then how does he really know that the sales person, or the person in charge of his operations, is not playing tricks on him? If the business is not producing management accounts regularly, how can the owner know what is happening in the course of the year and take remedial steps before it is too late? Business owners should insist on written partnership agreements and appointment letters for employees, but frequently fail to do so.

The cost of the related professional services can frighten a businessman, but he may not always have to pay exorbitantly for each and every piece of assistance. He will be amazed at the amount of professional advice that budding business people can receive free—initially from professional friends. As time goes on, he may offer them a retainer. They may also be offered payment in kind in the form of business products or an investment stake in the business or they may work for credit until the client's fortunes improve. Payments to professionals can be on a commission basis, that is, a percentage of whatever the professional does, sells, or makes. There may also be employee's share options schemes; some shares can be put aside for all the employees collectively or individually.

Pooling of resources. Most African businesses are so small that they cannot take advantage of economies of scale. At best, they operate on the fringe. They lack resources to compete aggressively in a more competitive business world. They cannot attract and keep professionals in sufficient numbers and for long periods; because they are not properly established or staffed, once the owners die the businesses also die. Furthermore, they cannot think or plan globally. Prospective foreign investors and trade partners have been disappointed by this fact. African businesses have to think, plan, and act on a big scale. We have to consider a region such as West Africa, or Africa as a whole, as our market.

Traditionally, Ghanaian business owners have relied on the following sources of financial capital for the expansion and growth of their businesses: the owner's personal savings, financial assistance from friends and relatives, or revenues generated internally by the business. Occasionally there is a fourth source, namely bank credit in the form of bank overdraft, loans, and guarantees. These sources of finance have serious limitations: the amounts raised are seldom substantial, and the monies come in slowly. Also, banks play it safe, requiring buildings and other forms of collateral as security.

To take full advantage of investment opportunities, entrepreneurs must be prepared to tap fully other sources of financial capital. Bankers are important assets, and business managers must learn to develop good relationships with them even when they do not need them. One day the bank may be useful. But managers should not leave their business at the mercy of their banks. Additional sources of finance are now available in Ghana and in an increasing number of African countries. This is the result of reforms in banking and nonbanking financial institutions as well as capital market reforms. These additional sources include leasing and hire purchase, venture capital, private placement, mergers and acquisitions, and public sale of shares or bonds.

Avoiding the get-rich-quick syndrome. In Ghana at least, many business people are tempted to get rich quick. In the process, they get into all sorts of troubles as they sacrifice quality and probity. The open secret in business is that quality will always win. Let us, therefore, do the right things and be patient. In pursuit of the many business opportunities, entrepreneurs should insist on quality, strive to expand their market share, and remain as technologically up-to-date as possible. In this way, business owners will earn the goodwill of their suppliers, distributors, customers, employees, financiers, and boards of directors. They will also earn the goodwill of governmental authorities such as the tax bureau and customs and regulatory bodies.

Export first, buy and sell last. To benefit significantly from the business opportunities in Africa, Africans have to think of exports first, agribusiness second, and manufacturing third. Importers' representation comes fourth, and buying and selling last. The reason is simple. If everybody is importing, where is the foreign exchange to pay for the imports? Again, if everybody is buying and selling, who will produce the goods to be bought?

Attitudes to holidays. The fact is that we have to revise our attitude to holidays. Whether as a result of precedent under labor laws or not, in the formal sector many employees have long paid holidays—at least 30 working days per year. On the other hand, in the United States, 14 days of holiday a year are common. In addition to the increasing number of statutory holidays in Africa, there are weekdays when people in certain localities are, according to customary taboos, not allowed to work on their farms. Long funeral celebrations can also be counterproductive for private sector development.

The Christian Church in Africa and Poverty Reduction

The Church can address poverty challenges by providing material technical assistance or needed social amenities—schools, clinics, water, toilets—as it has done over the centuries. On the other hand, the Church, through Christian private business or investment subsidiaries, or in joint venture with others, can also set up farms, businesses, and so forth, in order to create jobs, income, and goods. This the Church has done on a limited scale to date.

The Church has been in Africa since its foundation. It knows the terrain and has firm roots on the continent. It has networks for communication and social action that usually reach the remotest corners of society. The Church, as an institution, has time-tested hierarchical structures with clear lines of ethical and social authority. Its values are well respected as are its disciplinary processes and sanctions. The Church has a large following in Africa to the extent that the continent is now regarded as the epicenter of the Christian faith in the world. The Church in Africa has a strong, distinct voice. It has influence; it commands attention; it is credible.

The Church has an undeniable track record of achievement:

- In preservation of African culture, music, folklore, and language through developing writing systems for African languages
- In African human resource development (by establishing educational institutions and providing other social services)
- In development of value systems and promotion of respect for human life and dignity

The Church has survived countless political ideologies, civil strife, political parties, and successive governments in Africa—and sometimes complete chaos in the civil societies where it operates. It has often been the sole surviving voice of reason and restraint or even the sole mediator in internecine strife. Because it is a microcosm of African societies, the Church has within its membership the poverty, deprivation, and want that is in evidence all over Africa; so it is naturally concerned about these issues. On the other hand, the Church in Africa also has within its membership multifaceted skills and potentially huge financial resources.

What the Church seeks from the Bretton Woods institutions is formal partnership arrangements in which these assets can be tapped and, with requisite leverage from such institutions, deployed to even greater benefit of the African continent. In other words, in addition to channelling funds and technical support through governments and government agencies, the Bretton Woods institutions will do well to consider channelling part of their resources through the Church in Africa, to complement the Church's own resources for use in fighting poverty in Africa. Such resources would be used partly to provide services and infrastructure to alleviate poverty in targeted areas and partly as seed capital for private investment in those areas.

Appendix: Characteristics of Poverty in Ghana

Low Production
Lack of access to land and assets
Low productivity inputs
Weak agricultural technology
Lack of access to credit and capital
Pricing and marketing constraints
Adverse climatic factors
Low soil fertility
Small farm sizes
Lack of research and extension services
Low productivity

Low Income
Lack of marketable skills/untrained labor
Lack of employment

Lack of small enterprise credit
Lack of farm-to-market transport
Low wages
Lack of income-generating opportunities

Unplanned and Uncontrolled Human Settlements
Lack of threshold population for service delivery
Isolated settlements
Lack of access to land
Environmental sanitation problems
High residential densities
Inadequate transportation network
Unaffordable housing rents
Slums
Lack of access to affordable housing finance

Environmental Degradation
Farming in environmentally sensitive areas
Soil nutrient depletion
Overgrazed and depleted ranges
Deforestation and fuelwood shortage
Poor environmental sanitation
Bush fires

Poor Health
Food insecurity
Poor nutrition
Lack of access to potable water
Poor access to health facilities (because of cost and distance)
Inadequate health services
Unsanitary conditions

Water
Poor water quality
Waterborne diseases
Inadequate maintenance
Long distances to fetch water
Inability to pay for potable water

Low Level or Lack of Education
Low primary enrollment rate
Poor quality of education
Inadequate resources
Inability to pay school fees
Inadequate classrooms
Limited facilities
Poor access (because of cost and distance)
Absenteeism by teachers

14

Poverty Alleviation and the Role of Microcredit in Africa

Makonen Getu

Despite its natural wealth and human resources, Africa is the poorest continent in the world. Thirty of the world's 40 poorest countries are in Africa, and more than 50 percent of the continent's 600 million people suffer from absolute poverty. Over the last five decades, the International Monetary Fund and the World Bank, which were set up in the 1940s to help with reconstruction of the war-torn European economies, have been actively involved in the developing world. Since the early 1980s, the World Bank has promoted structural adjustment programs (SAPs) in more than two-thirds of Sub-Saharan African countries. As part of these programs, economies have been liberalized, state-owned economic enterprises privatized, local currencies devalued, subsidies withdrawn, and bureaucracies downsized. Multiparty democratic elections have been held, and anticorruption and antiinefficiency measures have been taken. The ultimate purpose of implementing SAPs has been to alleviate or reduce Africa's ever-growing poverty.

However, the overall results have been disappointing. Although basic improvements have been made in GDP growth, efficiency, and democratization, most Sub-Saharan African countries have remained socially, economically, and politically poor and weak after 15 to 20 years of implementing SAPs.[1]

This paper provides an overview of microenterprise development, discusses its socioeconomic impact on the poor, and suggests some meaningful and effective ways to enhance the microenterprise development industry.

Essentials of Microenterprise Development

Microenterprise development (MED) involves providing credit and financial services and related training to poor microentrepreneurs to enable them to enhance their businesses and create employment and income for themselves and their communities. MED is, therefore, an intervention aimed at poverty alleviation and development. It is not charity, nor is it a subsidized program.

MED practitioners promote microcredit programs on the premise that the poor are creditworthy. Their problem is not lack of thriftiness and creativity; it is lack of opportunity. Because formal banking and other financial institutions are structured to serve small and large businesses in the formal sector, those who operate in the informal sector are excluded and marginalized. They rely on loans from relatives, or on local moneylenders who often charge exorbitant interest rates. It is thus difficult for them to increase capital and improve technology in order to grow their businesses and create more employment and income. By offering credit, training, and services to poor microentrepreneurs, MED helps them overcome these constraints. The conviction is that the poor will be able to run profitable businesses, repay their loans, become self-sufficient (after some repeated loans), and eventually liberate themselves from poverty (Reed and Morser 1998: 2–4).

Unlike the subsidized, mainly rural, credit schemes run by governments in the 1960s and early 1970s, MED programs run purely on business principles. Loans are given on the basis of systematic appraisal of applications to determine which business proposals are viable. Commercial interest rates as well as administrative and processing fees, including late payment fees, are charged. Loan terms are deliberately designed to take short cycles of 4 to 6 months for the first few loans and then from 12 to 36 months for "mature" loans. The cycles are designed to make repayments easier and circulation of loan funds faster and wider.

Since the mid-1970s, the microcredit/microfinance industry has gone through a process of evolution. Particularly in the 1990s, more diversified and qualified lending products, loan tracking and reporting systems, governance tools, and internationally accepted best-practice standards have been developed. The aim has been to achieve financial excellence and lasting impact (Reed and Morser 1998: 2–4). Some of the major common standards that have evolved over the last 20 to 25 years are described below.

Outreach

Microfinance institutions (MFIs) are expected to reach out to increasing numbers of poor microentrepreneurs. The more clients an MFI serves, the better the coverage. However, outreach is not only about numbers; it is also about depth. It is about reaching poorer areas and poorer people. This, in turn, involves larger programs, larger loan funds, and more complex technology and systems. Many MFIs have committed themselves to the Microcredit Summit goal of reaching out to 100 million poor households, especially female-headed households, by the year 2002.[2]

Quality

Quality implies efficiency in portfolio management and deals with the rates of loan recovery and the cost of lending. At the moment, the best-practice standards include 5 percent arrears rate, 10 percent loan portfolio at-risk rate, and US$0.20 per dollar lent. The greater the number of clients handled by a loan officer, the better, as it is a good indicator of productivity and efficiency. The industry applies a combination of individual, solidarity group, and trust/village banks approaches. The client–loan officer ratio, therefore, varies from product to product.[3]

Impact

All MFIs want to see their programs result in significant and sustainable socioeconomic changes among the poor. The emphasis varies among players. Some emphasize the economic aspect and tend to take a minimalist approach. Others look at the whole person and try to encourage holistic transformation in the people they serve. Opportunity International's goal, for example, is not only to increase the amount of money in the pockets of the poor but also to "enable the poor to become agents of transformation in their communities" (Opportunity International 1998: 4). The aim is to use microcredit as a means of facilitating deeper economic, social, political, and spiritual changes among the poor. This is a view shared, particularly, by all Christian MFIs.

Sustainability

Sustainability has to do with the viability of the MFIs themselves as lending institutions. MFIs need to move toward self-sufficiency in order to continue serving poor people for a longer period of time. Currently, most MFIs depend on donor grants, but the aim is to reduce and ultimately eliminate that dependency. The progress toward achieving this goal is measured by the level of operational and financial sustainability achieved by MFIs. The income generated through interests and fees is meant to cover the repayment of loan funds, operating expenses, administrative expenses, expected loan losses, and return on capital. When interest and fee incomes cover operational and actual financial costs, MFIs reach operational sustainability. When these incomes cover all expenses, including inflation, financial sustainability is achieved.

The higher the ratios and the shorter the time it takes to achieve operational and financial sustainability, the better. MFIs are expected to reach 100 percent operational sustainability during the first three to five years of operation and financial sustainability within five to seven years. The pressure to move toward sustainability has led to the current drive to help nongovernmental MFIs evolve into private financial institutions that obtain commercial loans and take deposits as a means of raising more loan capital other than grants (Campion and White 1999: 3).

Although a good number of the leading MFIs now implementing best-practice MED as described above emerged in the early 1970s, most of the MFIs in Africa are relatively new. Most of them entered the industry after the mid-1980s, mainly in the 1990s. Many more are still entering the market. The accumulated experience in the field and hence the overall capacity is therefore very limited. However, as will be seen below, they have achieved much in the limited time they have been in existence.

The Role of MED: What Microcredit Does for Poor People

Positive changes in a number of areas occur in African economies in general and among the poor in particular as a result of MED interventions.[4]

From Having Little or No Access to Having Credit Opportunity
The poor are powerless partly because they lack access to credit and means of production. They are ignored by the formal financial sector on the grounds that they are "not creditworthy."

Microcredit challenges this conventional negative perception of the poor. As described above, best-practice MED takes the view that the poor do not lack ability but only opportunity. The poor are recognized as creditworthy and bankable and are given credit and related services. This positive recognition is empowering in itself.

From Dependency to Self-Reliance

The poor have little or no uncommitted money. They have too little surplus income to improve their businesses or their household economies. Very often they depend on loans or assistance from relatives, friends, and neighbors to meet their business and consumption needs. They borrow and borrow with shame and pain on their faces.

Microcredit enables poor people to expand and grow their businesses, create employment, and generate income for themselves and their communities. The increased personal and household incomes enable them to invest in their businesses and household assets. They are freed from the bondage caused by lack of savings, reduce their dependency, and increase their self-reliance.

From Enslavement by Local Moneylenders to Freedom

In the absence of credit opportunities, the poor frequently must resort to borrowing from local usurers at exploitative interest rates that are destructive. Microcredit has helped the poor reduce their dependency on local moneylenders. This is liberating and empowering.

From Bad to Better Education, Health, Housing, Clothing, and Food Security

With microcredit, poor families can send their children to school and pay for the requirements that go with it. They can send not only one or two children, but all their children of school age. They become able to pay for medical care when necessary and can obtain timely care for both prevention and treatment. Housing and clothing conditions are improved. Microcredit also enables the poor to have adequate food, to eat better-quality food, and to store more food for disaster times. Food shortage decreases and the quality of nutrition improves. This is another area of empowerment.

From Low to Higher Self-Esteem and Dignity

The poor frequently have low self-esteem. They may see themselves as having little value to society, and others may also see them this way, causing them to lose social respect and dignity.

Microcredit enables the poor to use their ability and creativity to run businesses, develop innovative products, provide services, and create employment. They may even begin to make financial contributions to community projects, make short-term loans to others, and sell on credit. All these lead to a positive appreciation of the role that poor people play in society, increasing their self-esteem and dignity.

From Silence to Increased Voice

In the absence of freedom of expression, the poor are often silent, and even when they speak, little attention is given to them.

When the poor form groups and receive four to eight weeks of orientation, and when they are exposed to ongoing interaction with one another and with credit officers, the level of their political information and awareness increases. This helps them to know their basic social rights and obligations. They then can begin to exert pressure through lobbying, advocacy, and negotiations with local and national authorities to provide the necessary services. As they act collectively, they begin to be heard and to influence the course of development in their communities.[5]

From Marginalization to Integration

Because of their low economic status, low self-esteem, and limited political awareness, poor people do not tend to take an active part in political affairs. For the most part they participate in electing well-off activists and rarely run for political office themselves. The poor are often excluded by the political system.

As they begin to develop confidence through the material, political, and organizational changes that follow from involvement in MED, they dare to run in elections, winning positions in political institutions at the community level. They then move from the periphery to the center.

From Gender Inequality to Gender Equity

Among the poor, women are the most disadvantaged and powerless. For cultural and other reasons, they have limited control over resources, including land, credit, and other assets. They are often financially dependent on their husbands.

The majority (up to 80–90 percent, and in some cases up to 100 percent) of microfinance clients are women. Microcredit enables them to increase their access to credit and to own increased assets, including housing and land. This in turn allows them to reduce their dependence on their husbands, thereby lessening the "gender gap" at the household level. Although some findings seem to indicate that microcredit results in less family time and an increased workload for women, family relationships have seen general improvement. Some women have also been able to participate in local elections and gain seats on local councils, or have taken leading positions in women's and other local committees.

From Immoral to Moral Values

Some poor people turn to crime, including stealing or prostitution, in order to survive.

By creating productive alternatives, microcredit has helped to reduce such vices and to enhance moral values among the poor. The poor involved in microcredit have been empowered to say no to and give up such humiliating and immoral activities.

From Hopelessness and Fear to Hope and Courage

The poor face many obstacles in their lives. Superstition and witchcraft practices leave some in fear and bondage. The crippling effect of poverty today and the uncertainty about tomorrow often reduce them to hopelessness.

Through direct and indirect witnessing, Christian MFIs have enabled many of their clients to become followers of Christ, thereby liberating them from the bondage of sin and fear. This has helped many poor men and women and their families to become hopeful and courageous. Because of what they have been able to achieve through microcredit, the poor have begun to see their future as bright. The days of daydreaming and "I can't do it" perceptions are gone. The poor have begun to realize their potential and appreciate their opportunities positively. They have begun walking with their heads up as capable people and not as hopeless people.

From Being Easy Victims to Preventing HIV/AIDS

It is estimated that 20–30 percent of the population in most Sub-Saharan African countries are infected with HIV/AIDS. Millions are dying each year, leaving large numbers of orphans. Many studies of HIV/AIDS have found a strong linkage between poverty and AIDS. The main victims of increased poverty are women, youth (especially girls), and unemployed people.

MED has served and is likely to continue serving as a critical intervention in preventing the spread of AIDS in Africa, primarily through employment creation and income generation. MED offers employment opportunities to women who are unemployed and likely to become sex workers. It also offers income to women who otherwise cannot say no to dangerous sex because of their economic vulnerability. Noninfected people are enabled to provide material support to relatives and dependents with AIDS. In other cases AIDS patients themselves are helped to run businesses to generate their own income.

From Micro to Macro

In many cases, MED clients have moved from micro to small and medium businesses. They have moved from informal to formal ventures. The increased number of machines and workers as well as capital that MED clients are investing in their businesses and the rate of diversification indicate that these businesses are moving from micro to macro levels. With the increased effective demand and technology and innovation taking place in the industry, it is likely that MED will serve as the breeding place for homegrown industrialization and national economic development. In the absence of foreign capital, and given the meager domestic private investment, it is likely that the MED industry will be the motor force of Africa's future development.

In summary, it can be said that microenterprise development has enabled the poor to experience radical changes in their lives and in their communities. As a result of the financial gains, they have been able to break the shackles of their poverty. As a result of the improved standard of living they have achieved and the contributions they have made in their communities, they have earned social respect and dignity. As a result of training, organizing, and exposure, they have gained increased political awareness and can participate in affairs that affect their destiny. They have also improved their spiritual and moral values. Without any doubt, it can be said that the poor have been transformed and empowered through their participation in MED programs.

What Governments, Donors, and the Church Should Do

In view of the challenges and constraints faced by microfinance institutions and their clients, governments and donors can take a number of steps to promote the MED industry.

Market Distortions

Although a number of senior government leaders have taken part in the three global microcredit summits where commitments to best-practice MED have been made, the subsidy mentality is still prevalent. Some donors and governments are still bound by the old belief that the poor cannot pay commercial interest rates, and this tends to distort the best-practice principles the microcredit industry is trying to apply in the financial market. This is particularly true in cases where governments are implementing public credit schemes with political motives. Also, in cases where credit activities are undertaken as part of integrated programs funded by donors, the tendency is for clients to be charged uneconomic rates with relaxed repayment requirements, thereby creating market distortions in the areas where this occurs. Local churches and some Christian organizations involved in MED also tend to be uncomfortable with charging commercial interest rates. This practice is rooted in the old "handout" mentality and contradicts best-practice principles that call for charging commercial interest rates with no tolerance for arrears.

The poor are not only able but also happy and proud to repay their loans with commercial interest rates and on time. They want to do business on the basis of equal partnership and not take handouts that undermine their integrity. Any government/donor distortions, regardless of good intentions, are likely to tarnish the image of best-practice MED and thereby make it difficult to maintain quality. Governments, donors, and the Church should therefore refrain from taking measures that will distort the market in the microcredit industry. Rather, they should develop policies that are in line with best-practice principles that promote "hand up," not handout, practices.

Funding

MFIs need larger amounts of loan capital, qualified human resources (staff and boards of directors alike), and improved systems to be able to reach out to more poor people and more remote areas, and to ensure financial excellence (quality portfolio management) and durable impact. This will require putting in place state-of-the-art loan tracking systems and recruiting qualified and experienced board members, managers, and staff with ongoing internal training activities. It will also require lending to more poor people, training them, and spending quality time with clients rather than meeting them only to disburse and collect loans.

Despite their will and commitment to build capacity and expand their programs, most MFIs are constrained by lack of adequate funding. Donors have tended to become more selective and restrictive in their giving.

Donors are seldom willing to spend much money on capacity building, research, and innovation in MFIs. What portion of SAP loans, for example, go toward microenterprise development? Whatever the amount, what are the mechanisms put in place to ensure effective delivery? Although the Consultative Group to Assist the Poorest (CGAP) was established on World Bank initiative in 1995, how much in loan funds has this program brought to Africa, and where? It is good that the Africa Capacity Building Facility has recently been established with the cooperation of CGAP and the British government to provide technical assistance to MFIs in Eastern and Southern Africa. It is hoped that this will make a significant contribution to promotion of the microcredit industry in Africa.

Governments have restrictive regulatory and control systems that do not allow MFIs to mobilize savings and deposits from the public or clients for on-lending. Many mature MFIs are at the stage of converting to or establishing banks and/or financial institutions for this very purpose. This requires committed support by governments and donors to facilitate effective transformations. Donors, governments, and financial institutions could help to enhance the MED industry by creating enabling macroeconomic environments, improving infrastructural facilities, and providing grants and concessionary loans to MFIs.

Measurement

In the microcredit world, where the core business is receiving money (from lenders and donors), disbursing money (to borrowers), and collecting money (repayments from clients), measurement issues occupy a major place. Donors, practitioners, and clients all want to measure their performance, results, and the impacts they are making through their activities. They want to see figures. This is not a bad thing, but good indicators have to be selected to measure progress and impact, and to determine the long-term direction.

Problems arise, however, when the focus is only on numbers. These problems worsen when only quantifiable variables are appreciated and unquantifiable ones are suspect. This practice reduces the meaning of life and hence the issues of poverty to the question of having or not having material possessions. Measuring only those variables that are observable and tangible focuses on things that serve the body. It emanates from the belief that the solution to basic human misery is material, and that when the poor improve their production, health, and education, and increase their income, they have been led to a "superior" life.

The full picture of life, however, goes beyond physical possessions. It is not only to have but also to be and to become that gives life a deeper meaning. *Having* is about externals, while *being* concerns the inner person. We need to be loved and to love. We need to be emotionally healthy and spiritually right. Material prosperity on its own cannot make life meaningful. Without the satisfaction of nonmaterial needs, it is unlikely that we can lead whole-person lives. A great and troubling vacuum will always be with us. The nonmaterial dimension of performance and impact measurement is important for faith-based MFIs.

Donors, governments, researchers, and policymakers should go beyond measuring only the quantifiable when evaluating impact. They should begin to take nonmeasurable factors such as the spiritual, emotional, relational, deliverance, moral, and cultural issues of life into account so as to be able to appreciate the total transformation experienced by the poor. This will help to justify allocating resources to these aspects of MED and to enhance transformational development through microcredit.

Perception

Generally speaking, as we are taught we think and as we think we act. Our perception of MED determines how we treat, facilitate, and implement microcredit programs. Currently, most donors and governments see MED as a "survival" intervention and a short-term solution to poverty. Very rarely is it seen as a long-term development strategy. Very little attention and emphasis is given to it in the multiyear strategic development plans of governments and donors. The limited analysis of MED-related activities and the amount of resources allocated to them are indicative of this.

In Africa—where the informal sector employs 70 percent of the urban labor force on average, where foreign direct investment is difficult to attract, and where domestic private investment is insignificant—the potential contribution of MED to efficiency and equity has been insufficiently recognized.

Historically, industrial economies have grown through businesses that moved from micro to small and from small to large ventures. The microcredit industry has witnessed that the poor are growing their businesses in volume, technology, employment, and diversification from "survival" to developmental levels. Some have moved from employing only one or two workers to employing 50 or more and from engaging a portfolio of US$300 to engaging US$15,000 or more. They have moved from using one or two machines to 20 machines, from operating with one or two outlets to 5 or 10 outlets, and from one or two locations to several. Overall, MED enhances two cardinal aspects of national economic development: purchasing power and national effective demand, on the one hand, and savings and domestic investment, on the other.

In other words, in Africa, where indigenous accumulation (investment) is still weak and foreign capitalists generally uninterested, the potential of MED in producing future industrialists, manufacturers, exporters, and traders should not be overlooked. In the long term, the microcredit industry is likely to be the foundation of indigenous or "homegrown" (independent) industrialization and national economic development.

Another important aspect of holistic development that is often ignored by non-Christian players is the spiritual dimension. In view of the critical place that spiritual factors hold in people's lives, it is important that organizations recognize that investment in spiritual transformation is part of national development.

Donors, therefore, should lift the pressure they put on Christian organizations to curtail their spiritual activities under the pretext that religion and development are two separate entities. On the contrary, donors should recognize the dialectical relationship between spiritual and physical aspects of development and even provide support and encouragement to organizations and individuals involved in the promotion of spiritual development. It is time that spiritual considerations are included when designing and evaluating development projects in the same way that gender, environmental, and, lately, AIDS aspects are considered. It is time for spiritual issues to be included on the development agenda, and for donors to engage spiritual specialists in the same way they have done for gender, environment, and AIDS specialists.

Coalitions

We are not only in the era of intensive globalization; we are also in an era of coalitions. Nations are entering into regional and global economic and geopolitical coalitions at an unprecedented rate. Multinational corporations, airlines, and telecommunications companies are doing the same on a continuous basis. MFIs are not an exception to the trend.

Realizing the importance of coordination, knowledge sharing, resource mobilization, and synergizing in strengthening the concerted effort of the industry, MFIs have begun establishing global, regional, and national networks and coalitions. The Microcredit Summit mobilizing all MFIs, the Christian Microenterprise Summit mobilizing Christian development organizations, and the SEEP Network are among the global coalitions that have been formed with the spirit of promoting the MED industry in unity.

The Church can and should play a significant role in enhancing the MED industry as part of its mission to facilitate transformational change in people's lives. As an institution, the Church has a wide constituency and social influence. The more people become obedient to God and apply Christian principles, the better the prospects for best-practice MED. Through its Christian teaching, the Church could create a stronger presence of good stewardship, accountability, reliability, and integrity. These are important ingredients of best-practice MED because they promote financial discipline among clients.

A study carried out by the USAID Best Practice Project in December 1999 found that a good number of MFIs have been affected by the AIDS epidemic, which has claimed the lives of many of their staff and clients. Because they work in deprived communities and mainly serve women, among whom the rate of HIV infection is much higher than among men, MFIs may be more exposed to the effects of HIV/AIDS than society at large (Versluysen 1999: 1).

The HIV/AIDS epidemic is an economic, spiritual, and moral problem. The more spiritual people become, the less sexual immorality there is. Under normal conditions, a spiritually and morally grounded woman or man will not make sexual contact with another partner outside marriage. It is an immoral and hence a sinful act. The spiritual transformation that the Church facilitates in communities is highly likely to contribute to the reduction of the HIV/AIDS epidemic and hence encourage the promotion of MED. The Church can do this not only through its teaching of the gospel but also through credit activities related to MED. When getting involved in MED, it is important that the Church recognize that it is not an MFI, nor should it attempt to become one. It should collaborate with and seek technical assistance from experienced Christian MFIs.

It is important, therefore, that donors and governments properly appreciate the role of the Church in the promotion of MED and poverty alleviation, including spiritual poverty, and try to cooperate with the Church. This includes engaging in dialogue with the Church, and making available financial resources to the Church that will enable it to contribute to policy formulation and poverty alleviation in meaningful ways.

Conclusions

As an antipoverty intervention, MED has played a positive role by creating employment and generating income among the poor, especially women. More broadly, microcredit has proved to be an effective tool for facilitating transformation among the poor and empowering them to influence their own destinies.

It is time, therefore, to stop treating MED as a survival intervention and a short-term solution to poverty, and to view it instead as a long-term development strategy and a potential source of capital accumulation. It is time for MED to be given stronger financial and technical support to ensure that it is implemented in such a way that the poor are holistically transformed and empowered.

Notes

1. Many critics of SAPs have attributed Africa's failure to World Bank policies and conditions "imposed" upon countries implementing SAPs. My view is that Africa's failure is a combined result of many external and internal factors, including SAPs.

2. The declaration of the Microcredit Summit was signed by about 3,000 participants (practitioners, donors, government leaders, private sector representatives) who attended the first Microcredit Summit held in Washington, D.C. in 1997.

3. The various ratios were calculated and published by the SEEP (Small Enterprise Education and Promotion) Network and by Calmeadow, a Canadian NGO specializing in microfinance.

4. The positive changes that have taken place among the poor as a result of their participation in microenterprise programs have been documented by various studies, including impact evaluation reports. See, for example, the

impact studies issued by the AIMS project (Assessing the Impact of Microenterprise Services) of the U.S. Agency for International Development's Office of Microenterprise Development.

5. Here is an example. A client who was a member of a loan group in Botswana was rearing and selling chickens, and had a near monopoly in her community. Eventually, the school administration decided to sell chickens they had raised for educational purposes in the market. The prices they charged were lower than the client's, and she lost customers as a result. She reported to her group that she was not making money because the school's participation in the market had depressed the price for chickens. The group leaders went to the school administration to lobby, telling them that they should not distort the market by selling subsidized products. The school administration responded to their request positively (Getu 1995: 15).

Bibliography

Campion, A., and V. White. 1999. "Institutional Metamorphosis: Transformation of Microfinance NGOs into Regulated Financial Institutions." Occasional Paper 4. The MicroFinance Network, Washington, D.C.

Christen, R. C. 1997. "Banking Services for the Poor: Managing for Financial Success." ACCION International, Washington, D.C.

Getu, M. 1995. "Microenterprise Development in Theory and Practice." World Vision Australia, Melbourne.

Microcredit Summit Secretariat. 1997. "Microcredit Summit Declaration." Washington, D.C.

Opportunity International. 1998. "Network Five-Year Vision Statement." Chicago.

———. 1999. *Annual Report 1999.* Chicago.

Reed, L., and S. Cheston. 2000. "Measuring Transformation: Assessing and Improving the Impact of Microcredit." *Journal of Microfinance* 1 (1).

Reed, L., and T. Morser. 1998. "The Market for Funding of Microenterprise Development Trends." Processed.

Thurman, E. 1995. "Is Interest Christian?" *Opportunity International Update.*

Versluysen, E. 1999. "East and Southern African Microfinance Institutions and the AIDS Epidemic." U.S. Agency for International Development, Washington, D.C.

15

Microfinance for Poverty Reduction: Leading Issues

Shimwaayi Muntemba

Microfinance picked up in Africa in the 1980s. By the late 1980s and early 1990s, the World Bank saw microfinance as a way of contributing to its mission of poverty reduction. With support from Swiss Development Cooperation, the Bank began a review of what had happened up to then and the impact microfinance was having on poverty reduction. A program, Banking with the Poor, focused on microfinance institutions (MFIs) in Africa and Latin America, seeking to draw out best practices.

Within this context, the Swiss development agency also agreed to support a new project, Action Research on Sustainable Microfinance Institutions in Africa. Its main objectives were to document best practices and innovations, help MFIs learn from each other, facilitate network building, and provide a mechanism for the Africa Region of the Bank to support MFIs that reach the poor.

The shift toward building networks responded to the view that networks are effective tools for:

- Sharing emerging information on best practices
- Developing standards for the industry, such as standard interest rates and performance indicators
- Developing modules to facilitate implementation of best practices and innovations
- Optimizing human and financial resources
- Playing effective advocacy roles in relation to government and central or commercial banks, encouraging them to create an environment conducive to the growth of the microfinance industry

- Through dialogue, assisting governments to accept microfinance as an integral part of the national financial systems.

This work was piloted in Kenya and Ghana and soon included Cameroon, Ethiopia, Zambia, and Mozambique, while Uganda and Malawi received marginal support. The information that the program created was shared with networks in other countries through workshops, newsletters, and publications on documented best practices. As the networks grew, the program began to focus on enabling them to build their capacities and professionalize themselves so they could become important tools for helping their members move toward sustainability.

Leading Issues Facing Microfinance

A number of significant issues have come up during implementation of the program. They include:

Microfinance and the very poor. Can microfinance reach and serve the poorest clients? This critical issue has preoccupied the Africa Region at the Bank in recent months. It probably calls for identification of the various categories of the poor, so that in the short and probably medium term the very poor can qualify for assistance.

Grants versus credit. This has proved to be an issue with economic, social, and political dimensions. Where grants or highly subsidized loans are given, they are viewed as enemies of microfinance that could actually thwart its growth.

Microfinance in rural, especially very remote, areas. MFIs shy away from agriculture, in particular small farms. This has been the case even with regard to rural banks. Moreover, serving rural and remote areas in much of Africa is costly at best and impossible at worst because of missing infrastructure, markets, and other components.

Microfinance in post-conflict situations. Can it work and should it be encouraged, and if so, in what form?

Sustainability. Given the fragility and weak base of both the institutions and their clients, this is a key question.

Markets for MFIs and for rural clients in particular. Some networks are developing ways of linking rural clients to urban clients in order to help create or improve markets for rural entrepreneurs.

The gender dimension of microfinance. In some cases up to 90 percent of the clients are women, yet MFIs often use tools and mechanisms that are not gender-neutral or welcoming to women.

These issues are preoccupying a number of networks in Africa, which see answers to them as critical to the growth of the microfinance industry and to the sustainability of their member institutions.

16

Creating a Climate for Private Sector Investment

Gordon O. F. Johnson

Attracting private sector investment is critically important for lifting people out of poverty. Indeed, it is more important than investment in public, human, or social capital. Key to attracting private investment is creating the *climate* that both domestic and foreign investors seek.

Poor people need and want solutions to the same problems that concern investors, both local and foreign. A climate that attracts investment, therefore, is also a climate that can best help to alleviate poverty, given the right context.

Lessons from My Experience

In 1955 I helped start a new private company where I worked for 30 years. It grew to employ 400 people, with US$30 million in sales revenue and net income over US$1 million. It had customers in 90 countries, subsidiaries in 3 countries, and licensees in 2 more. Based on my experience, I offer four observations that may suggest how best to work with private sector investors.

The "profit motive." It is not the profit motive that drives a businessman as much as the *fear of what will happen* to him and his company if the company does not make a profit. Profits are necessary for survival, to finance growth, and to attract new capital investment. They also benefit customers by attracting competitors to the field and generating new technology. A successful business must have a "mission" that goes well beyond simply making a profit if the firm is to attract good employees and grow by serving its customers better.

Who's in charge? Every new employee who joined our company had to learn that the real "boss" over all of us was the customer! If customers were unwilling to pay more than what it cost us to serve them, they were telling us they did not need us and we could go out of business without being missed. They had to pay us *voluntarily* for what we did for them and were free to stop paying if we did not deliver their money's worth. This meant that we had to listen very hard to our customers before telling them what we could do for them.

Small companies can compete. We knew we could not compete in our bigger rivals' core business areas. Instead we concentrated on niche markets, where our continuing focus on product quality, customer service, and people training allowed us to do better than our larger competitors.

Divide a big problem into parts. A big problem can often seem overwhelming. A good approach is to divide it into smaller parts and work on these one at a time. For example, a "sick business" can be treated like an accident case, in three stages: (a) stop the bleeding (that is, stop the financial losses), (b) nurse the victim back to normal health (that is, make it profitable), and (c) start training to compete (that is, develop a vision and plan for future growth).

Another example is privatizing a state-owned enterprise. This can also be divided into three separate problems: (a) redundant employees, (b) excess indebtedness, and (c) long-term viability. Almost every state-owned enterprise has too many employees. Rather than considering them as a single group, consider the needs of different age groups and develop different options for each group. Older employees can be offered early retirement; middle-aged employees can be helped to start small businesses; and young employees can be offered more training.

Privatizing Public Sector Corporations

In 1984 I cofounded the Center for Privatization in Washington, D.C., as a contractor and adviser to USAID. Before I retired, we had fielded more than 150 consultants on projects in 50 countries.

Privatizing state enterprises turned out to be complex as it is an ongoing political process rather than a series of business projects. If done well it can be a boon to the citizens of the country, including the poor, but if done badly, only the elite will benefit. Countries with healthy, open, transparent privatization programs usually have a climate that attracts private investment. Those that carry out the process in secret, with deals "under the table," usually do not have a healthy climate for investors.

State enterprises are often insensitive to their customers, particularly the poor, and are affected by nepotism, political patronage, overstaffing, and favoritism in hiring, promotions, and procurements. They are often late in paying their bills and in publishing audited financial reports. Budget cuts in government often result in state enterprises with obsolete, underutilized, and poorly maintained assets, and minimal investments in customer service, product quality control, and human resource development. Many of the problems that we found in state-owned enterprises stemmed from the conflict of interest inherent in trying to achieve political and social objectives as well as economic objectives. It is very difficult for a good manager of a state enterprise to serve both his government minister and his customers, when the minister enters into management decisions for the enterprise. It is even more difficult if the minister interferes for political reasons or for personal gain.

The private sector operates with a different incentive system which, because it tends to be result-based rather than mistake-based, encourages risk taking and early decisionmaking before a problem escalates. Government and the private sector differ markedly in their decisionmaking processes, their willingness to tolerate mistakes, and their ability to reward successful risk taking. They also differ markedly in their ability to attract investment capital. Mixed arrangements, such as public-private partnerships, can work but they require a clear-cut division of responsibility and rewards from the outset. But an economy in which government has a major controlling role in the business sector has an unattractive climate for most investors, including investors who live in the country.

The Importance of Private Investment for the Poor

Private investment does not mean simply a flow of money into a stock market, though stock markets can be important vehicles for local companies to raise equity capital. The most important investors are those, *both local and foreign*, who invest for the long term, building new plants and establishing new services. In the case of foreign investors, we especially want to encourage investments made in partnership with local investors and entrepreneurs.

Why is private investment vitally important in helping the poor and alleviating poverty? There are four major functions that private investment can play:

New jobs and better-paid jobs. Creating new and better jobs is at the heart of poverty reduction. We want to create these opportunities through customers paying voluntarily for products and services. Such opportunities may need to be supported initially by loans and subsidies such as SME programs, microfinance, and agricultural credit for small farmers.

Enhanced incomes and new jobs have a multiplier effect. Additional incomes boost demand for consumer products and services, which in turn leads to more national and local business activity, investment, and job creation. Many of these secondary jobs will require fewer skills and thus can help the poor gain entry into more remunerative markets for these products or labor services.

Increasing productivity and competitiveness. Investment in new facilities, plants, and equipment, and in training makes workers more productive and more competitive in global markets and raises their standard of living. In the case of foreign investors, their investment can also broaden management know-how and skills, bringing in new technology and providing access to new markets. The resulting higher productivity and competitiveness can then lead to expanded production, creating even higher income levels and new employment opportunities.

Reducing crime and violence. More jobs mean lower unemployment, which takes urban youth off the streets, provides income for family support, and helps to build a society with less crime and violence. The poor are major beneficiaries of reductions in crime and violence as they are its major victims.

Eliminating the brain drain. A country that attracts investment, raises labor productivity, and creates jobs is a more attractive place to live. An economy that drives away its best and brightest citizens through emigration, on the other hand, has a discouraging future. Declines in the economy hit the poor sooner and harder than they hit the elite.

What Kind of Society Attracts Investors?

Investors make their decisions first and foremost on trust, which depends on both the perceived climate and on judgments about the people the investor is dealing with. Other things being equal, investors will go where the investment climate seems most favorable and where it appears most likely that this climate will continue. There is usually a tendency for investors to invest within their own countries based on their local knowledge—unless risk is perceived as unacceptably high.

Where private investors perceive low risk and have high trust, they will accept a relatively low rate of return. Where the enterprise is high-risk *and* the climate is high-risk, investors will require an exorbitant and probably unacceptable return. Investors can go elsewhere to look for a more favorable risk-return ratio for their investment. The poor in a country that fails to attract investors are the ones who suffer most.

There is no shortage of private investment capital in the world today, and there is no shortage of capital looking for opportunities to invest in Africa. This investment will mostly go elsewhere, however, unless the climate for investment improves.

- Investors and the poor have many similar needs and desires. I suggest that there are three pillars of a civil society on which everything else must rest:

The rule of law. A society without fair and understandable laws to protect lives and property is a threat. People cannot live happily, or in a civil relationship with each other, amid uncertainty as to what is the law.

An independent judiciary. The rule of law is fair and effective only if there is an honest, independent, impartial judiciary to pass judgment in case of disputes and infringements. Without this, people will be unable to place their trust in the law and the level of uncertainty, again, will be high.

Independent media. The best means of ensuring the effective rule of law and an independent judiciary is transparency in the process, and the key to this is a free and independent press.

Other important features of a society that is attractive to investors and offers hope to the poor are:

Political and economic stability. This implies stability of the political system (including the assurance of peaceful transitions of power) as well as low inflation and a stable rate of exchange for the country's currency.

Honesty. Investors look for a low level of corruption, bribery, and bias in the society, plus use of accepted accounting principles and procedures for financial statements. A government needs to have transparency as a guiding principle for its policies and actions, and should strive to create transparency in the private sector (for example, by requiring full disclosure of financial information by publicly quoted enterprises to protect investors).

Low rates of crime and violence. This reflects rising levels of prosperity in the recent past.

Healthy and educated people. This reflects rising investments, especially by the state, also made possible by rising prosperity.

Acceptable infrastructure. Includes adequate roads, ports, water, power, and most importantly, telecommunications.

Local investors' behavior. If local investors are investing their own money outside the country, outside investors are likely to do the same. Capital leaving the country is a "red flag" for foreign investors, warning them to ask, "What do local investors know that we should also know before we invest?"

This is an especially important factor to consider for Africa. The National Bureau of Economic Research, studying reasons for the economic decline of Sub-Saharan Africa, observed that "Africa's wealth owners have relocated 37 percent of their wealth outside the continent. This compares to a ratio of 17 percent in Latin America and only 3 percent in East Asia . . . If Africa reduced its capital flight to that of Asia, its capital stock would increase by a half" (Freeman and Lindauer 1999, citing Collier and Gunning 1997).

Economic Freedom

Finally, economic freedom is key to creating an environment that attracts investors and allows poor people a chance to rise out of poverty. "People . . . tend to undertake hard work and investment only if they have a probability of enjoying the fruits of their efforts" (O'Driscoll, Holmes, and Kirkpatrick 2000). We read repeatedly in *Voices of the Poor* that the poor may work hard, but others benefit unfairly from their work; the system in which they live and work and raise their children is skewed against them; and they lack economic freedom (Narayan and others 2000).

What do we mean by "economic freedom"? A number of research organizations are engaged in defining this, but the two most comprehensive indexes come from the Fraser Institute, based in Canada, and The Heritage Foundation/*Wall Street Journal.* The Fraser Institute publishes *Economic Freedom of the World* (Gwartney and Lawson 2000), assisted by a network of institutes in 55 countries. The authors rate 123 countries using quantitative variables that allow them to construct country ratings back to 1970 for 57 of those nations, tracking changes in economic freedom over three decades. Their index is based on 23 components grouped in seven major areas:

- Size of government
- Economic structure and use of markets
- Monetary policy and price stability
- Freedom to use alternative currencies
- Legal structure and security of private ownership
- Freedom to trade with foreigners
- Freedom of exchange in capital markets

The Heritage Foundation and the *Wall Street Journal* together publish the *Index of Economic Freedom* (O'Driscoll, Holmes, and Kirkpatrick 2000). It contains chapters by their staff members as well as researchers from Harvard University, Atlas Economic Research Foundation, and the Libertad y Desarrollo Institute in Santiago, Chile. They measure how well 161 countries score on a list of 50 independent variables that have been divided into the following 10 broad factors of economic freedom:

- Trade policy
- Fiscal burden of government
- Government intervention in the economy
- Monetary policy
- Capital flows and foreign investment
- Banking
- Wages and prices
- Property rights
- Regulation
- Black markets

Both studies rely extensively on data from international sources, primarily the World Bank, the International Monetary Fund, the World Trade Organization, and the OECD, and they come to similar conclusions and country rankings. Both indexes give higher ratings to countries with institutions and policies more consistent with price stability, rule of law and secure property rights, smaller government (smaller expenditures and lower taxes), free trade (lower tariffs and fewer nontariff trade barriers), and greater reliance on markets (few government enterprises and less regulation).

The authors of the Heritage/*Wall Street Journal* study define economic freedom as "the absence of government coercion or constraint on the production, distribution or consumption of goods and services." For the authors of the Fraser study, the core ingredients of economic freedom are "personal choice, protection of private property, and freedom of exchange."

In a chapter in the Heritage study on "The Rule of Law, Democracy and Economic Performance," Robert J. Barro of Harvard University observes: "Basic reforms that improve institutions provide one of the best routes for transforming a country over the long run from poverty to prosperity." On the issue of the relative importance of democracy for achieving economic growth, he concludes:

> For a country that starts with weak institutions—little democracy and little rule of law—an increase in democracy is less important than an expression of the rule of law as a stimulus for economic growth and investment . . . If there is a limited amount of energy that can be used to accomplish institutional reforms, then it is much better spent in a poor country by attempting to implement the rule of law—or, more generally, property rights and free markets. (O'Driscoll, Holmes, and Kirkpatrick 2000)

Chapter 3 of the Heritage study analyzes the relationship between economic freedom and corruption. Their analytical framework shows that "over-expanded and over-regulatory government structures create incentives for corruption by encouraging the seeking of privileges." It should be obvious that it is not normally the poor who are successful in seeking these special privileges. The authors point out that "economic freedom has little value if corruption in government means that only a few will enjoy it." They conclude that "the higher the level of economic freedom, the lower the likelihood of encountering corrupt government practices."

Changing the Investment Climate

Creating a climate for investment through systemic change is a long, frustrating, and arduous process with many risks for those who attempt it. The needs of individual countries, the probable obstacles to change, and the potential supporters of reform vary widely. Nevertheless, I offer several general suggestions for creating a climate for investment.

Push for Transparency in the System

A leadership that insists on transparency in all its transactions is highly likely to be a leadership that people can trust. There may still be disagreements, but at least there will be a climate of trust. In the absence of trust, leaders are forced to spend precious resources on military support in order to stay in office.

Most bad things happen in secret. One leading businessman pointed out that making ethical decisions is simple: "You don't need lawyers writing codes of ethics," he said. "You only have to ask yourself, How would this look on TV?" If a decisionmaker is willing to have the details of a transaction laid out for everyone to see, the chances are high that it will be an honest decision made in the best interests of most people concerned. It is the secret decisions and under-the-table deals that should cause the greatest worry.

Public awareness of all the facts is the best bulwark against corrupt practices in high places. Most corrupt leaders maintain their power not only by having a strong military but also by preventing citizens from being fully informed. Areas of greatest sensitivity, where transparent policies and practices are most needed, include government procurement and contracting, privatization processes and transactions, and government oversight commissions and audit institutions.

Identify and Support Champions of Reform

Without political will at the top, it is very difficult to bring about change. Politicians are not necessarily courageous individuals, but they can be courageous if given strong support and encouragement. Support by foreigners is likely to be counterproductive. The necessary support and encouragement must come from fellow citizens who are champions of reform. Without this, outside development assistance is likely to perpetuate the status quo.

Even when a country's leadership is unwilling to listen and actively resists calls for reforms, it is important to begin the process of encouraging and recognizing the champions of reform. When the time comes for a change in leadership, the window of opportunity will be open for new leaders receptive to good ideas that have the support of the people and have been thought through ahead of time.

New Laws Only as Last-Resort Solutions

Many think that problems can be solved by passing new laws, but there is a danger in this approach. New laws increase litigation. Additional laws and litigation not only increase the burden on the judiciary but also on citizens and businesses who must comply. They also provide employment for lawyers. This may benefit lawyers and those who can afford to pay them, but may not benefit the poor who lack access to the legal system.

Where new laws are needed, laws that allow people and markets to decide what is best for themselves are likely to be more help to the poor than laws that work against letting people and markets decide. For example, laws that provide for some form of direct subsidy (such as vouchers, scholarships, or food stamps) to help poor people afford a needed product or service are likely to be more cost-effective and fair than laws that establish government agencies to provide that product or service. Government agencies that decide who among the poor will benefit tend to become new centers of power over poor people with accompanying increases in favoritism and corruption.

Pass Power to the People: Follow God's Example!

The suggestion to pass power to the people is in reality a calling to follow God's example. After all, God created us with free will, and if we are created in his image, then we should be willing to take some of the same risk he took when he created us. Most of the parables in the Bible present God as a father image, a shepherd, a landowner, a master of the manor, or some other authority figure. Systems of government in biblical times were highly authoritarian, and authority figures for God fitted the scene.

But I would like to suggest that God can also be envisaged as an entrepreneur because an entrepreneur is a risk taker, and God showed himself to be the biggest risk taker of all time when he created man with free will. This is the great mystery. God created the universe, but he gave up power when he created mankind with free will. He will still guide us in his way if we seek it, but he created us free to make mistakes!

God took the biggest risk of all when he sent us his only Son. He sent Jesus to change mankind and to help his followers to change the world. Jesus gave us a model to follow when he chose mainly the poor of the world to be his followers and when he trained these recruits to train others. God's Son bypassed the complexity of our laws and the bureaucracy that developed around them. He gave us two command-ments in their place, and relied on our judgment to decide how best to carry them out. Jesus also taught many parables that show us how to carry out those two commandments and how to avoid or minimize "mistakes" and wrong ideas.

Invest in People's Assets Rather than Their Needs

In the parable of the workers in the field (Matthew 20), the landowner pays the late afternoon workers, who worked only an hour, the same wage as those who came early and worked through the heat of the noon. As a businessman I could never understand this parable, though I knew there had to be a message here somewhere. On the surface it seemed to me this was a sure way to destroy morale. In my business "equal pay for equal work" is essential to maintain peace among work-ers, between male and female, young and old, senior and newly hired.

Earlier this year, a sermon preached in my local church by the Rev. Stephen Wade indicated an entirely new way to look at this parable. In summary, the exposition was: Jesus tells us that God is concerned to invest in you and in me as assets, rather than to invest in the needs and self-interest that we think to be legitimately our own. "Take what be-longs to you and go," says the landowner. "I choose to give to the last the same as I give to you." The point is theological, and it is that in the Kingdom of Heaven we are all assets, we are all beloved and precious.

I have a friend up in Boston, Massachusetts, who is a philanthropist. He gives away money, mostly to poor neighborhoods. Those who have worked in outreach ministries or other helping enterprises know that most people who seek to be helpful to marginalized people begin their work with what is commonly called a needs assessment. The idea is to locate the needs in a community, and to try to figure out how to meet those needs. But need-based solutions to people's problems only per-petuate needs. They make needy people more dependent on those who seem equally in need of offering help. Everybody ends up in need. Better to start in a different place . . . Locate the assets in people. Where is their hope? Where is their energy? Where is their initiative and prom-ise? Invest in people's assets rather than their needs, and you will change the world.

So that's what my friend does. He begins his work with what he calls an "asset map," rather than a needs assessment. Then he gathers together representatives of many asset maps, to share what is exciting to each of them. Good news and initiative feeds on itself.

And then he holds a contest: Those who have the most innovative entrepreneurial plan for deploying the assets in their community or neighborhood get the largest grant of money from my friend's foundation. Asset-based philanthropy is very exciting stuff! It gets people thinking like Jesus . . . thinking about one another as assets to be invested in, rather than as needs to be taken care of. The point is economic and social as well as theological.

The Problem with Power Over Others Is Corruption

It was Lord Acton, the English "historian of freedom," who wrote in the last century that "Power tends to corrupt, and absolute power corrupts absolutely." The proof of this dictum has been demonstrated over and over and it is still true today. Yet there are many well-intentioned people who still feel that it is important to have power over others in order to help them.

But as we are created in God's image, can we not learn to give up power as he did? In politics, can we learn that government should be the servant of the people, rather than people the servants of government and those who control the government? In economics, can we learn that people need to be free to make economic decisions for themselves through increasing incomes earned from, and spent in, free and fair markets?

Rev. Avery Dulles, S.J., professor of theology at Fordham University, observed recently that the United States in the present century has been fluctuating between two extremes represented by the state and the marketplace. "We seem to be caught between the seductions of the welfare state and libertarian capitalism. The one consistently pursued, leads to the 'animal farm' of state socialism; the other to the anarchic jungle of social Darwinism. To transcend the dilemma, it is necessary to recognize that politicization and commercialization are not the only alternatives."

He goes on to point out that "the moral-cultural system is the presupposition of both the political and the commercial systems." Our values and beliefs, as expressed in our culture, must be brought into the dialogue between proponents of the state and proponents of the marketplace. There must be a third balancing factor between politicization and commercialization. He then quotes from Pope John

Paul II's encyclical *Centesimus Annus:* "At the heart of every culture lies the attitude that a person takes to the greatest mystery: the mystery of God."

The churches can play a vital role in efforts to make a real difference in the lives of the poor. One of the ways to begin a partnership between the Bank and the Church could be to work together to encourage meaningful dialogues within African countries to deal with opportunities for, and obstacles to, economic freedom. The dialogues would involve not only national leaders, but also the poor and the entrepreneurs and would-be entrepreneurs of those societies, to allow their hopes and aspirations to be heard.

Money, Minds, and Markets

What do the Bank and the churches represent to the people in Africa? The Bank probably represents "money"—and the opportunity to do good with that money. The churches of Africa, on the other hand, represent the "minds" of the people of Africa, particularly the poor to whom they minister (box 16.1).

As I thought about "money" and "minds," something seemed to be missing. It dawned on me that I was missing "markets." Markets are the means for minds to express the people's priorities and preferences in a commercial system. Money is the medium that allows markets to function. Markets bring freedom of choice. Both must be guided by the values and belief system of the society's culture. Minds, representing

---

BOX 16.1 Money and Minds

MONEY	MINDS
The World Bank	The churches
Material wealth	God: spiritual wealth
Government decisions	People decisions
Grant money	Parishioner gifts/tithing
Taxpayers' cash	Customers' cash
Involuntary payments	Voluntary payments
Top-down control	Freedom

the values and beliefs of the culture, must mediate between the control that accompanies money and the freedom that accompanies markets.

These three M's by themselves still need to be linked together in a relationship of trust, and they need a foundation, before they can become the vital parts of a civil economy. I suggest that the underlying foundation for this pyramid is the rule of law and the linking element required for a trusting relationship between the parts is transparency. These five elements comprise a *schematic for civil economy*. All five elements must play their role in creating a climate to attract investment.

If there were easy answers to these problems, we would have solved them long ago. But there are no easy answers. Nor can we sit back and expect governments to solve these problems. When governments act, even with the best of intentions, unexpected and unintended things tend to happen: the law of unintended consequences comes into play. The solutions lie with the people in each country. The following three points are useful starting points for the struggles that lie ahead:

- Trust depends on transparency.
- Take risks to try to change the system.
- Strive for economic freedom.

References

Collier, P., and J. W. Gunning. 1997. "Explaining African Economics." Working Paper 97-2. Center for the Study of African Economics, Oxford University.

Dulles, A. 1999. "Centesimus Annus and the Renewal of Culture." *Journal of Markets and Morality.* Spring.

Freeman, R. B., and D. Lindauer. 1999. "Why Not Africa?" Working Paper 6942. National Bureau of Economic Research, Cambridge, Mass.

Gwartney, J., and R. Lawson. 2000. *Economic Freedom of the World: 2000 Annual Report.* Vancouver: Fraser Institute.

Narayan, Deepa, Raj Patel, Kai Schafft, Anne Rademacher, and Sarah Koch-Schulte. 2000. *Can Anyone Hear Us? Voices of the Poor.* New York: Oxford University Press.

O'Driscoll, G. P., K. Holmes, and M. Kirkpatrick. 2000. *2000 Index of Economic Freedom.* Washington, D.C.: Heritage Foundation; New York: Wall Street Journal.

Web Addresses

The key organizations referred to in the text are:

The Fraser Institute: **www.fraserinstitute.ca**

The Economic Freedom Network: **www.freetheworld.com**

The Heritage Foundation: **www.heritage.org**

In addition, important work is also being done on specific aspects of economic freedom by:

Freedom House (for measures of democracy, including electoral rights and civil liberties): **www.freedomhouse.org**

Political risk services (for two independent risk rating systems for investors and international businesses): **www.prsgroup.com** or **www.countrydata.com**

Transparency International (for indexes of both corruption and bribery): **www.transparency.org**

Part 7

Faith in Development: Roles of the Churches

17

The Role of the Christian Faith in Development

Molefe Tsele

It is inadmissible that the Church's missionary activity should be indifferent to the needs and aspirations of developing countries and, because of its religious orientation, neglect the basic duties of human charity . . . We for ourselves, in our encyclical *Popularum Progressio*, have stressed the duty of resolutely and intelligently fostering the growth of economic, cultural, social and spiritual well-being amongst peoples, especially those of the so-called Third World.

— Pope Paul VI

It is not many books that make men learned, nor even reading. But a good book frequently read, no matter how small it is, that makes a man learned and godly.

— Martin Luther, "An Open Letter to the Christian Nobility of the German Nation"

In the present polarized climate it is neither an easy nor an uncontroversial decision to choose to enter into dialogue, and possible partnership, with the World Bank. Indeed, for better or for worse, the World Bank and its Bretton Woods cousin, the International Monetary Fund (IMF), have left an indelible mark on the political and economic landscape of Africa. We are justified in asking whether Africa is today better off or worse off after two decades of experimentation with World Bank structural adjustment programs and IMF stabilization policies. In the same breath, we need to interrogate the claim by the churches that, given resources, they could have done better. This study does not take a position for or against the World Bank/IMF policies, especially their market liberalization ideology. Our primary intention, rather, is to assist in formulating a perspective of development that can contribute toward a new era of cooperation with the World Bank with the goal of eradicating poverty in Africa. It is in this regard that we as the Church need to define our entry point to this collaborative enterprise.

Africa at the Present Historical Conjuncture

The current condition of Africa is nowhere better articulated than by the leaders who gathered in Arusha, Tanzania, in 1990 to deliberate on the state of the continent. They adopted the African Charter for Popular Participation in Development and Transformation, which summarized the leaders' thinking as follows:

> We are united in our conviction that the crisis currently engulfing Africa is not only an economic crisis but also a human, legal, political and social crisis of unprecedented and unacceptable proportions manifested not only in abysmal declines in economic indicators and trends, but more tragically and glaringly in the suffering, hardship and impoverishment of the vast majority of African people. (African Charter 1990: 17)

Numerous testimonies have been recorded about the state of the continent. Its malaise has proven hard to cure and cannot be reduced to a single cause. The problems include sponsored wars involving young children; unending regional conflicts; the growing debt burden of many countries; collapsing infrastructure, academic institutions, and health services; a growing army of unemployed young people; and the devastation of entire communities by the HIV/AIDS epidemic. Indeed, the list is endless, and it seems that with every passing year it grows larger and more complex.

The reality is that Africa is worse off today than it was 20 years ago. And with the growing winds of globalization and neoliberal free-market capitalism, the indications are that Africa's marginalization and poverty will worsen. The outlook therefore calls for a serious review, rather than a business-as-usual approach. We do not need more of the same: that is, we need not more World Bank engagement in Africa, but a different kind of engagement.

As Bryant L. Myers observes, the poverty of Africa can be viewed as "entanglement." This is a situation where interconnected systems result in a "poverty trap." You cannot disentangle yourself from one without dealing with its interrelationship with the others. In that complex situation, material poverty, physical weakness, isolation, vulnerability, powerlessness, and spiritual poverty all work to reinforce the chains of poverty.

In light of this, we argue that the religious community in general and the Church in particular must be called to account for its absence from the forums that seek solutions to Africa's crises. Central to Africa's recovery is a rethinking of the development model. In other words, without religion as its base, development will be reduced to an appendage of capitalist ideology and, therefore, will not offer much to the poor in Africa. As will be demonstrated, we need to embrace a new path of development, one that is driven by the need to achieve significant impact on the overall quality of life of the poor.

Revisiting the Development Debate

The concept of development, since its emergence in development and political studies in the 1950s and early 1960s, has not been without controversy. The modern theory of development dates to the end of World War II, a time when many war-torn countries were reconstructing themselves. During this period the concept came to be synonymous with economic reconstruction and growth. In its classical sense, development theory focused on the level of production and resulting national income in order to categorize a given country's economy. Within this model, five stages or levels of development have been delineated (Rostow 1960):

1. Traditional society: low technological knowledge
2. Developing stage: agricultural productivity increases
3. Take-off: industrialization takes place
4. Maturity: modern technology takes root
5. Mass consumption society: the ultimate goal

According to this model, African countries are somewhere between the second and third stages, and, depending on the politics they adopt, they can either hobble or fast-track their development process. While this version of development is no longer mainstream thinking, it continues to linger in the work of some theorists. Like the modernity project that accompanies it, "development" has come to be associated with the Western or European mission of bringing progress to a backward country. So-called development assistance from Western governments consists of support to poor Third World countries that are supposed to need help so that their economies can enter the take-off stage. Radical critics of this development theory, especially in Latin America, preferred to speak of "underdevelopment," suggesting a negative causal connection between the Third World economies and those of industrial (developed) countries.

The "stages of growth" theory assumed a linear historical process that links all nations' histories and experiences on a single plane, putting some ahead while others lag behind. Development thus becomes an alienating and humiliating process for poorer countries that must helplessly await being developed, much as children who are "empty" must be taught or "filled up" by a teacher.

Liberation theologians were quick to point out that this philosophy needs to be challenged on two crucial points. First, the solution for poor countries does not lie in mimicking rich countries. Second, the advantages the rich countries currently enjoy are a consequence, directly or indirectly, of their historic relationship with the Third World. In the words of Herb Addo and his collaborators:

> What became known as development studies, or modernization, concerned itself largely with one question, which was how the internal condition of societies of the periphery could be made similar to those of the center societies. This question was considered adequate to all intents and purposes, because it was held that development or modernization had to do with how the non-European world could be Europeanized. . . . This was the axiom from which all deductions flowed. The scientific answer was that, to DEVELOP, the non-European areas must change to look like Europe by imitating Europe and European history. (Addo and others 1985)

Somewhat echoing this critical concern, but emanating from another experience, was the work of Gustavo Gutiérrez, Latin American father of liberation theology. He stated:

> The poor countries are not interested in modeling themselves after the rich countries, amongst other reasons because they are

increasingly more convinced that the status of the latter is the fruit of injustice and coercion. (Gutiérrez 1973)

Here, more than arguing for a link between the development of the rich and the underdevelopment of the South, a differentiation is made between the two processes. Development comes to acquire a different quality; it becomes a transformative and liberating process that goes beyond material and financial advancement to overcome other deficits including cultural, social, political, and ecological ones. The crucial issues here are, first, that development must of necessity be related to particular contexts, and second, that it must be comprehensively construed in relation to the diverse factors that affect the totality of human existence.

In theorizing about development there have been significant shifts from a primarily economic growth model to one that takes into account several factors, not least of which is the moral dimension. It is crucial that as we embark on discussing the problem of development, we begin by raising these concerns. We hope that by declaring these problems up front, we can move toward a new way of talking the development language that is not trapped in a one-dimensional view of societies, but redefines the terms of engagement toward a model that goes beyond the current teachings.

We need to assert that from the African perspective, which is a perspective we subscribe to, our model of development has to be more than a catching up exercise, more than a struggle to climb the development ladder to the commanding heights already reached by countries in the North. We must state from the beginning that our development project is concerned with something qualitatively different, something that has to do with the totality of our social well-being. This kind of development seeks to achieve a more human society and greater equity in the distribution and sharing of resources. In particular, we need to measure development by its ability to sustain healthy and dignified standards of living without excessive destruction or abuse of people and ecosystems.

It is within this context that current United Nations indicators for development include diverse factors such as literacy, life span, infant mortality rate, income inequality, and access to health care and clean water. They extend to questions of women's political participation and, recently, consumption, pollution, and environmental waste. The United Nations Development Programme describes developing as a "process of enlarging people's choices. This is achieved by expanding human capabilities and functioning. At all levels of development the three essential capabilities for human development are for people to lead long and healthy lives; to be knowledgeable; and to have access to the resources needed for a decent standard of living"(UNDP 1998).

We need to make the same claim—that all peoples and nations are in a state of development. Indeed, a country may even grow in a negative direction, toward underdevelopment, or it may be lopsided in the sense of being economically advanced while remaining backward in its social and moral systems. It is the nature of life that no species can be said to have arrived at the zenith of its development; neither is it spared the possibility of degenerating below its present stage of development. Similar possibilities seem to face countries and people.

Having placed on record those preliminary concerns, we should now formulate our task, which is to critically examine the role of Christianity in development. In probing the role of religion, our concern goes beyond both the ethics and the theology of development. Ethics seeks to probe the principles undergirding development work; and the theology of development is an enquiry into the soteriological claims of development. Our present task is to explore the contribution the Church can make to the enterprise, the unique role of religion. Our view is that, at its core, development is about people and thus about values. Obviously we are not engaging in a frivolous argument; on the contrary, our polemic has vested interests. We want to stake a legitimate place for faith as part of the Church's option for the poor, but also to liberate the development enterprise from its secular and material captivity and crisis.

Faith-Based Approaches to Development

Missionaries or Agency Workers?
Most African Christians are products of missionary theological traditions that came to us incorporating a variety of development activities, such as education, hospitals, and agriculture. Even though these traditions later were largely taken over by governments as our countries won their struggles for political and economic independence, the Church often continues to be active in development work, especially in education and health.

However, our reality at present is that we are no longer the sole players, and, in some respects, neither are we the best players. The field is crowded, and the ministry of many churches in the field of development work has suffered an acute identity crisis. We are not the only ones who move in after floods and similar natural disasters, nor are we the only ones talking about development. For example, the Nobel Peace Prize for 1999 was awarded to the nongovernmental organization Médecins Sans Frontières (Doctors Without Borders). These are people who move in wherever medical care is needed, irrespective of religious or political affiliation.

As we seek to strengthen our legitimacy in this domain, we have an obligation to demonstrate that the Church brings something substantive, and that our commitment is driven by different motives. Otherwise, why not simply hand over the work to international development agencies and concentrate our attention on Church growth? To use contemporary commercial criteria for measuring complementarity, what added value do we generate? What will be missing if we are not development aid players ?

I argue that it is only by reintroducing faith-inspired motives in development, which seek to restore the dignity of our work and which in turn make people subjects in their own human restoration project, that the Church's development enterprise can become authentic. We are not saviors of the poor. We are servants, vulnerable and fallible, yet convinced that it is not the fate of the poor to remain in poverty, nor is it their fault. In other words, to the extent that development does not seek transformation and liberation of the poor from conditions of dependency and structures of oppression, it is ideological and thus its authenticity is in doubt. Thus, redefinition of the content and goals of development is itself part of the task of defining the role of faith in development.

Introducing Value-Based Development

Development is not an end in itself, nor is it a mere business that can be measured in relation to a "bottom line." It is about people, societies, and life. It would be misleading to assume that development programs have no particular value basis. In fact, there are rules and norms that guide program activities. Most of the programs are based on values of efficiency, prudent use of economic resources, in some instances some form of mutuality or consultation between donors and recipients, particular norms of accountability to donors, and specific criteria for selection and sectoral concentration policies such as a preference for rural/women over urban/male. Within ethical theory we talk of ethical systems that are premised on given rules and norms, what are known as rule-based ethics. Without lessening the usefulness of the rules, the Church is operating from a value system that says we must not be enslaved by rules, that rules are there to serve human beings and not the other way around. In particular, we are reminded that rules are socially constructed and reflect the dominant values of society.

Working with the poor is an endeavor that tests the values of a given society. Whenever one does good there is the temptation to forget the humanity of the recipient and believe in the good of the giver. Development touches the core or the soul of the other. It cannot be done in a detached manner, without being involved. It is not like fixing motor vehicles. It is about restoring the humanity of those who have been robbed of it by wars, natural disasters, or oppressive systems. That is why it requires empathy.

A Christian approach to development entails a passionate involvement with the objects of development, turning them into subjects of their own lives. In our view, more harm than good can result from handling development work impersonally. An inherent danger of development work, primarily because it unavoidably affects the personhood of both recipients and donors, is that unless careful attention is paid to the inherent dignity of agents, it can result in damaged or distorted social relations. In particular, what is called for is spirituality in development that sets the context of the interaction, restraining the donor from assuming a godlike attitude and keeping the recipient from being reduced to a mere case or number.

Enriching Development through the Faith Dimension
There is without doubt growing realization in various quarters that the faith dimension should be added to development work. As part of the World Bank study on poverty in the twenty-first century, a consultation was held in Johannesburg early this year where the major areas of debate were poverty measurement and definition. It was revealing that among economists, cultural anthropologists, and sociologists alike there was agreement that any measurement and definition that does not include the religious dimension is inadequate. This theoretical shift is very significant, especially for the Church, since it legitimizes its role in

development. We must register a particular concern about tendencies in mainstream development for aid workers to approach this field as nothing more than a profession, as scientific and businesslike as any profession, like accounting or law. Having been commercialized and professionalized, development ceases to be about people and becomes a business of targets and measurable outcomes.

But no matter how advanced materially a country may be, without the dimension of religious experience and values that progress cannot pass for development. Take the example of Russia, which has more engineers per head than most Western nations and is able to send human beings into space. Clearly, in terms of stages of development, Russia can be said to have passed the take-off stage. Yet it has hundreds of people sleeping under bridges, and is receiving aid from the IMF and World Bank as if it were a Third World country. Another example is that of India, which is the only country that both exports medical doctors to the rest of the world and has nuclear capacity. Yet poverty in India is desperate by comparison with other developing countries. What this means is that development is not simply the number of BMWs driving around our capital cities, but is about the balanced development of a country's people.

Africa needs more engineers and other university graduates, yet we must also have societies that value their people, that seek the fulfillment and dignity of their members. When that happens, we are on the road to real development. This is a plea for the churches to save development from its captivity by professionals. Maybe because the Church failed to execute the work diligently, it is now being done by professionals. Our view is that they also must not reduce it to just a profession.

Human Actors, Not Messiahs

It is the inherent temptation of all human beings to make history, to solve big problems, to be remembered beyond our earthly lives, to seek immortality. In a sense there is a hidden struggle to be messiahs in our own way, be it small or large. The temptation is greater for those of us who have the power and can use it to change people's lives. We are tempted to become redeemers and thus commit the fundamental error of playing God. Development workers, like political liberators, tend to forget that they are human after all, and that there are some problems that simply are beyond our capacity to solve. We are not the Mr. Fix-It of societies' woes. A faith-based approach in this area is crucial insofar as it reminds us that we are dealing with a problem that is a composite outcome and made up of multiple layers of issues, not only economic failures. Introducing the religious dimension into development refocuses the problem and thus lays the basis for addressing it adequately. In a sense, we are not the only power players, and we need to admit our limitation. However, this should be no excuse for inaction.

The Act Is as Good as the End Made Possible

Doing development work is by definition a medium- to long-term project whose end results may not be enjoyed immediately. One is reminded of the task of building a cathedral. In the city of Uppsala in Sweden, there is a cathedral that took close to a hundred years to build. The original architect and builders knew that it would not be finished in their lifetimes. A story is told of how some building stones were transported from the southern part of Sweden; it took winter and spring to cart each load to the building site. After 50 years of building, after all the first generation had died, work continued in the hands of a new generation. Today you see the cathedral towering over Uppsala University, and you marvel at the faith of the people involved, especially those who began the project, but also those who inherited the unfinished idea and brought it to finality.

One lesson that comes out of this is that it really does not matter whether one lives to enjoy the fruits of development labor, since the reward is both in the act and in the end. Obviously, like the building of the cathedral, the act must have an objective; it is not activity for its own sake. Faith thus adds the notion that development is both a collaborative venture and a process. As we plant the seeds of growth for a future generation, we may not live to see them grow into productive members of their society, but our humble contribution is crucial.

When we thus insist on the involvement of the churches in development work—when we remind development workers that the Church has been with communities and will remain with them long after a particular development agency's policy has changed or it has left the scene entirely—we are making a valid point. Development is a work of faith and love that is undertaken without the assurance that we will live to see and enjoy its fruits. As with life, one can never claim to have arrived or to have reached the final stage. The German theologian Eberhard Jungel made a distinction between two stages of life: *being* and *becoming*. The same can be said about development, and it is this dimension that religion should reintroduce in the development debate.

Personhood: Ubuntu

Consistency and unity are the cornerstone of ethical behavior. This unity becomes the basis for doing and being: your actions reflect who you are and you are defined by your actions. A disintegrated person cannot act with consistency, and thus cannot act ethically. Integrity of personhood is a definition of identity, of who we are. By taking seriously the being of ethical agents, we are showing respect to their personhood. In some African languages, this is called *Ubuntu*. It may go by other names in other traditions. At the root of this principle is the confession that there inheres in every person a core of being who cannot be reduced to nothingness; that all of us, despite our apparent differences, are united at a deeper level where our commonality as persons with histories, experiences, and destinies are located. A religious approach to development takes Ubuntu as its primary operating guide. This means one works in the spirit and conduct that reflects this inner respect for the dignity of the other, especially the recipient of our goodness. Ubuntu is a moral force as much as it is a guiding philosophy for interpersonal relationships.

Development Work as Options for the Poor

The churches are involved in development work because they are primarily involved with the poor. If there is any social group that lives, understands, and identifies with the poor in Africa, it is the Church. In South Africa statistics show that other than the post office, no institution has as many local branches as the Church. It is found in the most remote parts of the country. When the Church talks of the poor, it is talking of its own members. It is the Church with the poor and of the poor. It is trusted by the poor: they understand its language, motives, and leadership.

It is this familiarity that gives the churches an advantage. In a sense they have earned it by accompanying the poor in their lives. When nonchurch development workers arrive, poor communities are suspicious of their motives, and cannot count on them becoming a permanent feature of their communities. In our view, the churches should use this identity to their advantage. They can be better conduits and channels for development aid and effective practitioners, since they have the value basis for that kind of work. Whether we like it or not, politicians run for office, and however good they may be they still cannot separate what they do from winning the next election. However, the local church minister has to learn to do development work across denominational lines. In Africa, wars do not discriminate between Catholics and Anglicans. We need to serve our people ecumenically, without favor to ethnic or denominational allegiance. In doing that, we will truly have created a new option for the poor.

Development as a Mission of the Church

Many Christians see development as a dangerous thin edge of the social gospel. They worry that before long, the Church will have deviated from the real issue, which is saving people for the Kingdom. They counsel those who busy themselves with matters of poverty alleviation to tread with care lest they forget the real prize. We must counter this attitude by strong affirmation that human, social, and economic development is not alien to the Christian concept of mission, even though it is true that mission cannot be reduced to poverty alleviation. A holistic understanding of mission reaffirms that God is not only concerned with the supranatural, but is active to humanize the world as we know it, and that his power is active in the secular life of humankind. The mission of God is to this world. Addressing this issue, Carl Braaten wrote:

> As long as Christian faith is oriented by the history of promise and eschatological significance of Christ, there will be a Christian mission in world history. . . . The universal scope of history of promise posits the whole world as the horizon of its mission. . . . The world is not something that can be added on. The world stands within the horizon of mission from the beginning, or simply comes too late to prevent evangelistic backlash from ecclesiastical retrenchment. . . .
>
> The doctrine of the Church needs to be reconceived within the horizon of the eschatological mission of God in world history. (Braaten 1977: 54)

Development therefore is not something that churches are busy with apologetically, or by default. It is the work of God, part of God's own mission to the world. Mission churches understood this when they first came to Africa, and they have experience of such work.

Like any work of God, development work requires spirituality. It is hard these days to define what spirituality means, especially with the arrival of New Age spirituality. But the main point is that spirituality entails an aspect of transcendence, a dimension beyond human capacity and rationality. It includes such realms as rituals and sacraments. For our purpose we can say that to be involved in development work is to partake in the work of God, and that we need to do that by being in constant relationship with the source of our being and deity. This work thus requires prayer, intercession, and support. One cannot underestimate the need for divine support in this work. Seeking to fight systems and structures that bring death and misery to people is not without its dangers. It is tempting to withdraw into our comfortable zones, free from the controversies that come with engagement with the world. Indeed, many church leaders have opted for the uncontroversial offices of preaching, pastoral care, and so forth. But if we understand that development is not a work of our choosing, and that we are not alone, but can count on the life-giving power of God, then development ministry becomes a way of thanksgiving, a joy of participation in the world but working with God to fight poverty.

In summary, both the World Bank and the churches in Africa have a contribution to make and therefore can enhance the fight against poverty by entering into principled partnerships. Ideologically we may still be a distance apart, and some may even caution the Church not to come within an inch of the World Bank for fear of being co-opted. We are reminded of the ministry of Jesus, who showed that no ideology, religious or political, should stop us from doing good to those in need. Our view is that our differences notwithstanding, we need to work together in the fight against poverty in Africa. To do that, we start by affirming the strategic contribution the churches bring to the partnership. In our view, Christian institutions are rooted within their communities; they have developed a credible leadership that is familiar with the needs of the poor; and they are familiar with the cultures, histories, and contexts of the people. Religious communities approach their development work from a unique perspective that reinforces the moral and ethical value systems of those communities.

A similar pattern can be found in the emergence of Christian development agencies in Europe at the end of World War II, such as EZE and Miserior in Germany, HEKS in Switzerland, and DanChurch Aid and Norwegian Church Aid in Scandinavia. This was motivated by the realization that churches were well placed to do development work in partnership with their governments' overseas development ministries.

As we embark on this new partnership it will be necessary to spell out its principles and framework. For churches in particular, it must also be asked how they can best serve all the poor in their communities, not simply those within their folds. In other words, development aid in the hands of the churches should not be used to further disempower some or all the poor and strengthen the local pastor and his flock. History has taught us that there is the risk of this happening.

Conclusion

The Church in Africa does not have the luxury of choosing whether to participate in or disengage from the field of development. More than any other continent, ours has to account for the well-being of its people. We are a continent in crisis; we have not even fully come to terms with the real proportions of that crisis. The evidence we see daily in the horrors and misery faced by our people should inspire us to become unconventional, more daring, and less çautious. Africa and its people have endured centuries of neglect, plunder, and abuse. All of us, especially the churches, have not worked hard enough to unleash the full potential of our human assets. As a generation of poor, landless urban dwellers hands over its meager inheritance to its unemployed, unskilled children, all indications are that the standards of living enjoyed by our rural-based parents will remain the envy of the coming generation. Their hopes and dreams will be simply to reach those standards, and the chances are slim that even those wishes will be answered. This underlines how much we need a Church that is committed to addressing the crisis of poverty and human neglect.

If we are to mount a formidable challenge to the crisis as defined, we cannot resort to the tried and tested models of development and economic reforms that have been with us for the last two decades. We need to embrace a new model that is premised on the realization that unless religion and religious institutions become active players on this field, we are doomed to repeat the same social and economic failures already experienced. The lesson of the past three decades for Africa is that political independence, however valuable, will not be sufficient until it permeates popular structures and systems of the entire African social life.

By the same token, we must boldly declare that macroeconomic fundamentals on their own cannot resolve the development conundrum. We do not need more of the World Bank, but a different and a new World Bank. The failures of structural adjustment programs have not come about because these programs are dispensed in too-moderate doses. We have had an overdose of such programs, but still the problems have become acute. Sensibly, this means we must require that the international financial institutions change the way they deal with Africa.

It is time for the religious communities to engage, and this should start from the perspective that development must be value-based and oriented to human beings. In our view, the only way of being a true religion in our African context is by becoming development agents. The Scripture gave us a fundamental lesson in teaching that "Man shall not live by bread alone, but by every word of God" (Luke 4:4). Even though this text has been misused to justify the unimportant, what is true here is that Jesus rejects the ultimate supremacy of economics for life. He posits an alternative view, one that says: Economics yes, but something extra. It is this something extra, the religious dimension, that we argue has been missing in development work. Let us conclude by listening again to what the Arusha charter says about the centrality of human beings as agents in development:

> In our sincere view, popular participation is both a means and an end. As an instrument of development, popular participation provides the driving force for collective commitment for the determination of people-based development processes and willingness by the people to undertake sacrifices and expand their social energies for its execution. As an end in itself, popular participation is the fundamental right of the people, to fully and effectively participate in the determination of the decisions which affect their lives at all levels and at all times. (African Charter 1990)

References

Addo, H., S. Amin, G. Aseniero, A. G. Frank, M. Friberg, F. Frobel, J. Heinrich, B. Hettne, O. Kreye, and H. Seki. 1985. *Development as Social Transformation: Reflections on the Global Problematique.* London: Hodder and Stoughton.

"African Charter for Popular Participation in Development and Transformation." 1990. Adopted by the International Conference on Popular Participation in the Recovery and Development Process in Africa. Arusha, Tanzania, February 12–16.

Blomström, Magnus, and Björn Hettne. 1984. *Development Theory in Transition: The Dependency Debate and Beyond: Third World Responses.* London: Zed Books.

Braaten, Carl E. 1977. *The Flaming Center: A Theology for the Christian Mission.* Philadelphia: Fortress Press.

Gutiérrez, Gustavo. 1973. *A Theology of Liberation: History, Politics, and Salvation.* Translated and edited by Sister Caridad Inga and John Eagleson. Maryknoll, N.Y.: Orbis Books.

Luther, Martin. [1520] 1965. *Treatise on Good Works.* Vol. 44 of *Luther's Works.* Philadelphia: Fortress Press.

Myers, Bryant L. 1999. *Walking with the Poor: Principles and Practices of Transformational Development.* Maryknoll, N.Y.: Orbis Books and World Vision International.

Niebuhr, H. Richard. 1963. *The Responsible Self: An Essay in Christian Moral Philosophy.* New York: Harper and Row.

Rostow, W. W. 1960. *The Stages of Economic Growth.* Cambridge: Cambridge University Press.

UNDP (United Nations Development Programme). 1998. *Human Development Report 1998.* New York: Oxford University Press.

18

The Role of the Church in Poverty Alleviation in Africa

Julius Oladipo

The issue of the reduction of mass poverty in Africa requires urgent worldwide attention. A wide range of institutions have roles to play: the southern and northern governments, international development finance institutions, international and local NGOs, the private sector, and the Church (the universal Church and the churches in Africa). The focus of this paper is on the distinctive position of the Church in Africa in this task of poverty alleviation. The emphasis here is that the Church deserves a prominent role in the process of economic and social development (and particularly in the social service sectors).

Stabilization and structural adjustment measures adopted in African countries have usually led to a reduction in government involvement in social services delivery. The expectation is that private enterprise and personal expenditures will make up the difference. This leads, typically, to the exclusion of the poor. This paper presents the credentials of the Church as a candidate that should be supported and enabled to fill the gap.

The definition of poverty given by the United Nations Development Programme is adopted here. It states that poverty is a lack of productive resources, income, and capacities that contributes to individual and/or group isolation, vulnerability, and powerlessness; to economic, political, and social discrimination; and to participation in unsustainable livelihoods (UNDP 1996). Poverty has various manifestations, including hunger and malnutrition, ill health, and limited or no access to education, health care, and safe residential and occupational environments. It has both *absolute* and *relative* dimensions. A distinction is also made between *structural* (or chronic) poverty and *transient* poverty. Officially defined poverty lines identify absolute levels of poverty, while relative poverty refers to an individual's or a group's position in relation to others. Structural poverty is rooted in socio-economic and political institutions, is experienced over the long term, and is often transferred across generations. In contrast, transient poverty is due to cyclical or temporary factors and is experienced over shorter periods of time.

My focus is on absolute, structural poverty. Alleviation of the effects of disasters and emergencies is an important subject, but is usually distinguished from the goals of socioeconomic development. By all official measures of absolute poverty, the people of the Sub-Saharan African countries form the bulk of the world's poor.

An effective solution to a problem must be based on good diagnosis. Early theories that sought to explain causes of poverty took rather narrow perspectives. It is now being recognized that the causes of poverty are complex and sometimes even contradictory. Political, economic, and social institutions and processes are implicated in the production and perpetuation of poverty. Based on this view of the multidimensional nature of the causes of poverty, holistic approaches to poverty alleviation are being promoted. However, what is now known as holistic development has been the approach of the Church from its inception in Africa. Whenever we think of a mission station in any part of Africa, the following specific features come to mind: a church, a school, a health clinic, and a vegetable garden or farm. There is also the characteristic campaign of the church agents against the social ills of the time, which in earlier days centered on harmful traditional practices.

Strategic Advantages of the Church in Poverty Alleviation

Several of the ideal features of the Church give it an advantageous position in working for sustainable development. The Church is rooted in the community. It is present not just in urban areas but also, and particularly, in the remote rural areas, including even areas of conflict where many other NGOs are unable to operate. It draws its voluntary membership from any and all segments of the local population and knows the local situation well. It is familiar with people's needs. With these advantages, it has potential strength for speedy, effective community mobilization and influence.

The Church is nonpartisan. The Church serves the whole society, the family, the community, and even the government. It serves the rich and the poor. It usually spans ethnic and other dividing lines (although it may be excluded from access where another world faith claims precedence). The Church is not in a position to take power, nor is it interested in such struggles; hence it is not in competition with established political and traditional structures.

The Church is a stable institution. Political institutions are dogged by worries about the next election, and autocratic leaders are sleepless for fear of being unseated. Most nongovernmental organizations face uncertainties with changes in leadership and funding. But attachment to biblical absolutes and age-old traditions ensures minimal disruptions to the organization of the Church. Leadership succession generally does not upset the established structures or procedures. Membership is lifelong.

The Church has a regular and predictable system. It is known who makes decisions. The resources are clear. There are regular meetings of membership with fixed meeting places.

The Church conforms to a moral order. Church agents subscribe to a system of checks and balances, enforcement of which is facilitated by intrinsic personal motivation. In practice, its personnel are by and large people of integrity. Comparatively speaking, the Church has high credibility, even in skeptical modern society. Also, the traditional African awe of religion means the Church is held in high esteem, and is even expected to serve as the conscience of society. Moral authority is conferred on it that obligates it to speak out about society's ills.

The Church has a strong value base of concern for poor and marginalized groups that is supported by its biblical mission and that inspires commitment from its leaders, members, and development staff.

The Church has a long and established history of doing socioeconomic development work to benefit all needy people. The track record of the Church in development is discussed below.

The Church has a culture of volunteerism. People offer themselves to God in selfless service to humankind. Church members are committed to a culture of giving in cash and in kind—skills, labor, financial and material contributions. Among the membership, there is a pool of voluntary professional expertise from which the Church can draw for technical services. Even the salaried staff generally take their regular work as a calling and often go beyond the normal call of duty.

The Church has among its intangible assets the capacity to imbue the poor with hope, a necessary ingredient for them to keep on going until improvement is effected. The Church lives on faith and hope and it endeavors to infuse hope in all the people it serves.

The Church has an existing structure and mechanisms for initiating new activities. Its associations—women's groups, men's groups, youth groups, and children's groups—serve as effective contacts and vision-carriers among their counterparts in the community. Generally, physical premises (such as meeting halls) and other facilities are available that hasten start-up processes.

The Church is part of a wider global institutional structure, with extensive interpersonal linkages, resource transfers, and opportunities for discussion, training, and so forth, at the international level. These linkages are reinforced by the image of "the Body of Christ" transcending national, racial, and other boundaries, and can be drawn on when needed for solidarity and support.

The Basis of the Church's Service to the Poor

The theological and philosophical development of the ministry of the Church is discussed by Molefe Tsele (see chapter 17). Here, I only make a brief comment to underscore the point that the Church is a legitimate player and not just stumbling into development work. Defining the role of the Church in development requires, first, defining the goal and content of development (see, for example, Samuel and Sugden 1987). Also required is an understanding of the mission of the Church.

There have been many efforts to define development; each of the various approaches to development work necessarily stems from the particular definition adopted. The "economic growth" perspective has dominated the public discourse, although over the last decade there has been some rethinking. That is, there has been a shift from an economic growth model to one that takes into account several factors, particularly the moral and equity dimensions. It can be argued that the shift in viewpoint has not yet brought about major changes in official approaches to development. However, it has been accepted in principle that development interventions ought to "wear a human face"; that is, at the policymaking stage, the possible effects of policies on the vulnerable groups in society ought to be considered. There is also global agreement that the yardstick for measuring development ought to be a society's ability to sustain a healthy and dignified standard of living without abuse of others or destruction of ecosystems.

The Christian "stewardship" view of development decries the unbridled quest for economic gain in which no one cares about who or what is hurt in the process. This view hinges on the passage where God places humankind in "the Garden of Eden" to both work it and take care of it (Genesis 2:15). It emphasizes responsible and accountable use of God-given resources (see, for example, Bragg 1987).

True development improves the total person in a holistic manner. This is summed up in the meaning of *shalom*. That is the goal of development, from the Christian perspective.

A basic reason for the Church's involvement in development is contained in the declaration of Jesus concerning his mission (Luke 4:18–19): bringing "good news" to the poor. And his mission is our mission. The fact that humankind is created in the "image of God" also signifies that each person is entitled to a decent and dignified living. It is with this in mind that Kinoti (1994) has said, "The wretchedness of the African people dishonors their Creator . . . And we must overcome the disgrace of being the poorest people on earth." For the Christian, development work is not an optional matter. The Christian is commanded to demonstrate her/his faith in good works. Hence, socioeconomic development is an imperative sphere of engagement for the Church.

The Church's Track Record in Poverty Alleviation

The European voyages of world discovery were motivated by religion, commerce, and political expansionism. The effects of the three motives are indelible. The indisputably bright part of history is that Christian missionaries brought the message of spiritual redemption and they also ministered to the physical needs of the people. In many places, they introduced new staple crops and the use of animal power for farming. In most African countries, formal education, vocational skills training, and modern health care services were pioneered by the Church. The management of these services subsequently passed from the missionaries to nationals.

Many of the national leaders in African countries were educated in Christian schools. Nevertheless, in line with Western secular trends, these leaders decided that government can and should run these services on its own. In many African countries, the government took over church schools and hospitals. The result is well known. In many countries, when the government took over the schools, the Church stepped up vocational training for youths, for instance by introducing the concept of "village polytechnics." The Church has also made a significant contribution in providing safe water to rural communities by means of boreholes, hand-dug wells, protection of springs, and rainwater harvesting techniques.

The leaders of the Church have taken their prophetic role very seriously. In almost every country in Africa, the voice of the Church has been loud, clear, and consistent against the ills in society. The Church played a major role in the dismantling of apartheid. When oppressed by a dictator—military or civilian—citizens have usually looked to the Church to speak out on their behalf. And the Church has been alert to the onerous responsibility, in some cases at the cost of its leaders' lives.

Civic education and election monitoring are recent additions to the work of the Church in many countries, and they have been proving so effective that unpopular political leaders have realized that they can no longer mislead and exploit the populace.

The voice of the Church has been loud in the campaign to cancel the debt of the poorest indebted countries (for example, see Gitari 1999). In recent years, the debt crisis has worsened the already grievous conditions of the poor countries. A large proportion of the limited foreign exchange goes into debt service. The reality is that in some cases the net flow of funds is now from developing to developed nations. The view that the creditor countries should be held responsible for their part in creating the problem underscores the moral dimension of the issue. "Cushioning" involves offering indebted countries additional but softer loans. An "improved" version being proposed is to let some proportion of debt service payments be retained in the debtor countries as grants for poverty alleviation. The plea of many churches is that what poor African countries need now is total debt cancellation and not half-way responses.

Much is known about the development work of the Church in Africa, but only in a general way. Statistics are very scarce. Various denominations and Christian NGOs produce separate reports for each country they work in. Collation of information on all this work is overdue.

The Church's Core Competencies for Development Ministry

It is obvious that the issue of alleviating mass poverty in Africa calls for radical but carefully thought out strategies. The approaches have to be multipronged to be effective. There are economic, sociocultural, and moral/advocacy dimensions. Also, every effort has to address the root causes of poverty rather than merely treating symptoms. In this section, we discuss those aspects of the development potential of the Church in Africa that are yet to be adequately explored.

In the economic dimension, there are both the macro- and the microeconomic levels. Until recently, it was not thought that the Church has anything to contribute at the macro level. Now that bad governance is understood as a major factor that contributes to deepening poverty, all agents that are in a position to help secure positive changes in the polity are being recognized as important.

Good governance is important for sound formulation and implementation of economic policy. Here, the Church has recently taken up the role of "conscientizing" the citizenry to elect competent leaders and is engaging in election monitoring to ensure that the people's choice is respected. Through its ongoing prophetic ministry, the Church speaks out on any manifestation of poor policies or blatant misrule. Also, the Church has often been called upon to serve as an informal arbitrator in trade disputes, particularly nationwide strikes.

However, there are other areas in which the potential of the Church needs to be more purposively harnessed. In almost all African countries, the constitutions inherited at independence are inadequate for addressing contemporary challenges. The principles on which nationhood should be based are only vaguely stated. The role defined for government is all-pervasive and far outstrips its capacity even if there is the will to deliver. The framework for making leaders consistently accountable to the citizenry is invariably lacking. Elections are based on the winner-takes-all principle rather than on power sharing. Provisions for smooth leadership succession are generally inadequate. Accordingly, the need for constitutional reform is widespread. The Church is getting involved in the movement for reform, and it needs to be supported and strengthened in this role.

Guiding governance, in addition to the written constitution, should be the expressed will of the people. While the Church needs to continue in civic education for the governed, there is also a need to raise the consciousness of political leaders. The Church should be enabled to convene, particularly at the district level, workshops involving party leaders across the political spectrum, with local traditional and religious leaders in attendance, as forums where principles and procedures of good governance would be discussed.

Also, the civic education program should go beyond enlightening people about the electoral process. Communities must be able to demand accountability from their local elected leaders. Obviously, when these leaders blame their poor performance on the national government, they are declaring themselves irrelevant and hence not qualified for reelection. However, people should not just keep quiet and wait for the next election time. In this regard, to lead the way in assertiveness, the heads of the Church's development departments, who in most countries are members of the government's district development committees, should insist on being de facto members contributing to the formulation and monitoring of the official district development budgets.

Most of the objectionable policies or practices of government could be corrected at the outset if popular protests took place before they were officially adopted. The leaders of the Church should have a proactive approach to their prophetic ministry. This would require, among other things, sources of information in the government policymaking offices that would allow the leaders and their professional advisers time to discuss the best way the Church should react to any particular matter.

It is recognized that certain regulatory features of world trade have worked unfairly against developing countries and are among the factors that have contributed to the current scale of poverty in Africa. The Church in Africa needs actively to join the lobby that has been demanding redress in this sphere. It should work with its external supporters in the campaigns for a just world trade order and for debt cancellation.

Microeconomics is a major area of the Church's development ministry. However, there is much room for improvement. Although it is accepted that development efforts should address the systematic causes of poverty, the choice and design of interventions has often not focused on that goal. Most community development programs attempt to offer relief to the poorest of the poor rather than to change livelihood opportunities for the whole mass of the poor. Lambs, kids, and heifers are being given to poor and marginalized households. Self-help groups are being assisted here and there. However, the whole mass of poor people in the village is not affected. Programs that relieve the tragic suffering of the poorest of the poor should not be neglected, but the Church should recognize its capability to influence the whole village by introducing sustainable livelihoods that can be adopted widely.

The household cash flow problem is a basic issue. The common practice is for small farmers to sell off their produce at giveaway prices during the harvest season to obtain cash for children's school fees and other family expenses, only to buy grain at much higher retail prices later in the year. Even where food production is not a problem, good output retention in the household is problematic. There are traditional granaries to store the grain, but they are now used less. It is pointless, therefore, to promote the adoption of "appropriate technology" granaries in such a context. The Church needs to design effective ways of addressing the household cash liquidity problem.

Rural savings and credit schemes are relevant in this regard. The services of the few microfinance NGOs currently operating in Africa are generally not accessible to the many would-be new entrants. The goal of the rural savings and credit schemes of the Church is to build up novices in microenterprise to a level where they can use the services of specialized microfinance NGOs. However, there is a need for the Church to adopt more effective activities in these schemes. Involvement of resource persons with relevant expertise would be very helpful.

As it has done in the past—for example, with coffee and cotton innovation in East Africa—the Church in Africa can mobilize the people to adopt sustainable innovations. Which innovations can the whole village embrace that will make a difference in the standard of living? For example, sericulture is one very promising possibility; there are many other viable ideas waiting for adoption.

Food security is a major theme in the Church's development ministry. Increased production is frequently a great need. However, influencing people's dietary choices is probably a more basic requirement. The globalization of dietary patterns is leading the African family to substitute imported foods for the traditional staples, which wastes scarce foreign currency among other things. Where drought-resistant crops are appropriate the Church could make a significant impact. In some semi-arid and arid areas where sorghum, millet, and cassava are the traditional staple crops, modern tastes have changed to rice and spaghetti and the motivation for cultivating the former staples has waned. With new varieties and production techniques, the Church may be in a position to revive interest in them. There is also the need to diversify the staple crops. There could be more sharing of crops across the tropics than has currently taken place. African soils can produce a much wider variety of foodstuffs than are cultivated at present. Irish potatoes were introduced by the missionaries and widely embraced in many higher-altitude areas. The Church can do this again with other products.

The Church has been promoting the adoption of appropriate small-scale irrigation technology on family farms, but only as a marginal activity and not in a vigorous manner. Small- and micro-scale irrigation and water harvesting technologies have barely started to be used in Sub-Saharan Africa, despite the fact that their viability has been clearly demonstrated in South Asia where they have been widely adopted. This is an area for urgent consideration in the anticipated poverty-focused discussions between the Church and the World Bank.

The Church has great strengths in promoting the formation of self-help groups and in enhancing their capacity for self-actualization. The development ministry organs of the Church should expand into formation and facilitation of cooperatives and associations built around the objectives of marketing and input supply. They should work for the emergence of local processing facilities that add value to the primary products of each local economy. The Church could spearhead preprocessing for export and also promote linkages with already existing fairtrade organizations in the North that are promoting direct exports from small producers in the developing countries.

There is the need to recognize the potentially competitive position of small-scale African farmers in high-value commodity trade, already demonstrated in, for example, tea, coffee, and cocoa production. The world is kept supplied steadily with tobacco (and other controversial crops) essentially by small farmers. Rural cooperatives are an effective organ for pooling the limited output of the individual small farms into large exportable volumes. The basic requirement is to focus on a high-value crop and establish linkage with overseas nonexploitative buyers—facilitated, possibly, by contacts within the universal Church as well as by some Christian-owned commercial agencies.

The Church can play a great part in the promotion and diversification of export production. As Belshaw (1999) has noted: "The range of high-value products that have a growing world market has been tapped by only a few African countries to date. Product types include tropical fruits; flowers and vegetables of all types in the northern winter months; nuts; spices; livestock products; medicinal plants and aromatics."

The Church has been working extensively on household income-generating activities, but its efforts need to be more imaginative. Village groups are assisted in poultry, pig, or bee-keeping enterprises. Everyone in the village adopts the idea. Soon, they discover that they have insufficient outlets to absorb the output. Then the Church is blamed for having not done a thorough feasibility study. The same question of demand applies to vocational skills training. Scores of youths in a village learn carpentry and masonry, but the village perhaps does not need more than two carpenters and three masons. Similarly, the Church women's vocational center annually graduates, say, five tailors, six embroiders, and seven craftswomen into the village. The sewing machine left up on a shelf testifies to the low returns from such training. It is evident that the Church's development organs have the capacity to enhance skills. The question is: Which types of skills do the villagers require for sustainable livelihoods? Increased attention should be given to that issue.

The above observations relate to some of the economic dimensions of the Church's role. Next, competencies of the Church in the sociocultural sphere are discussed. Awareness creation is a necessary activity and is one of the areas in which the Church is roundly competent. Being rooted in the community, having a multidimensional knowledge of its people, and being regarded as a credible institution are significant assets.

Social cohesion is a basic issue in Africa. It sets the atmosphere for productive engagement. It is an important component of development and is an area in which the Church has much proven capacity. Land disputes within and between communities, ethnic clashes, and civil wars continue to augment the miseries of the poor. The Church needs to introduce, as a widespread program, regular intercommunity forums in which issues are discussed and steps are taken toward joint planning and implementation of development and civic projects. Because it is known to be nonpartisan and because it already has credibility with the people, the Church is usually in a better position than the political leaders to initiate and facilitate these discussions. Similarly, youths of different ethnic groups could be brought closer through carefully designed interethnic cultural and vocational activities.

Land is a common matter of concern in almost all African countries. It is a thorny issue that politicians prefer to keep off the agenda. Here, the Church can play a key role: at the least, the Church can convene local forums for redressing incessant communal land disputes. Also, the plight of peoples living in arid, famine-prone regions requires systematic discussion. Reclaiming the hard land, as Israel has done, is not an option open to poor countries. Forcible resettlement is unacceptable, as is the situation in which part of the population become perpetual receivers of relief handouts. The Church could negotiate the voluntary relocation of new farm households to underused areas once these are provided with adequate production and social infrastructure.

The capacity of the Church in running institutional social services, particularly health care services and schools, is widely appreciated in Africa. The Church can be counted on to deliver health care and educational services effectively and in a sustainable manner. In health care, greater emphasis is being placed on preventive services, relative to curative medicine. Governments and the Church have been active in this category because private health care providers can earn limited profit in this area. Now that governments are reducing their involvement, the Church is poised to be the main player in that arena. The possible advantages of Church-state and Church-private partnerships should also be examined in specific situations.

Cost-sharing has been promoted both as a requirement for the financial viability of the service institution and as a factor in protecting those who receive services from the dependency syndrome. However, there is concern everywhere about how to help the poor afford even relatively low fees. Health insurance is being discussed, but has not been widely explored; while it should receive increased attention, only social (subsidized) insurance would seem to be suitable for the poor. Such a conclusion would emphasize the importance of the discussion above on raising the productivity and incomes of the poor.

The Church is involved in campaigning against traditional harmful practices and restrictive beliefs. So far, however, this has merely been regarded as another activity of the development department, rather than as one that involves the whole mobilization potential of Church. It seems that Church leaders will need to take extra time to study the particular and often local issues and start playing their full role as agents of change. The Church has immense but only partially tapped potential in this area. Some African traditions, such as those involving high bride prices and expensive weddings and funerals, make the poverty situation worse. The Church is in a position to influence communities to devise appropriate adjustments in conformity with current realities.

Family planning or child spacing is a theme in the socioeconomic program of the Church. Less rapid population growth is an important factor in poverty alleviation. Also, the scourge of HIV/AIDS is a matter of increasing concern to the Church (see chapter 12).

The sociocultural dimension has several components, including giving attention to the waning communal spirit, the increasing instability of marriage relations, the problem of street children, the widening generation gap, gender issues, and so forth. In all these areas the Church, by its mission, has primary interest, is eminently competent, and can work effectively given the will and resources.

The moral guidance and advocacy dimensions are indisputably central to the mission of the Church. The prophetic role of the Church makes it not only the conscience of society but also a testimony and witness to the values and ethics of the kingdom of God. A concern with justice is at the center of poverty alleviation, and the Church is characteristically equipped for advocacy. For example, the marginalization of women is a matter of importance in the poverty situation in Africa. The role that the Church is playing and is further capable of playing is discussed by Agnes Abuom (see chapter 11).

Constraints Facing the Management of the Church's Development Ministry

The Church is faced with some basic challenges in its development ministry, which need to be recognized and urgently addressed. Most of these are probably features of the general working culture of the Church in Africa. As the Church wants to play a greater role, it needs to prioritize its use of resources. International partners need to note the top-priority areas for capacity-building support.

In the Church's system, policymaking organs and reference committees are usually dominated by clergy, despite the availability of appropriate practicing professionals within and outside the churches' membership. Also, involvement of women in decisionmaking has rarely moved beyond tokenism. Furthermore, while the Church has been known to target its services to the whole community without discrimination, inclusion of nonmembers on project management committees is not yet a common feature. The increasingly accepted concept of participatory management enjoins that these facets be considered.

While the Church recognizes the importance of having appropriate professional expertise for the technical aspects of its sectoral services such as health care, schools, and water supply construction, Church leaders generally appreciate less fully the place of professionalism in management aspects. Also, multisectoral approaches to community development require a level of expertise and intellectual capacity that is not yet fully appreciated.

Some Church leaders have not made a distinction between a project that has been set up to serve the people and one intended to earn profit for running the Church's internal administration. When a hospital or a school is required to pay an annual "quota" into the Church's administrative fund, that is no different from expecting dividends from shares in a commercial venture. The goals of poverty-focused development can hardly be attained when expecting such services to bring dividends.

It has already been mentioned that in general the Church can be credited for integrity, but it should be noted that occasionally the temptation to dip into designated donor funds to meet other genuine unfunded needs is not resisted. Misapplication of funds needs to be detected and rooted out as a form of financial indiscipline. While the state of financial management in the Church in Africa is improving progressively, there are still cases of weak financial systems and procedures where fraud goes undetected far too long. While excessive documentation is the bane of government service, the lack of paperwork is a pervasive weakness in the Church's working environment in Africa. "Don't you trust me?" is the common reply when someone is asked to put things in writing or to back up financial transactions with documentary evidence.

There is a general tendency to be slow in implementing decisions. Although things move faster in the Church's working environment than in government, there is much room for improvement in developing a sense of urgency about what needs to be done. Speed of response needs to be greatly improved.

Transport and communication are areas of widespread need. The Church tends to target its services to underserved people in geographically remote locations with poor communication and access, where the population is sparse and scattered over wide areas. Because of the poor state of roads, vehicle maintenance is a common problem. But a maintenance culture is not yet widespread; it is an irony that physical assets obtained with scarce funds are left to deteriorate through poor or absent maintenance procedures.

The Church in Partnership Relationships

It is not unhealthy for the Church in Africa to continue to have external funding support for its development ministry. What is not desirable is for the Church to expect external funding for meeting its own internal "club needs." Church members should provide the funds for the internal administration of the Church. They should fund the synod conferences and other administrative meetings. But in its ministry to the poor, the Church in Africa should not feel ashamed to continue to solicit external funding support. It should see it as providing a service to the donors—by signposting them to worthy causes that deserve their funding support and by providing efficient and effective management of these funds to improve the lives and prospects of the poor. Sustainability should be promoted widely as a thematic priority, but we should all be clear about what is meant by "sustainability of social services." By their nature, long-term or welfare services to the poor can hardly be financially self-sufficient. Anywhere in the world, not-for-profit service or charity organizations typically depend on donor funds.

A significant feature of the Church's development work in Africa is that it has been carried out in close partnership with international funding agencies and NGO support organizations. The two sides bring their distinctive strengths together to serve the poor—the African churches' contribution being in the aspects of needs identification and project management while the international Church provides funds and technical support. The possibility of entering into a working relationship with the official aid institutions, especially the World Bank, is currently being discussed; these funders could benefit from the experience that the Church has acquired in its existing partnerships.

The World Bank has been perceived in different ways. For example, Mohammed Yunus, the founder of Grameen Bank, presents his own perception of the World Bank's relation to a borrowing country as follows:

> They give you money. They give you all the ideas, expertise and everything else. Your job is to follow the yellow lines, the green lines, the red lines, read the instructions at each stop and follow them. The World Bank is eager to assume all the responsibilities. They don't want to leave any responsibility to the borrower, except the responsibility for the failure of the project. (quoted in Hodson 1997)

The Church is not familiar with such a relationship where its only role in formulation of agreements is to sign on the dotted line. The need for negotiation of positions is obvious.

With reference to the early stage of a particular Bank-funded project, Hodson (1997) states:

> Through frequent supervision missions the Bank tried to ensure that the project design was closely followed. The level of micro-management of the project at times reached ridiculous levels with 15-member supervisory missions leaving hundreds of pages of notes and instructions, much of it based on an inadequate understanding of the situation.

The donors that provide aid grants to the Church prefer, in the language of development, to be referred to as "partners." Although most of them are still grappling with the implications of that position, its importance is recognized in principle. The Church cherishes partnership based on mutual understanding, mutual respect, and mutual accountability.

The business community—the commercial and manufacturing sector—is virtually dormant in social development in Africa. But the theme of social responsibility is currently being promoted worldwide. The Church leaders in a district could come together and approach the profitable companies and factories in their locality to fund some specific community projects. The potential of involving such local donors has not been adequately tapped. In addition to benefiting workers, suppliers, consumers, owners, and government (through taxes paid directly and indirectly), these businesses should be feeding back some returns to strengthen their local communities.

This paper intentionally has not given any definition of "the Church." For the partnership relationships to be effective, fruitful, and sustainable, the Church needs to recognize and maintain its identity. There is ongoing debate about whether or not the Church is an NGO. The Church is an active and significant player in development; however, this is only a part of its mandate. A basic requirement for good partnership is to know and respect each other's distinctive qualities and peculiarities and also to collaborate on the common ground.

Bibliography

Asante, R. K. O. 1998. "Sustainability of Church Hospitals in Developing Countries: A Search for Criteria for Success." Geneva: World Council of Churches.

Belshaw, D. 1999. "Poverty Reduction in Sub-Saharan Africa in the Context of the Decline of the Welfare State: The Strategic Role of the Church." *Transformation* 16 (4): 114–18.

Bragg, W. G. 1987. "From Development to Transformation." In V. Samuel and C. Sugden, eds., *The Church in Response to Human Need.* Grand Rapids, Mich.: W. B. Eerdmans.

Gitari, D. M. 1999. "Development Opportunities and Challenges in Africa: Effects of International Debt Crisis on the Sub-Saharan Region." Processed.

Global Coalition for Africa. 1999. *Global Coalition for Africa: Documents on Development, Democracy and Debt.* The Hague: Netherlands Ministry of Foreign Affairs.

Goold, L., W. Ogara, and R. James. 1998. "Churches and Organisational Development: Churches and Organisational Development in Africa: Directions and Dilemmas for Northern NGOs." INTRAC Occasional Papers Series 20. Oxford, U.K.: International Training and Research Centre and CORAT-Africa.

Hodson, R. 1997. "Elephant Loose in the Jungle: The World Bank and NGOs in Sri Lanka." In D. Hulme and M. Edwards, eds., *NGOs, States and Donors: Too Close for Comfort?* Basingstoke, U.K.: Save the Children Fund/MacMillan Press.

Hulme, D., and M. Edwards, eds. 1997. *NGOs, States and Donors: Too Close for Comfort?* Basingstoke, U.K.: Save the Children Fund/MacMillan Press.

Kinoti, G. 1994. "Hope for Africa—and What the Christian Can Do." Nairobi: African Institute for Scientific Research and Development.

Samuel, V., and C. Sugden, eds. 1987. *The Church in Response to Human Need.* Grand Rapids, Mich.: W. B. Eerdmans.

TAABCO/CORAT. 1998. "The Role and Contribution of Development Projects (run by Churches and Christian NGOs) to the Development of Civil Society:

Report of a Study Done for the Swedish Mission Council and Swedish Pentecostal Churches." Nairobi: Interlife.

World Bank. 1989. *Sub-Saharan Africa: From Crisis to Sustainable Growth: A Long-Term Perspective Study.* Washington, D.C.

UNDP (United Nations Development Programme). 1996. "Progress Against Poverty: A Report on Activities since Copenhagen. UNDP Progress Report." New York.

19

The World Bank and the Churches: Reflections at the Outset of a New Partnership

Vinay Samuel

The World Bank has recognized that to succeed in addressing poverty it needs to be in partnership with others previously excluded from the development community and its debates.

The Bank's President, Mr. Wolfensohn, has said that the World Bank has learned from its general experience that strengthening the organization, at both the central and local levels, is the first priority in tackling the challenge of human poverty. "Do we have all the answers? No. Success will only be achieved in partnership with others in the development community."

So the World Bank is set on a course of building coalitions for change. It has already attempted a degree of coalition with NGOs, but now has started to work with the Church as well.

The Context of Coming Together

The World Bank has mainly worked with and through governments. But some governments are part of the problem. Some issues cannot be resolved by governments acting in a top-down manner, without the agreement and enthusiasm of the people who need help. Such action has produced a sense of powerlessness and a desire for new solutions. The sense of powerlessness has to do with the way in which the "marketization" of cultures has devolved power to smaller groups: people who have money and connections.

There is a realization within the World Bank that finance and economics are not the only issues. This was shown through their study *Voices of the Poor*, in which 60,000 interviews were conducted in 60 countries by hundreds of interviewers and social scientists. The findings were presented to the CAPA–World Bank conference by Deepa Narayan, a social psychologist who has done research on poverty.

Despite the ambitious scale of the study, its methodology has limits, as other specialists—including many within the World Bank—have pointed out. One must also beware of jumping to easy conclusions, such as, "It was clear to us that the poor are experts on poverty." It sounds humble, generous, graceful, even Christian. But no poor people would claim to be "experts" on poverty. No poor person would say, "I know what the causes of my poverty are, I will deal with it, leave me alone." They will still need help in understanding their situations and overcoming them.

But, just as the World Bank is beginning to realize that there are realities other than finance and economics, so the churches, having focused on relationships, are now realizing that finance and economics are areas they must deal with.

Focus on the Poor, Not Just on Poverty

In the 1970s, the focus of development work was on helping the poor. In the 1980s, sound macroeconomic policy received primary attention. In the 1990s the emphasis was on poverty reduction through growth, not on the poor. The World Bank is now thinking again about the poor *as people*, rather than just about processes and projects that address poverty. So the *Voices of the Poor* project is enabling huge organizations to realize that the poor are people and adapt their approaches to poverty by seeking new partnerships and new solutions. This is a salutary lesson for development agencies. We may lose sight of the subjects—the poor. We may lose our passionate commitment to them. That is where the Church can feature so prominently. If you want to know where the poor are, ask where the Church is.

The Context of African Poverty

In the 1960s and early 1970s African countries showed a lot of promise, but that has all gone. Had they maintained their share of world markets they would have been able to earn an extra US$70 billion a year (and in three years repay their official debt). So people who were employed all their adult lives are now on the streets. In a market-dominated world, the primary human interaction is competition, not support and solidarity. Every day you are struggling in competition. You think about the poor say once a Sunday.

World Bank reports conclude that Africa's poverty is attributable to, among other things, loss of markets, bad governance, and population growth. There is a realization that markets and household economies are interdependent. There is inability to incorporate household economies and, more important, to deal with gender bias in the household economy. On average, women spend four times as many hours working in the household economy as men, and women are significant producers (as well as reproducers) in household economies. But control is by males, so household economies do not develop to the full potential they could reach under joint management. HIV/AIDS is another cause of widespread poverty (as well as human suffering), due to the deaths of adults at the peak of their productive abilities.

What Does the Church Bring to this Relationship with the World Bank?

The Church brings its presence. The Church is where the poor are. This has been an eye-opener for the World Bank.

The Church provides dignity to the poor. The greatest significance of the CAPA–World Bank conference was the realization of the Church's contribution to the dignity and self-worth of the poor. The voices of the poor are not the voices of helpless, powerless people, but the voices of people with dignity. Despite AIDS, the deaths of family members, the deprivations of poverty, poor people still deal with life and survive. The heart of addressing poverty is ensuring and building on this inherent dignity of the poor, and the Church facilitates this.

The poor to whom the gospel provides dignity through transformed lives are the ones who make a difference. The gospel tells the poor that they are related to a powerful almighty God who is sovereign. This is poor people's greatest asset. They also have relationships to communities, to people who will take care of them.

Dignity can be based on hope or on fatalism. Dignity based on fate is a stoic dignity: I accept what comes. But dignity based on hope says: I have been given hope by someone who is a Lord of this situation. There is a strong sense of hope and empowerment, giving rise to a sense of dignity and self-worth.

That is a key understanding that the Church brings to the table. It includes individual responsibility, community solidarity, and willingness to sacrifice for the common good. Such dignity is not imparted by economic growth. It is a prerequisite for addressing poverty, rather than the outcome of addressing poverty.

Dignity has a role to play in civil society. The key role of civil society in addressing poverty was rediscovered in the last 10 years. In the development of civil society, we can see people who contribute as participants and not as recipients only. Usually it is taken for granted that civil society is defined in Western democratic terms, as voluntary associations in which people participate as contributors or recipients. In churches the poor should be active participants. Such participation brings dignity to them.

The Church brings local relevance. Some NGO representatives are called "briefcase people." They are temporary residents who stay, at most, only as long as a project continues. The church brings a long-term presence and local incorporation in the community.

The Church brings a moral vision, based on its "big story." Development requires a moral vision, not just ethics, but a vision based on something that transcends the harsh realities of the poverty-reproducing situation. No moral vision can shape society without a transcendent reference point. People want society to be shaped by a moral vision—not just by economic, social, and political constructiveness. Freud suggested that an appeal to the transcendent showed evidence of immaturity. Marx suggested that such an appeal was an opiate. Rationalism was another source of attack. However, an exploratory undertaking such as science needs the security that transcendence brings. Willingness to take risks comes not from independence alone but from being part of a community where there is a grounding for personal security and wholeness together with encouragement to take risks in the sphere of the new and as-yet unknown. This is also true in the moral sphere for society.

What Can the World Bank Bring to the Church?

The World Bank brings enormous resources, professionalism, an understanding of markets, and finances. It also brings its own vulnerability and its interest in refashioning itself so that it can serve developing countries more effectively.

The Church lacks the capacity to act professionally across the holistic range of needs. It has been undermined by a culture of substandard financial accountability that flourished among some Western development agencies that had easy money from their governments. These agencies provided African churches with development money without accountability. There is a feeling among church leaders that our theology never made us accountable and professional. U.S. donors expect professional reports on what happens to their funds. If the churches are to work with the World Bank they have to develop their capacity more than they ever expected to. But will the Bank enter into partnership just with large churches? The really significant churches are local churches. The local leader is often a Pentecostal preacher. Development will have to be focused on those people.

The Church has also had an inadequate theology. It has moved in the circle of salvation. What operates in salvation is grace. On the other side are works, merit, and achievements. When grace operates, we think we should scrub out works, merit, and achievements. When we take this one-sided theology into daily life, we become suspicious of works, merit, and achievement and see them as not of grace, so we have a theology that undermines them. We need to recover all these properly. Sometimes, the Church has a sense of powerlessness in regard to poverty, feeling that we cannot eliminate or even reduce it.

What are the weaknesses of the World Bank? It is ill-acquainted with, and—because it is a global and nonconfessional organization— somewhat ill at ease with the transcendent. But without transcendence, the moral vision will not work. The idea of the integration of all aspects of development is itself a moral vision. But this needs transcendent rooting.

The World Bank has difficulty working with local and decentralized bodies. The Bank operates at the center and at the macroeconomic and sector ministry levels. The Church may think that the World Bank has huge resources. But its plans and programs are often disappointing when measured against practical reality.

Why Did the World Bank Turn Around?

The World Bank funded huge government programs, so therefore it was suspect in the eyes of the poor. The Bank has genuinely recognized its failure and knows that a gun is being held to its head.

There are different stakeholders in poverty-reduction efforts: governments, the poor, civil society (including faith-based organizations), and the private sector. Addressing poverty requires working with all of them.

Could the World Bank lean on governments and ask them to work with the Church? Callisto Madavo, who is Vice President of the Bank for Africa, spent two days with the conference. There was a clear message to governments: If you want to work with the World Bank, work with the Church also.

Africa needs huge amounts of direct and foreign private investment. Investment in China is currently US$59 billion a year. Investment in Sub-Saharan Africa is only US$2 billion and most of that goes to South Africa. Private investment could make the difference. It is true that local ingenuity has stagnated and local institutions have been neglected. But we cannot say that global investment is unnecessary. Who will invest in Africa so that it will grow? We must take the global very seriously. Local knowledge and leadership are the basic foundation but investment must take place as well. Africa has not produced adequate leaders who can develop both these aspects. Africa needs people who are successful in the global arena and happy to come back and play their role in the local arena. Global and local need to be negotiated by African entrepreneurs who have succeeded in the global and relate to the local effectively.

Has the Church been given an opportunity to build capacity? Civil society does not just automatically happen. Churches are much worse off than NGOs. The winners in this, as the money gets released, will be the professionalized northern NGOs. If the church builds capacity in Africa and says it is ready to absorb US$2 million, the northern NGOs will find themselves in a more competitive performance-driven arena.

We need a consciousness of accountability to neighbors. What will the local church do to restore dignity to the poor? Will they have a rehabilitated prostitute on the finance committee? Until we facilitate the dignity of the poor and especially of poor women, then the gospel is failing. The Church is actually a far greater resource for women than is realized. The failure of the churches is not as bad as secular society believes.

We need systems of accountability and values of transparency. No culture has those values automatically. We have to have working systems of structures, procedures, and values. Systems currently in Africa are often such that the villains get away with it.

A very moving poem about African women was read to the conference. It was entitled "Release Me." We need to be partners in releasing the poor to address poverty with dignity. This is an act of the gospel. Addressing poverty from a biblical perspective helps us understand the gospel, and this is complementary to the way that research in biblical studies helps us understand the gospel. The Church is to be a partner in helping people release the potential of Africa. The African poor when released will be those who make the difference. This is not the language of the powerful releasing the powerless. We need to go back to the Bible and its understanding of God's power and sovereignty. At the heart of the gospel, that which enables everyone to experience the power of God is at work in their lives. And the poor assist the richer in this release. The poor with the gospel have a sense of dignity and ability. They are not experts but are people with dignity. We do not release them, but are partners in their release.

Contributors

Agnes Abuom is Africa president of the World Council of Churches.

Tokunboh Adeyemo is general director of the Association of Evangelicals in Africa.

Yeboa Amoa is the managing director of the Ghana Stock Exchange.

Deryke Belshaw is professor emeritus of Development Studies, University of East Anglia, and director of the Institute for Development Research, Oxford Centre for Mission Studies, in the United Kingdom.

C. Mark Blackden is a lead economist in the World Bank's Africa Region.

Robert Calderisi is the World Bank's country director for Central Africa.

Makonen Getu is the director of Opportunity Center for Transformation Studies, Opportunity International.

Gordon O. F. Johnson is president of Johnson Associates in the United States.

Christopher Kolade is chairman of Cadbury's Nigeria and head of the President's Commission on Corruption in Nigeria.

Callisto Madavo is the World Bank's vice president for Africa.

Shimwaayi Muntemba is a senior social scientist in the World Bank's Africa Region.

Deepa Narayan is a senior adviser on poverty at the World Bank.

Bernard Ntahoturi is the Anglican bishop of Matana, Burundi and former chief of staff to the President of his country.

Peter Okaalet is regional director for East and Southern Africa of Medical Assistance Programs (MAP) International, based in Nairobi.

Julius Oladipo is director of research for Christian Organisation Research and Advisory Trust (CORAT) Africa, in Nairobi.

Vinay Samuel is executive director of the International Fellowship of Evangelical Mission Theologians (INFEMT).

John Shao is vice chancellor of Tumaini University in Tanzania.

Chris Sugden is executive director of the Oxford Centre for Mission Studies, Oxford, in the United Kingdom.

Molefe Tsele is chief executive officer of the Ecumenical Service for Socio-Economic Transformation (ESSET) in South Africa.

www.ingramcontent.com/pod-product-compliance
Lightning Source LLC
Chambersburg PA
CBHW020607270326
41927CB00005B/216